FINDING NORTH

ALSO BY GEORGE MICHELSEN FOY

Zero Decibels: The Quest for Absolute Silence

FINDING NORTH

How Navigation
Makes Us Human

George Michelsen Foy

FLATIRON
BOOKS
NEW YORK

www.flatironbooks.com

The Library of Congress Cataloging-in-Publication Data is available upon request.

ISBN 978-1-250-05268-1 (hardcover)
ISBN 978-1-250-05389-3 (e-book)

Our books may be purchased in bulk for promotional, educational, or business use. Please contact your local bookseller or the Macmillan Corporate and Premium Sales Department at (800) 221-7945, extension 5442, or by e-mail at MacmillanSpecialMarkets@macmillan.com.

First Edition: July 2016

10   9   8   7   6   5   4   3   2   1

to my family

CONTENTS

FINDING NORTH

CHAPTER ONE

Fear

This story starts with fear, as so many stories do, harking back forever to that moment when, confused by light, we are dragged out of our mothers into an unknown space and must sort out, among these alien forms, where we are.

"Where" is the primal question, rather than "when," "how," or "who" because for any animal, figuring out where to move in defense or attack relative to the forces around us has always been the first step to survival. From the start, staying alive has depended on navigation: the art of figuring out our position and in what direction to travel.

I HAVE A HISTORY OF not knowing true position. Recently, near the end of a long late-night drive that took me from New

York City to Route 195 in southeastern Massachusetts, I grew drowsy; pulling over at a rest area, I switched off the engine and quickly fell asleep. When I awoke I had not the slightest idea of where I was or how I had gotten there, to slouch in this tight, cold space in darkness. In that instant I could have been anywhere, I might have been kidnapped by aliens, I could have lost my memory and been shipped to Turkmenistan. In some ways, I was as helpless as a newborn once more. A strange terror gripped me then, and held me back from moving or calling out for what seemed like minutes, though it was probably only a few seconds. It was a panic somehow augmented by the emotional memory of similar situations, whose outcomes lay beyond the haze of fatigue, in a place I could not quite recall.

That feeling was matched by the desperation with which, as soon as panic furloughed my motor centers, I catalogued as quickly as possible what I could see or touch: steering wheel, windshield; and beyond the glass, a tall, highway-style lamppost, a dark stand of white pines. I remember the relief that washed over me when geophysical clues crossed lines on a mental map, suggesting a solid position and memories connected to them: car, rest area, highway. It was country that looked close to home, which as it turned out lay forty minutes to the east: home, where my brother, who was gravely ill, waited to see me.

LIVING IMPLIES CHANGE AND THUS movement, and since navigation is the art of computing where we are, where we've been, and where we are going, it's not an exaggeration to say that navigation in its myriad forms is not only a crucial survival tool but the prime expression of living. Of the generally accepted criteria for life, most imply knowing our current position and moving where we must to fulfill a particular goal. "We have a brain for one reason and one reason only," a Cambridge neuroscientist named Daniel Wolpert once stated, "to produce adaptable and complex movements." Producing movement means finding position and a direction in which to move. Our brains evolved by navigating.

Navigation is so basic, so present at all levels of our lives that, like the proverbial company of blind men touching various sectors of an elephant and coming up with different definitions—*it's an archway, a wall, a fire hose*—we rarely recognize the whole for what it is. We navigate when we search for Smith's office in a part of our workplace we've not visited before; we navigate when, on the East Coast, we think of e-mailing a friend in San Francisco, situating him mentally three thousand miles away in SoMa, in the darkness before dawn. Even waking up in a space we know well, requiring a glass of water at 3:00 A.M., we automatically use navigational skills to plot our journey: roll off the bed, stagger around the chest of drawers, the scattered jogging shoes, through a door, then turn left (fingers outstretched, touching a wall to guide us) down an unlit hallway to the kitchen tap. The process is so unconscious that if someone were to insist we were navigating within our own house we would probably scoff.

And yet, during our short voyage from bed to faucet, the

navigation and memory centers in our brains perform a suite of calculations: of distance, course, time in relation to known landmarks; whose complexity is not watered down by the fact that we're not aware of them. These calculations are the same in kind—and performed, relatively speaking, with similar efficiency—as those employed by a World War II navigator using parallel rulers, pencil, and map to chart a bomber's journey from southern England to Berlin and back.

THE INCIDENT ON ROUTE 195 has shaken me. Over my thirty-plus years of adult life, I have traveled frequently and awoken in many odd places: a cornfield in southwestern France, a brothel in Indonesia, a rooftop in Damascus, a subway train (after a night of imprudent celebration) in the Bronx; but as a rule I've always been certain of what, and who, I would see when my eyes opened.

As I think back, I decide it was not the waking-up part that shook me as much as the particular flavor of associated terror and its familiarity. For I have known such extreme and de-bilitating panic twice before, and both times it was linked to losing track of where I was.

THE MONTHS THAT FOLLOW ARE full of turmoil and loss. My brother dies, and my wife and children and I have to absorb the emotional shock, as well as legal and financial fallout, from his death. At times, waking from the day-to-day routine that absorbs our lives, remembering Louis is no longer here, I feel I have lost track of myself in a fashion similar to what happened on Route 195. Is it despite or because of this that I become increasingly determined to examine not only the origins of my own propensity for navigational breakdown but everything else about this skill that so defines us?

I am not overly thrilled with the idea of exploring such personal navigational panic. I decide, therefore, to start my research at the furthest remove from the consciousness spectrum, at the level of a developing cell and how it knows which part of the body it's meant to reside in. I learn, after sifting through scientific papers from Germany, Israel, Taiwan, that one of the top researchers in the field works in the same college at which I teach; and I make an appointment, therefore, with Dr. Stephen Small at New York University in Manhattan.

To meet Small I must travel and therefore navigate. Driving from our house in southeastern Massachusetts I follow Route 195 west and then, in Providence, Rhode Island, alter course toward New York City. My car is not fitted with a Global Positioning System receiver, or GPS, so I match the Jeep's compass readout to the sun as our star swings southwest. Once in Manhattan I recognize the landscape and have little trouble finding my way to a street near the White Horse Tavern in Greenwich Village; parking there, I walk south and east to NYU's campus in Washington Square. This process of recognizing landmarks and geographical patterns and matching them to a map in the head is known to scientists as "path integration." It's the basis of a skill we usually refer to as sense of direction.

Stephen Small's work focuses on the sense of direction

as well, though at a more primal level. As chair of NYU's department of biology he runs a laboratory that seeks to understand how a given cell in a fetus navigates its way to become part of the left eye, the liver, a right toe.

Small is six foot three, lean, full of energy. He has an engaging grin, an easy manner, and close-cropped gray hair. He greets me in a corner office on the top floor of NYU's Silver Building. From this godlike vantage point over the West Village I observe the tourists in Washington Square wandering small as lice. Small leads me to his laboratory, the Center for Developmental Biology, on an adjoining floor of the Brown Building.

The lab is sealed behind thick metal doors. The space inside, defined by institutional walls painted gray and white, contains stacks of shelves laden with glass jars, tubes, vials, all numbered and color coded; workbenches below bear microscopes, computers, more vials. The monitor lights of diminutive machines blink in broken rhythm. Dozens of grad students labor at adjusting things I can't make out.

Small performs many of his experiments on drosophila, the common fruit fly, because they grow out of large embryos that are easy to mess with physically. Millions of drosophila participate, unconscious conscripts, in the lab's work at any given time. A room chilled to sixty-four degrees Fahrenheit slows the average life cycle of test insects. From one of that room's shelves, Small takes down a glass vial roughly two and a half inches long.

Inside are the formative years of a fruit fly's life. Drosophila teenagers, brown dashes barely a millimeter in length, crawl rebelliously around the top. "Can you see those tiny white dots?" he asks, pointing toward the bottom. "Those are embryos. Do you have a good slide?" he asks an assistant who, after much flipping through boxes, hands him a thin glass rectangle. Small places this slide under the light of a nearby microscope and motions me over. "Look at this," he says. "It's beautiful."

It is, indeed, lovely. Several hundred fruit-fly embryos swim in the empty ocean of magnified glass. Each embryo is an oval containing thousands of tiny dots, and every dot is a nucleus. Each nucleus is filled with a specific amount of a protein called Bicoid. The nuclei at one end have accumulated so much Bicoid that they appear almost black, but the concentration in each nucleus thins progressively toward the embryo's other pole, forming a remarkably even gradient of light to dark. The effect resembles a winter's sunset when snow clouds are so thick that the sky changes smoothly from light silver above, where the sun's rays still strike, to an increasing darkness where night gathers at the horizon. But this is a winterscape painted by Seurat, and every dot has a crucial job.

"You're looking at a morphogen gradient," Small tells me. It's the most visually striking expression of a position-finding mechanism based on recognizing varying levels of protein concentration. The developing cell, following a route-map written into its DNA, will navigate to the embryo's periphery, where different levels of Bicoid: higher near the source, lower farther away; already exist. It's as if the cell were a saloon patron, trying to find a place at the counter with a crowd at one end that thins progressively toward the other; his experience will depend on the number of people interacting at the section of bar where he happens to wind up. In the same way, the position the cell finds on the periphery—and thus, the precise concentration of morphogen—will determine which structure of the growing insect is formed at that exact point in space.

Another microscope illuminates embryos at a more advanced stage of development. Here every embryo contains a series of dark stripes aligned at right angles to the embryo's long axis. The striped patterns resemble a bar code trapped in a clear balloon; they are composed of cells that, having navigated to a particular position on the gradient, will develop into wing, or eye, or feeler, accordingly.

The work of Small and others like him is vitally important to the same extent that navigation is essential to normal life. If developing cells travel as they're supposed to, toward the various sectors of a morphogen gradient, the embryo will develop into a normal fruit fly or dog or human. If not, monsters result. At this early stage of life, bad navigation in the form of a wayward cell, a skewed gradient, can cause grave genetic defects in the fetus. Small's research, in the long run, should enable us to understand how those defects come to be and how to prevent them.

But normal embryo or monster, the cell won't care. It has zero consciousness and no choice in what happens.

I GET LOST, IN A casual sort of way, as I leave Small's lab. The Silver and Brown Buildings were originally separate, and though now conjoined they retain different floor levels so that the uppermost floor of Silver stands six feet higher than the top floor of Brown. Out of sheer laziness I opt not to climb back to Silver and descend to the next level, only to find the exit there locked. An open door on the floor below leads to a confusing array of hallways and locked doors, and soon I lose all sense of direction.

I remember now that, before NYU took them over, the uppermost floors of Brown were home to the Triangle Shirtwaist Factory. The fact carries with it a buzz of shock. If I were trying to find a place that epitomizes how dangerous it is to lose the ability to navigate, I could not have chosen one more appropriate.

Triangle Shirtwaist was a sweatshop that employed almost five hundred workers, mostly young women and girls, some as young as thirteen, in the manufacture of men's clothes. When fire broke out in the sweatshop at 4:15 P.M. on March 25, 1911, the flames spread at terrifying speed, gorging themselves on heaps of scrap cotton, through the top three floors of what is now the Brown Building.

The sweatshop's owners, Max Blanck and Isaac Harris, knew the factory well enough to find their way to the roof, with kids, governess, and foreman in tow, and from there they fled to an adjoining building to safety. It appears, based on survivors' testimony, that a number of workers could also have climbed to the roof ahead of the flames and smoke, but they had never been shown anything beyond their work stations and few of them knew the territory well enough to find their way out. The location of two emergency exits was obvious; those doors had been locked to prevent workers from taking unauthorized breaks or pilfering. Unable to navigate their way around the fire, 146 died, either burned to death inside the building or killed when they jumped to escape the flames: crushed on the sidewalk below or gruesomely impaled on the spikes of a wrought-iron fence that surrounded Brown at the time.

Eventually I find my way back to the stairs, to Silver, and take the elevator down. I am not psychic, nor do I believe in ghosts or spirits, but the memory of that fire, the screams of terrified girls it brings back, echo in my brain as I walk into the honking, in-ya-face, buttery, breezy, hot-dog-smelling sunlight of a late-summer afternoon in New York. In Washington Square I find a bench where I can sit and read the notes I scrawled while interviewing Small and think about what they imply.

Morphogens have no concept of whether they've navigated well or badly or what the consequences of poor navigation will be. Cells, lacking consciousness, have no choice in what they do, and therefore cannot know the fear, however latent, that comes when faced with a decision: sprint right or left to escape the flames? Assume, or not, a strong north wind drifting the aircraft southward as the pilot charts a course for Berlin?

Humans, on the other hand, have always defined themselves to a large extent by the knowledge required to fix position and venture farther afield, whether in exploration, trade, or war. This skill was acquired, often at great cost, by people who discovered new lands or figured out novel ways of observing the stars. They then added their knowledge to a body of navigational lore, oral or written, which enabled the next generation to make fresh discoveries. Although this conscious, venturesome aspect of human navigation might seem self-evident, it highlights the great difference between the French mother ten feet away from me examining her smartphone's GPS function and the pigeons her three-year-old is chasing.

The navigational tools employed by certain pigeons, as well as by myriad other creatures such as the Arctic tern or American eel, are elegant, precise. And all are instinctive, as mechanical and hardwired as the morphogen's; they guide life-forms having no idea of why, whether, or how they are guided. Whereas humans, with our weighty brains and fine reasoning skills, have lost our instinctive ability to navigate, which surely we possessed at some earlier stage of evolution.

I wonder if the price our species paid for becoming conscious was the loss of an ability to navigate instinctively. Or else, flipping the causal equation, was losing our instinctive skills, and the consequent need to invent navigational tools, what caused us to become conscious in the first place? Could it be that the fear attendant on judging where to go is not merely an awkward side effect but an important component of our need to move?

If that's the case, I think, it might be important to reassess the impact of such devices as the GPS-enabled cell phone with which the French *maman* is still obsessed. GPS and similar technologies over the last twenty years have rendered the hardwon navigational skills of individual humans obsolete. Every one of us has, with little notice and no training, become the navigational superior of Ferdinand Magellan, James Cook,

Sacagawea. For the price of a smartphone or an Internet connection, we can be led with astonishing precision to any point on the globe, and we don't need to know a single detail about how it's done.

But does such ease come at a cost? Will putting all our faith in GPS and related technologies diminish us in some way? Does the ensuing inability to get lost somehow sap our ability to seek and find new directions, geographical and otherwise? And is navigational fear—the panic that gripped me in the rest area, even the inchoate terror of a newborn—something we actually need in order to start exploring, and keep at it too, whether it be deep space or the flight paths of quarks? It seems vitally important that we investigate how these changes affect our lives.

Evening is advancing on Washington Square. The sun, now an hour from setting, draws shadows from buildings to the west, and the advancing dark pushes sunbathers toward Brooklyn. I stand, charged with a sense of urgency that draws its strength in part from the fear I felt before.

CHAPTER TWO

The *Stavanger Paquet*

I teach creative writing, and when my students ask me what they should write about I tell them, "Go to your blackest fear and use that." This is not therapy, I hasten to add, but a way to get to the heart of what good writing is about, which is breaking down barriers, personal and otherwise, in order to understand and convey what makes you tick, how other people work. It's easy advice to give: I have found, from experience, it is somewhat harder to follow.

What got me started in this project, however, was navigational fear, and I can't progress much further without tackling it. In this, at least, I have a precise position from which to start.

So I go home. Home means driving northeast, back to my family's house on the south shore of Cape Cod. If one views the Cape as an arm crooked in a rude gesture at the Atlantic, with Provincetown the upraised fist and the mainland providing shoulder, you would find me under the lower flab. The house overlooks Nantucket Sound, a body of water bounded by the peninsula to the north and the islands of Martha's Vineyard and Nantucket to the southwest and southeast, respectively. It's a tiny sea with big issues: shallow, complicated, chock-full of sandbars, rinsed by tidal currents, swept often by gusty winds; a hard place to navigate safely. Between light mirrored off the ocean and the filtering effect of sand, scrub pine, and salt marsh along its shores, Nantucket Sound is as luminous, as tricky, as lovely a stretch of salt water as you will find anywhere.

Once home, I pour myself a rum drink and sit in my father's favorite chair by the fireplace, under a granite lintel that my grandfather carved into a bas-relief of waves and Viking *drakkars* laboring, under a great burden of historical inaccuracy, into heavy seas with dragon heads and shields mounted. This house is where my brother and I came after we were born in Cape Cod Hospital, a few miles to the east. In the sunporch next door to the living room is where my brother died six months ago, fighting to breathe, propped in a mechanical bed while his nurse Tina, with utmost care and compassion, leaked liquid morphine through pipettes into his mouth. As he slipped into a coma he could see—although I'm not sure he was looking at them—seagulls cruising as they scanned for crabs, sunlight rippling off the corrugated blue of home water.

My first son, Olivier, who died at the age of one month from the kind of heart defect that can be caused by skewed morphogens, is buried in the back garden, under a cedar, next to cement gateposts molded for reasons no one can fathom into likenesses of Nefertiti and Ramses II. I wonder to what extent loss is something that expresses itself navigationally as we take bearings back to a person we loved and where we saw him last: in an apartment, a café, an intensive care unit, a grave?

This is speculation only, fueled by rum. My eyes, which usually are drawn by a large oil painting over the fireplace that shows stormy mid-Atlantic seas and nothing else, keep straying to a much smaller picture at the room's other end, a *giclée* print of a ship pounding through seas as big as those in the oil painting.

She is a black-painted wooden ship, single-masted, maybe a hundred feet long, with two square sails and a rectangular mainsail. The wind seems strong enough to shred the Norwegian flag snapping from the mainsail's top. Tiny men in top hats standing watch on deck appear somewhat concerned, though that could just be my imagination, which already knows their fate. Or are they worried their hats will be stolen by the wind? The ship's name is painted in yellow on her transom. Under the image the same name is repeated: *Stavanger Paquet,* and next to that, in convoluted Gothic script: Capt. H. Michelsen.

Here is the deepest root of my fear. And this is how the story goes.

IN THE MID-NINETEENTH CENTURY, the *Stavanger Paquet* ran a regular or "packet" route between southern Norway and Germany. She carried general cargo as well as passengers, usually emigrants traveling to America from German ports. Her captain, Halvor Michelsen, was my great-great-grandfather. On one of her trips, in 1844—here I must fall back on family lore, which has the peculiar characteristic of being as powerful as it is uncorroborated, the two characteristics, in fact, likely reinforcing each other—it was thought she went off course, possibly in fog or storm. I remember my mother pausing here for dramatic effect as she told this tale to Louis and me when we were very young, when all this was myth on the same order as Hansel and Gretel. At that point, she continued, possibly because of Halvor's navigational error (which our mother implied was not blameworthy, just the kind of thing that happened at sea), the ship, being too far from port to seek shelter, either foundered in storm waves or broke up on rocks. The crew launched a boat. Halvor ran back to his cabin to rescue the ship's log and was trapped. He went down with the ship. Nothing was left of him but his sea chest, which washed ashore some time later.

On the day he was lost, Halvor's wife, my great-great-grandmother, packed away her good china, put on a black dress, and announced that her husband had come to her in a dream and told her he was dead. When a ship carrying the survivors docked in Stavanger Harbor, flag at half-mast, the vision was confirmed.

That wasn't the end of it. The Michelsens, perhaps, were not the best navigators in the world, but they were nothing if not stubborn: they had always been a seagoing family and the boys were expected to ship out. Halvor's only child, Thomas, followed the family tradition and became an officer on the biggest ship sailing out of Stavanger, a square-rigged three-master named the *Drot,* working the South Asia run. He was washed overboard, our mother said, in another North Sea gale. At this point Halvor's daughter-in-law, Thomas's wife, decided that family tradition be damned, enough was enough: her sons were not going to sea. For my grandfather, Frederic Michelsen, she found a job at a local shipyard where, because he was fifteen and not big, he proved useful for working inside the tight steel tunnels where shafts that turned the propellers would spin. When he got sick of being a prop monkey, Frederic hopped a ship and emigrated to America.

AS I STAND EXAMINING the *Paquet* painting at close range I reflect how strange it is, given the history, that as a kid I always wanted to go to sea. And I did work on ships and fishing boats, although that did not become my career. Was there some perverse coding in the Michelsen genes that made us susceptible to venturing into ocean spaces to see if we could find our way around?

I realize that the sort of trouble Halvor and Thomas got into—excepting, so far at least, the fatal conclusion—has visited me at sea at one point or another. I have screwed up navigationally: I have come very close to going overboard, dying alone in the kind of soughing wavescape that pervades many paintings in this house.

It's hardly surprising, therefore, that the root of my navigational angst should lie in stories of Halvor and Thomas, which fused together as legends will, especially in the mind of a child, to become a myth of origins centered around disorientation in trackless oceans: around drowning alone.

Perhaps the best way to exorcise these ghosts is to figure out what happened to *Paquet,* where she sank and how: to find the wreck, if possible. We still have cousins in Norway who might have information on what happened, although the ship disappeared well over a century ago.

I own a sextant, which my mother, possibly defying her grandmother's influence, presented to me when I graduated from college. I decide now that part of the effort should include a test, a reenactment of the kind of trip Halvor routinely undertook as master of a sailing cargo ship. I'll sail offshore, a similar distance, perhaps from Cape Cod to Maine—to Isle au Haut maybe, or Mount Desert Island. I will use only the tools he used: compass, chart, and sextant.

I don't own a hundred-ton wooden coaster, but I have a sloop that will serve as test vessel.

THE NEXT AFTERNOON I GO out to the sloop. She is moored in North Bay, just under a mile from the nearest boat landing in my village. This is a long row in a rough dinghy, but I don't mind. It's one of those early autumn days in New England that seem to weep from the tension between, on one hand, the warm palette of colors rioting in salt marsh, in woodland; on the other, reminders in the slight chill, the trimmed light, in the relatively small number of boats moored nearby, that winter is not far off and life had better get busy if it is to survive the season's harshness. Already yellowtails and ospreys have disappeared from the marsh, and arrowheads of geese honk as they pass overhead, not always southward.

When I reach the sloop I run the engine awhile to recharge the batteries. I don't have time for a real sail, but on impulse I let go the mooring and motor south, through two miles' worth of narrows and bay, to a strip of sand and beach grass called Sampson's Island which separates harbor from sea. There I drop anchor in nine feet of limpid water and start taking inventory of the boat, not with my usual eye to overnighting in Nantucket Harbor or Oak Bluffs but to figure out what must be done before I can travel offshore using Halvor's tools and methods.

I'll take a little time describing my boat for she, and our history together, are important to this story. Her name, first of all, is *Odyssey*. It's a common name for a boat, and not one I would not have chosen, but I bought her used and seagoing superstitions: never utter the word *pig* aboard, don't sail on Friday, don't rename your vessel; were passed on to me by my mother and uncle. In any event, I don't mind the association with Homer and the epic cruise various gods and witches imposed on Ulysses.

Odyssey is a fiberglass sloop, thirty-five feet long and ten wide, built by the Morgan Yacht company of Saint Petersburg, Florida, in 1971. Her hull is white with a red bottom. In layman's terms, this is a single-masted, well-proportioned sailboat with a sharp front, a back-end that slopes inward at the top, a big cabin. Moving from back to front as you leave the cockpit and descend the short companionway (or stairs) to the cabin, you will find on either side a narrow "pilot" bunk running back under the cockpit deck and then a navigation station to port (left) with a chart table and a Very High Frequency (VHF) transceiver.

In front of the nav station is a wide wooden saloon table with settees in a three-quarter circle around. A small galley with propane stove, sink, and food lockers lies opposite the table. Farther forward stands a wooden bulkhead that carries a small wood-burning stove. On this panel, in homage to her name, I have affixed a painting on plywood of Ulysses tied to the mast of his ship, avidly listening to the songs of sirens who dance naked on an island beach as his crew, all wearing headphones that presumably blast Zorba-style bouzouki tunes, row him out of temptation's range. Beyond the bulkhead lie a clothes locker, the head (bathroom), and finally a separate cabin with a double, V-shaped berth.

That's the official version. Unofficially, she's a bare-bones, superannuated, not very fast sailboat with minimal teak trim and a mainsail so old it has lost many of the airfoil qualities necessary to drive the boat forward. Her one modern feature is an almost-new thirty-horsepower Yanmar diesel I bought two years ago to replace the original model, which had rusted out. Nevertheless, Odyssey is theoretically big enough to cross the Atlantic and most probably can make the kind of limited offshore passage that was bread and butter for my ancestor's ship.

I start with a walk-through of the deck. The rigging seems in good shape. The cables supporting the mast are all shiny, with no corrosion visible. The seam between deck and hull leaks despite my best efforts to plug it with waterproof compound. . . . I worry, always, about those leaks. Boats like this one typically are built of sandwiched layers of resin-soaked glass fiber and balsa wood and the wood, if not kept perfectly dry, will rot, weakening the whole.

I descend the companionway, taking notes in a black sketchbook that serves as *Odyssey*'s log. The VHF radio is new but doesn't work because the wires linking it to the masthead antenna need repair. True to local tradition, the marine electrician who was supposed to connect antenna to radio decided last summer to go into early hibernation and has not been heard from since. My bigger concerns below are rot and corrosion. I cannot examine the balsa core without cutting into fiberglass structure, but I can check the bulkhead separating the boat's forward end from her main cabin. This is an important part of the hull's strength. I tap it all over with a hammer, and it seems solid enough. Then I pull up floorboards under the table in the main cabin, and find nightmare.

A powerful connection is forged between people who sail and the craft they float on. This is especially true of those like me who sail old, creaky boats single-handed. No matter how careful your planning you will at some point find yourself in a seascape lonely and crazy as that portrayed above my grandfather's fireplace, with waves higher and winds stronger than forecast; and then the wind screams, the hull groans in pain, jade-hued seawater washes across the decks, the rigging twangs, and you wonder yet again, will all this hold? Or will something finally crack, rudder, mast, keel, and you flailing, panicked at the end of the kind of chain reaction whereby stress creates rupture that causes more stress, each added problem thieving time and margin for error in bigger and bigger chunks, until suddenly the boat is gone and you are dumped in water too cold to live in, miles away from land?

It's the vision that assails me when I peer into *Odyssey*'s bilges. The cabin deck is built on a framework of angle irons and when I thrust my hand deep into the black space under the deck, when I feel up the angle irons, rust peels off in orange scabs the size of tea saucers, and the metal frames seem jagged and thin. One has even rusted through; it hangs, a metal stalactite, from the angle iron above.

Farther forward the angle irons give way to a longitudinal steel beam supported by three plates of steel. Though I can't see under the beam, it feels as if a good third of the metal has wasted away there. This is potentially grave, since these plates support the mast step, a metal cup holding the mast's butt in place, without which that forty-foot pole and all the web of rigging and sails attached would topple over, probably cracking off a goodly section of deck as it fell.

On my knees in the dark, with my hands metaphorically feeling up the void under *Odyssey*'s skirts, I wonder how much of finding our way around, on land as at sea, has to do with imagining what might happen—thoughts on the order of, where will I be if I climb that mountain near dusk, rather than go around? What will happen to me if I steer north instead of northeast, if I keep the sails full in storm and go faster into this subset of the unknown? Is disaster, in sum, always envisioned geographically, is it always navigational in the deepest sense?

I finish off my checklist and close the logbook, making a mental note to call my friend Ned, who is the latest offshoot of a Cape Cod boatbuilding family that has been fixing boats since Halvor's time. In the galley, I brew coffee, then bring my mug up to the cockpit to sit by the steering wheel. It's late afternoon now, the sun is cruising lower over the brutish McMansions populating the shores of this bay.

I will have to arrange hauling the boat, always a complicated affair. This is a chore that cannot happen soon since I have just scheduled a research trip. It's a voyage that will take longer than a mere drive to New York, will draw me farther afield. The incunabula of travel and boat repair swirl in my brain; but the sky is trending indigo to the east, painting a gradient of blue that deepens into purple toward the sunset.

I think of other times I've moored here, hot summer days when as Liz and I picnicked the children would leap, shrieking cannonballs into the warm water, arctic terns wheeling and crying in protest. Those terns who nest every summer on Sampson's are some of the greatest navigators of the animal world. Every year they fly from feeding grounds in the Arctic to krill grounds in the Antarctic, a round-trip of over twenty thousand miles. They are the only animal in the world to experience two summers annually, returning in between to the same few meters of waterfront on which they were hatched—Sampson's, in this case—and so on through the generations.

But the terns have gone by this time of year, their chicks long hatched and flown south. And now the first stars appear, and I think about breaking out the searchlight because my return to mooring must take place in darkness through channels I'll have to pick out with candlepower.

Suddenly I am anxious to be moving again. I fire up the engine, plug the searchlight into its power socket, and start hauling in the anchor.

CHAPTER THREE

Birds, Memory, and London Cabbies

As the jet flies east-northeast I look out the porthole to the coastline of Massachusetts dimming to dark fractals and rhizomes of pumpkin-colored lights under a sunset not unlike the one I saw a week before on *Odyssey.* I fight the impulse to fling off my seat belt, stand up and, pointing toward Cape Cod, yell "Hey look, I *live* there!" But none of my fellow passengers care about what's outside their portholes. They are absorbed in smartphone games, laptop spreadsheets, the cheap hues and laugh tracks of inflight entertainment. They don't even glance at other passengers.

Yet I am seeing something, albeit in my imagination. Below me on the Cape, in Plymouth and farther north as well lie the convoluted estuaries, marshes, and coastlines from which those terns I thought of on my boat depart on their intercontinental pilgrimages. I am still amazed by the paradox, that animals and even insects, whom we consider infinitely lower in intelligence and abilities, possess navigational skills so far superior to our own as to make humans seem, by comparison, spatial morons.

Seven hours later, not far from Paris in the international airport where I'm in transit for London, we spatial morons follow each other up gangways and down neon corridors past exactly the same cafés, newsstands, bank ads, and duty-free shops we passed in JFK: following signs, herded like kine to customs, baggage pickup, ground transportation, other airplanes. I am struck again by the power of this observation: most people don't care where they are. They have absolutely no conscious idea of or interest in the place where, through the continuing miracle of jets that fly only two hundred miles slower than the speed of sound, after a seven- or twelve-hour trip that would have taken their great-grandfathers months or years to complete, they have safely landed. From Hong Kong to São Paulo, Helsinki to Sydney, Honolulu to Stuttgart, everything is planned so the modern traveler is carried as effortlessly as an overnight parcel from point X to point Y. He has no need to lift his eyes from laptop or smartphone to understand anything about the location in which he happens to be. The Eurostar terminal where I catch a high-speed train to London is no different, since it's laid out on lines similar to an airport.

All of this contrasts greatly with the scene that greets my eyes when the next day I emerge from South Kensington Tube station and walk to the Royal Institute of Navigation, secreted within the larger headquarters of the Royal Geographical Society. The RGS building is a massive Gothic Victorian jewel, or monstrosity, depending on your taste in architecture: a four-story catchall of chimneys, redbrick walls, columns, pitched roofs, gables, mansards, and leaded windows situated opposite the Alexandra Gate of Hyde Park; arrogant in design and placement to suit the temperaments of those who built it, most of whom were colonizers, imperialists, militarists. But they were also people who believed in the idea of "where," even if "where" was only another place for Britain to discover, map, and exploit.

The Royal Institute of Navigation was founded at the tail end of that process of discovery. Its director, Captain Peter Chapman-Andrews, meets me in the lobby. He is an ex–Royal Navy officer, former navigator on Britain's last aircraft carrier and on the royal family's last yacht. He leads me through corridors that look like they were renovated for George V's coronation, past an exhibit of electronic instruments that probably came off a Suez-era destroyer, to a suite of tired offices that is the Institute of Navigation's home. As we sit and drink coffee a minor commotion occurs down the hallway, voices are raised in greeting, and the magic hedgehog of animal navigation bustles in.

Magic hedgehog is perhaps an awkward image, but it's what sneaks into my head when I meet Air Vice-Commodore (RAF, retired) Douglas "Pinky" Grocott. A scientific creature with the drive of the Energizer Bunny is another. Grocott is ninety-two years old, and the process of growing that ancient seems to have worked in two ways, bowing and shrinking his body to porcupine compactness as it refined his intelligence and inflated his curiosity. Pinky has a pointed face, with roseate cheeks usually bunched in a smile. His thin white hair is neatly combed back. He wears a gray suit, an RIN tie, polished shoes; he speaks in upper-middle-class Home Counties English at a clip that is rapid and enthusiastic yet still fails to match the celerity of his thoughts. I came to the RIN hoping to attend a meeting of the Animal Navigation Group, which Pinky oversees, for I had been charmed by the list of scientific papers written by its members on subjects like "Using the blind Mexican cave fish as a model to explore [how] a three-dimensional map of space can be built." It now transpires that the meeting *is* Pinky, and the ANG a virtual group of scientists and obsessive amateurs scattered around the world but linked daily by Internet and the organizational skills of the magic hedgehog sitting in a borrowed office at the RIN.

Watching him work as he sifts through entire hard drives of data and research papers, some not yet published, I realize that Pinky, old as he is, represents a new science built on a wired map of investigative relationships. Simultaneously, he epitomizes the traditional British philosophical values of skepticism, empiricism, obsession with evidence: values that I admire and associate very specifically with my former tutor at the University of London, P. F. Dawson.

Pinky stabs at a computer screen with one finger. "There, at this conference, a professor's paper said pigeons had magnetite crystals in their beaks that detected magnetic fields. Then David Keays in Vienna said, 'We've been thinking about this, we used an MRI to look at pigeon beaks and found out those spots cannot be connected to the brain, so they can't possibly detect magnetic fields.' It happens all the time. . . . Ideas are put up, then you've got to validate them, replicate the experiment." Other research to which Pinky points shows that Pacific salmon do possess magnetite crystals linked to the facial nerve and to the brain, with which they detect gradients in local magnetic fields. Each of these gradients corresponds to a location stored in their tiny salmon minds.

For almost two hours Pinky relentlessly guides me through studies he and his ANG colleagues collate online; and my buttocks, wedged in a cheap office chair, slowly lose sensation. My thoughts, under fathoms of raw data, start to run through hallucinations of drowning, till consciousness of where I am fades; till I feel as if I'm in some other land, not virtual but not brick-and-mortar, either: a navigational Neverland in which a clutch of Manx shearwaters, seabirds flown in the baggage hold of a jet from the island of Skokholm in Wales to Boston, Massachusetts, and there let go make their way back to Wales so quickly—in twelve days—that given their average speed it is a dead certainty they flew at night and must have used the stars to navigate.

It's a place where pied flycatchers, loosed in planetariums, hop in the direction of the very stars that mark their migratory path, even as snickering zoologists shift the optically generated constellations around to confuse them; where loggerhead turtles are fitted with head magnets that distort their navigational faculties, causing those reptiles to swim in circles while their unmolested brethren, reading Earth's magnetic field like a chart, find their way unerringly across the Pacific.

It's a world where my Arctic terns orient themselves by observing the sun and stars and perform basic time/speed calculations to figure out how far they've flown, probably by measuring the length of days; and where the children of Cape Cod eels, riding the Gulf Stream's great gyre around the Atlantic, track their way back to the bay where *Odyssey* lies moored, in part because they recognize what their parents' home smells like, what odors characterize the streams and ponds that feed fresh water into salt.

Pinky's world exists to prove—or so it seems to me, sitting numb-assed as he tirelessly shuffles data—the existence of a navigational supercreature that's capable of using all its senses to figure out, instinctively and precisely, where it is and where it's going. It is a critter that Pinky, for all his love of science, envies not a little. "Human navigation doesn't exist anymore," he insists. Modern technology has made it superfluous, which means people are now deteriorating in navigational terms compared to their animal cousins. Pinky observes me with steely gaze. "The question is," he asks abruptly, "do you want to control technology or be controlled by it?"

By evening Pinky has finally shut down his external drives and, with Chapman-Andrews, we have moved to an Italian restaurant in Mayfair, an establishment of soft scarlet settees and starched linen tablecloths which the vice commodore has been frequenting since 1978. The maître d' automatically serves him a Sicilian liqueur concoction called a Mafia salute. "Ships and planes and Victoria Line trains are all automated, all run by computer," Pinky notes, downing the drink. "The real navigators nowadays are in software houses."

Though Pinky's words make sense, I don't entirely agree with them. Or rather, I agree with the point he's making: the type of navigation he used as an RAF pilot ferrying B-29s from Canada to Britain in the 1940s has become obsolete; yet I'm equally secure in my conviction that what humans and all other life-forms do to find their way around on a daily basis can also be thought of as navigation. I wonder if it's because of my personal stake in the matter, the concern regarding my own path-finding abilities, that I feel so strongly humans can and must navigate, and that we do this, however crudely, when moving around our living rooms as when traveling around London.

THE FOLLOWING MORNING I RIDE the Underground to the Russell Square station in Bloomsbury. As soon as I leave the station, I get lost. The problem is that I used to live in London, I loved living here; because of this, through some calculus that works on an emotional as opposed to a day-to-day, practical level, I harbor the illusion that it's still my city, I can slot right back into life here and know my way around. It's been a long time, though, and I miss a landmark on Queen Anne's Walk, perhaps heading unconsciously to Brunswick Square two hundred feet farther east where as a student I once spent a week, in bed mostly, with a pretty Sarajevan named Kumra. Avoiding such daydreams, I backtrack to the Tube station, examine a map, and find my way at last to Queen Square, on the west side of which a modest brick building houses the University of London's Wellcome Trust Centre for Neuroimaging.

My appointment is with Professor Eleanor Maguire, a world leader in the study of the hippocampus and associated structures. This area of the brain is thought to be the command center, in mammals, for navigating space.

Professor Maguire is a neat, reserved woman with delicate features, blond hair, and a Hibernian accent almost rubbed out by living among the English. She leads me down a lift to a sterile underground area she nicknames the "coalface." It looks like a hospital emergency ward; everything is painted cream over blue linoleum floors. Signs that would shine red when lit read "MAG ON" over chunky doors. Through windows set in those doors I glimpse tiny rooms in which machines that resemble massive beauty-salon hair dryers are poised carnivorously over a dentist's chair, attended by control screens and wires. There are three of these rooms, flanked by larger laboratory chambers lined with benches supporting computer terminals whose cables disappear in the direction of the machines.

Each of these "hair dryers," Maguire tells me, is a functional magnetic resonance imaging unit, or fMRI. Her work consists in part of using these machines to scan the brains of patients who have sustained damage to different parts of the hippocampal formation and linking those trauma and lesions to behavioral difficulties, to problems with both navigation and memory. In imagining what she does here, I chart my own path through what is known about the innate navigational abilities of our species.

. . .

IMAGINE FIRST OF ALL the hippocampal formation, or HCF. The hippocampus itself is a double structure—we actually have one on each side of the brain—but taken as a whole it resembles an elongated horseshoe, composed of two long arms with a bulb at each end, wrapped around the brain's center.

One could say that the hippocampus ends in emotion, because the bulbs into which its tips fold are the amygdalae, known to process strong feelings. The hippocampus is packed tightly 'round by related structures with names like subiculum and entorhinal cortex. The entire formation is massively wired to both the olfactory bulb, which processes smell, and the cortex, which is our conscious brain.

That's the clinical description, but imagine what the hippocampus is really like: a pulsing, pinkish double eel coiled around the brain's core, comprising many millions of bundled neurons elegantly arranged to process impulses in linear fashion, shooting them back and forth to next-door organs as well.

Now imagine how it works. You are in a large space, one that is new to you: Queen Square, say, where I walked earlier on my way to meet Maguire. This is a rectangular park surrounded by tall wrought iron fencing; it's filled with lawns, groomed paths, plane trees, sculptures, benches. While you ramble you turn your head right and left, trying to orient yourself, and different areas in the hippocampus (in particular sectors known as CA1 through CA4) will start to fire as you see, touch, feel, or hear specific landmarks. Each of these neurons is picking up on a precise point: a statue of Queen Charlotte, a limb broken during the last storm, a trash bin; and is called a "place" cell as a result. Once you're past the landmark the place cell goes dark until the next time you come across that topographic feature.

The next neurons to come into play, probably in the entorhinal cortex, activate when they perceive patterns and other connective features of terrain, and in particular boundaries or axial lines, such as the path that encircles our square or the footways that cross it. These neurons are known as "grid" cells. Both kinds of cells are automatically fed data about where your head and eyes are looking, and in the course of this overall process they work together to sketch a mental map of Queen Square. In practice, the brain probably views the square as a series of scenes, perhaps something like serial stage sets. Those scenes are arranged in two ways: first, from the perspective of your own body, known to scientists as an "egocentric" point of view, in which one thinks of places as lying "behind me" or "to my right."

The second happens in relation not to one's own body but to other points in the landscape, as in "to the north" or "past the valley between two mountains." It is thus known as "allocentric," or "centered elsewhere." Grid cells are also involved in the process of "path integration," keeping track of movement, direction, and speed to estimate present position; a process with which I, as a former ship's officer, feel very familiar.

Having walked around the park for a few minutes, your mental chart now allows you to traverse it by counting off landmarks via place cells, which recognize this old man snoozing on a bench, that bronze statue of a mother cradling a child, a historical marker describing how the delightfully named fighter pilot Wulstan Joseph Tempest shot down a

Zeppelin pilot who bombed Queen Square in 1915. When you hit the peripheral path, your grid cells, picking up on a familiar boundary, prompt you to turn left or right to follow that line of path around the park's eastern limits. The grid cells keep track also of your walking speed, direction, and time elapsed so as to anticipate the northeast corner and get ready to change course. It's true you might go wrong—park wardens are cutting up a large branch fallen across the path, the smell of sawdust is sweet and strong; having to leave the path, not recognizing landmarks, you might get a bit lost, as I did earlier when overshooting the boundary mark of Queen Anne Walk. In this garden it's unlikely to cause you more than a spike in the attention graph, but in a riskier environment, high mountains, say, the awareness of being lost would be shot through the far end of the hippocampus to your amygdalae, where fear, panic, and other strong feelings are generated. "That's what happened to me," I tell Maguire, "when I was at sea. I lost my bearings and freaked out."

"Yes," she responds drily, "people do panic."

Talking to Maguire reinforces my sense of the beauty and delicacy of this system. And that's not even the best, most elegant part. The coolest part is this: our mammalian navigational structure is one and the same as the system that processes and controls memory.

Maguire explains how this works in her office, which overlooks the square's trees and pathways. Her MRI scans link damage in different parts of the navigational structures to measurable effects on patients' recall. "What's really striking is seeing patients so apparently normal, who then walk out and get a cup of tea and come back in and reintroduce themselves; they don't remember talking to me five minutes before." Damage to the hippocampus will obliterate not only navigating skills but whole landscapes of memory. If a patient suffers sufficient trauma to the CA1 area, all recollections gathered over the last two years will vanish as if they'd never existed. If both CA1 and CA3 areas are affected, the amnesia will reach back decades.

The hippocampal formation functions as a crucial triage center, according to John Skoyles, a professor of philosophy and neurology at London University. It holds index tags for the billions of memory units stored elsewhere in the brain, in particular the cortex. A given memory, being summoned, then triggers a cascade of related associations, all similarly triaged through the hippocampal formation: all, more than likely, referenced not only by their position within the brain but through memory of a place in the outside world where that memory occurred. For example, the name of a neighborhood, "Wapping," glimpsed on a map of London's Tube, cross-references immediately to the memory of a tiring walk many years ago in cold and drizzle. It then links to my brother, with whom I was walking, who was trying to shoot photographs of what remained of London's docklands while I wished only to find a pub on Wapping Wall called the Prospect of Whitby. And all of that sends a signal, probably much amplified in the amygdalae because of the emotional content, through vast wiring to different parts of the cortex where specific associations with pub places and brother places and wharf places live; all somehow gathered together by the HCF into one unique memory-geography spectacular that evokes Louis and old pubs and other loci like the sunporch where he died and the office in Queen Square where I sit now thinking about him.

I AM STILL THINKING BACK as I walk out of Queen Square— and is the imbrication of movement with recall a clue to why walking often seems to help with thought?—finding a way south to Holborn Tube station through my own landscape of memory. The felt-tip smell of London's underground railway adds its own downpour of associations to the Wapping image, reminding me powerfully of when I worked as laborer, sailor, ship's officer after I graduated from university; half a decade spent mostly with Christine, in Kilburn and Camden Town.

It seems likely that the immediate proximity to the HCF of both emotion and olfactory centers accounts for the Proust factor, the synergy of memory and taste, smell and place, that join to evoke a particularly sharp sensation of recall, an indication not only of the power of such synergy but of its importance in our evolution as mammals. In *Swann's Way,* it is not just the taste of a pastry dunked in lemon tea that triggers memory and narrative but the cascade of related spatial associations: Aunt Léonie's room, her garden pavilion, and then, "like a stage set . . . the house, the town, the square where I was sent before lunch, the streets where I went to market from morning till night and in all weathers, the paths we took if we had the time . . ."

Our early survival as vulnerable, furry mammals depended

on smelling the wind for predators and always knowing in which direction lay escape. The HCF must have developed accordingly. The olfactory and navigation-plus-memory centers are the only parts of our brains where new cells are manufactured throughout life. I wonder if this might be another sign of their evolutionary importance.

I NEVER USED TO TAKE cabs when I lived here, I was always too broke, but I hail one on this visit because London taxi drivers have a connection to how navigation and memory work in tandem. One might even argue that cabbies epitomize this characteristic, this memory-navigation force. The connection is due to something called "the Knowledge": the rule that drivers may only pick up fares within twelve miles of London's center, Charing Cross, if they have previously memorized every one of the twenty-three thousand streets, squares, lanes, culs-de-sac, roundabouts, mews, flyovers, and other features of the city's terrain. As if that were not enough, they also must pass a test proving they've memorized every possible and practicable route to and from those twenty-three thousand streets, squares, and so on, all the while keeping in mind one-way systems, landmarks, forbidden turns, names of theaters, plus all other details necessary to take a passenger where he wants to go. I ask my cabbie about the Knowledge and the memory skills it implies. "My mates get cheesed off at me ever since I learned the Knowledge," he says cheerfully. "I say, 'Remember that match two years ago at White Hart Lane, Spurs were down two goals to nil and we won in injury

time?' and they say, 'Wot you talkin' about?' And I say, 'Cab-
bie's memory—magic, right?'" Drivers like him train for the
Knowledge test at the Knowledge Point School in Islington,
North London.

I sign up for the school's introductory course. It takes place
on the upper floor of a modern, two-story brick building on
the Caledonian Road. Fifteen or so mopeds stand parked on
the pavement outside. Each has a plexiglass-covered map
holder bolted over the handlebars. The course is run by Derek
O'Reilly, a native Londoner with accent to match. He is maybe
fifty, with the kind of face and demeanor you'd like to find
yourself standing next to at a pub counter: friendly, funny, a
good talker, sharp dresser; he wears a neat suit with burgundy
shirt and tie. The potential recruits are about thirty in number, of which twenty-eight are male and just under half of
South Asian, East European, or West African origin. We sit
uneasily at long trestle tables while Derek tries to reassure
everybody that learning the Knowledge is feasible for all. The
statistics, however, are not encouraging: learning London well
enough to pass the test takes a minimum of two years. "The
tragedy is," says Derek, "five out of seven will pack it in."

But Derek has a system. He has divided the map of London
into round areas that he calls "bullet points," each centered
on a square, roundabout, or crossroad. There are 320 points,
with roughly ten thousand routes between. To stand a chance
of passing the test, Derek continues, we must each buy a
250-cc moped similar to the ones outside and memorize all
the bullet areas, then the interconnecting routes by driving
every mile, day in, day out, in all weather, around across and

through. "You will drive, on average, one hundred thousand miles," Derek continues and adds, not unkindly, "You'll have to learn to start learning again."

I can't help thinking that the bullet points on his map look like the specific coordinates where place cells fire, while the routes approximate the kind of axial lines our grid cells pick up on, and build mental maps of, and across which they measure speed and distance.

Derek chats with me between classes. Eleanor Maguire, aware of the massive bolus of information that trainee cab drivers must ingest to learn London, scanned the brains of cabbies and found parts of their hippocampus were significantly larger than those of normal people. Derek's head doesn't seem bigger to me. What impresses me on the other hand is his passion, not for the Knowledge per se—though he's proud of the bullet/route system he developed—but for his city. He's in love with the sights and smells, places and sounds of the Smoke. It's how I felt once about London; still feel about it when I get past the Thatcherization, the wannabe-American "build-a-minimall fill-it-with-chain-stores" ethic that has wrecked so many of the city's hamlets and high streets.

Londoners, Derek insists, have lost touch with their city. "Tell me, which [railway] station is further north, Victoria or Waterloo? A Londoner will tell you Victoria, because it's on the north bank and Waterloo's on the south. That's because they don't understand the river. The river curves, you see?" He traces its course with one hand, caressing the northward arc the river describes. The words of Edmund Spenser, quoted by T. S. Eliot—"Sweet Thames run softly, till I sing my song"—come unbidden to mind, as does another line I once memorized from *The Waste Land*: "Unreal city; in the brown fog of a London dawn / a crowd flowed over London Bridge . . . up the hill and down King William Street." And I wonder if all writers, like Eliot and Joyce, Durrell and Homer, in one way or another navigate their fictions geographically, as Eliot's crowds navigated this city?

Perhaps it would be best to keep "navigate" in the past tense, because how we move around the city is changing. "There's a new phenomenon happening with GPS, with smartphones," Derek tells me. "People are relying on the machine telling them where they are, where they are going, and as a result they don't feel the need to learn London. . . . I get young people now in my cab, they don't talk to me! Just hand me the phone with the address of the place they want to go. . . . I said to one girl, 'You're going to Dalston. Do you even know what part of the city that is? Do you have any idea where you're going?' She didn't—she couldn't care less." Derek seems genuinely outraged by this behavior.

I sympathize with Derek. Something in his tone—the way he takes it personally, the way he identifies with the arteries of his town, how he simply doesn't understand why anyone could ignore a place so complex and alive—reminds me of Maguire's work, of the identity between memory and navigation, of how devastating it must be to lose both.

Later, as I leave the Knowledge Point building, walking up the Caledonian Road into Islington, where I last saw Christine, a sadness overcomes me, because Chris and I parted on bad terms, and I never heard again from the first woman I ever lived with. I have no idea what happened to her; I have tried but can't find her online. And it seems as if my life in London with the people I loved there is a country I gave up thoughtlessly, without realizing that by giving away the territory I was also abandoning the part of myself that *was* the territory. Those memories, of Chris and Kumra, of university and the Tube and working as laborer in the Jubilee Line tunnels, are not just window dressing or core samples of my habits and taste; they *are* the very stuff and substance of my life. The details of nursing at my mother's breast, what I saw holding my father's hand, how I played with my brother, how I lived with Chris, are what made me, not the other way around. We are what we remember, consciously or no. Turn that into a logical flow, the way electric impulses stream sequentially in the hippocampus, and you arrive at a fairly mind-boggling equation: human identity equals memory; memory equals navigation; human identity therefore equals navigation.

Caledonian Road is long. I check my course against the sun, but of course I'm in London, capital of Atlantic drizzle, and there is no sun, no shadow which, in late afternoon, should be pointing east-northeast; only the silver-plated light that seems to drench everything in this town. I spot a café up ahead, one of the few that has not become a Denny's or McDonald's, and walk in, hungry for my own Proustian moment, to order tea and a kidney pie.

CHAPTER FOUR

Modeling Halvor

W hen I was ten, my brother and I became juvenile delinquents. We had a war going with some boys down the bay: in summer this consisted of naval battles in rowboats during which we would splash each other by smacking oars against the water while hurling vile threats, such as, "Wanna contribute to the *blood*-mobile, stupid?"

One winter, Louis and I escalated the conflict. We rowed my dinghy to a beach near the enemy's house and snapped rocks through the windows of an outbuilding. Someone yelled and came at us darkly through trees. Louis ran off down the beach, but I was not going to abandon my skiff, and I rowed at flank speed across the bay. There an old man named Chester Crosby caught up with me in a harbor tugboat. I remember, as I stood trembling on the floorboards of my skiff, Chet telling me gravely that he might not get around to calling the police just yet, but he sure as heck was going to tell my mother.

Quite a few years later Chet's grandson Ned boards *Odyssey* where I have tied her up at a dock south of the town drawbridge, near a boatyard the Crosby family started in the 1850s. Ned has carried on his family's tradition in a boat shop inland. He is in his midforties but still seems young to me, most likely because I was friends with his father, Eddy. I often used to hang out at Eddy's house, talking about boats and places we'd been on them, while Eddy lay on the couch with Ned, who was probably eleven or twelve at the time; father and son rubbing each other's feet, slowly, absentmindedly almost; a family ritual that made me long for a son with whom I could share such easy comfort. I have a son now and a daughter in college. I miss them every day we're not together.

Once in a while, my son lets me rub his feet.

It's another lovely day, later in the fall now, with a cool wind starting to gather up its scarves and get serious about blowing from the north. This is Ned's last chance to inspect *Odyssey* in the water, to get a feel for how she sits in her intended medium: she must be hauled out soon, before winter freezes the bays. Ned goes straight to potential trouble spots, quite a few of which I forgot about or just filed under "If it ain't broke, don't fix it." He checks the stainless steel wires that support the mast, then goes below and closely examines the bolted backing plates to which those wires are fastened, and that take the strain of wind-tautened rigging.

"There's water coming in, you can see the rust," he says, pointing at an orange stripe painted below the plate's bolts.

"It would be a good idea to back those out and check how much corrosion there is." He spends a long time crouched in the boat's guts, peering at bolts securing the mast step to its supports. "You'll want maybe to take half of those out. If they're fine, then you're OK."

I ask him what he thinks generally, if the sloop is sound enough for an offshore passage in potentially rough weather. I watch Ned's face the way you'd watch the expression of a doctor examining an x-ray of your chest. The Crosbys have a calm about them that is part Yankee imperturbability and part, it seems to me, a sort of boat mysticism based on the cosmic balance that underlies both sea-kindly craft and the swing of galaxies. Ned's great-great-grandfather Horace started build-ing boats when his dead father appeared in a dream and or-dered Horace to break out his adze and go forth and build water transport. I know Ned well enough to assume he is not awaiting word from his ancestors.

"There's good news and bad news," Ned says slowly. "The good news is, nothing seems compromised by water intrusion. [Given her age] she's frankly better than I expected." As well as pulling the bolts he pointed to earlier, I will need to chip out rust on steelwork underlying the mast step to make sure enough healthy metal remains to support the spar and all its angst of sail.

"The concern part—" Ned's face doesn't change, but I'll bet mine does. This is the bit that's always most important, the shadow on the x-ray, the sentence that begins "Unfortunately." "The concern part is her general strength." Apparently, Ned says, these Morgan 35s were built of fiberglass laid down without a balsa core—just straight resin and glass matting. Here, too, the good must be weighed against the bad. The fiberglass contains nothing that will rot. So her hull is sound: that's the positive news.

But the glass is a little thin, the sloop lightly built. Ned rubs his chin. "The question is, was she built strong enough to go offshore? Is the hull built rugged enough to take a knock-down?" Ned will have to wait till the boat is hauled to measure lower areas for water intrusion. We finally agree that if the lower hull is healthy, the mast supports solid enough, and the "chainplates" that anchor the rigging check out, an offshore trip does not seem too foolhardy a proposition.

THE HAUL-OUT IS SCHEDULED FOR later that morning. I had hoped for a quick foray into Nantucket Sound, a last sail before winter. But the rigging plays glockenspiel against the mast, the forecast is dicey: wind out of the north at twenty-five to thirty, gusting to thirty-five. Small-craft advisories are posted, which means sailing is officially discouraged. On the other hand, a north wind means I'll be sheltered to some extent by the Cape's landmass as I sail off its southern coast.

And I want to go out. Something quite deep in my character lusts to live again at the center of these forces, holding rudder balanced against water, sail against wind. It's not some romantic Masefield thing, no "I must go down to the seas again" crap is involved here. It feels directly physical, as if my muscles, tendons, bones need to stretch that way, my mind to look for direction across a horizon that is not chained down by anything but clouds. Because of research trips, I haven't sailed for well over a month, and I won't be able to do so again until spring at the earliest.

So I head out. Even in the bays, steering toward the cut that leads out to sea, the wind is strong and gusty. Most of the channel buoys have been removed because of impending ice, and I must be careful to steer down lines of dark water, which remind me of the axial lines Maguire talked about. I imagine for a few seconds my grid cells firing to line up shallow boundaries against deeper water.

Then the practicalities of sailing reclaim my attention. I decide not to fool around with the mainsail, which would involve prancing around on the foredeck, an activity that increases the chances of being knocked overboard; I have been particularly sensitive to this sort of risk since I was hooked by longline gear and dragged halfway over the side of my boat while fishing alone one February. I unfurl the big foresail. This is something I can do without leaving the cockpit. Immediately the wind gusts and even in West Bay, heading a little west of south, *Odyssey* heels under the pressure. We move swiftly out the cut.

The wind increases steadily, kicking up waves against the incoming tide. The sound of crushed water grows as the boat speeds up, and I feel the old excitement of being taken by wind that could lead you anywhere the salt sea touches. A wall of low clouds has been advancing from the northwest and now it covers most of the sky in smoothly darkening colors, from blue-white overhead to near purple at the horizon, a pattern that signals snow. I think, inevitably, of Halvor and the bad weather in which the *Stavanger Paquet* got lost. The clouds remind me of something else, which takes a minute or two of mnemonic floundering to recall, the tag labeled "cloud image" in the hippocampus presumably shooting out electronic impulses to different areas of the cortex till it comes up with the association I was looking for: Stephen Small's lab at NYU and the gradient of morphogens, light on top turning smoothly toward dark at the bottom.

The wind now blows twenty knots. The dodger—a sort of half tent, made of blue canvas snapped onto aluminum struts, which protects the helmsman from spray—tore in an earlier wind, and now half of it flaps so badly I have to tie the canvas down with a line. Here is one more repair that needs doing before I undertake a trip of any length. I steer just south of Succonesset Point for the rising loom of Oak Bluffs on Martha's Vineyard. This course will give me a couple of miles, or twenty minutes of sailing at this speed, before I have to turn away from further shallows. My memory churns out another association, this one easy to trace. In this place, under these circumstances, it's a normal link, part of the library of navigational fears that have been obsessing me lately.

IN LATE AUGUST SIX YEARS ago, I sailed to Tashmoo, a harbor on the northwest flank of Martha's Vineyard, opposite the Elizabeth Islands. I anchored there, walked to Oak Bluffs, and spent half the night drinking with friends. The next day I was feeling the effects of a bad hangover, but I had to get back to the Cape so as to relieve my spouse who, understandably, needed a break from child-minding after I'd enjoyed twenty-four hours off. It was tricky weather. The wind was gusting to thirty knots, thunderstorms were galloping in from the west. Like today, a small-craft advisory had been posted, and as I rounded the island's northwest corner the swells grew. I found that as soon as I stopped steering *Odyssey* swung broadside to the wind, and then waves sluiced the decks and sails banged and tangled in dramatic fashion.

Dealing with sails and steering I was unable to take visual bearings. I couldn't even estimate how far I might have traveled since the last landmark, and that was a problem. This estimate, known by the somewhat sinister term of "dead reckoning," consists of working out a simple equation: distance traveled equals time divided by speed; and plotting the miles you've run since your last known position along a given course (altered, perhaps, by current, wind effects, and so forth) to find where you are now. It's a crucial backup in situations when, for whatever reason, it's impossible to fix your position by landmarks or other means.

On that trip I had no time to work out my dead reckoning. In the haze of past Coronas, under the thrust of this half gale, I figured I was sailing faster than usual, and believed I was looking at a coastline, with pale strand and large houses, much closer to home.

But as I crashed along eastward the land changed in ways

it shouldn't have, and now that I thought back the timing seemed wrong. I couldn't be seeing the big houses on Oyster Harbors less than an hour after leaving Tashmoo. I realized then I did not know where I was. This part of Nantucket Sound was particularly rife with sandbars, and a long shoal called Hedge Fence closely paralleled my intended course. Hedge Fence was, and is, a treacherous piece of ground that has wrecked many ships over the years, including the *Port Hunter,* a British steamer that, disoriented in fog, hit a tug and sank in 1922.

And the panic happened then, just as it did in that rest area on Route 195. My stomach turned, my knees lost torque. Even now, after uncounted sails successfully navigated in these waters, memory summons a sensation that registers as gut-kneading, physical.

Today, on this sail in autumn, I don't get lost. I am not going far, after all. I toy with the idea of continuing: to Nantucket, for example, twenty-two miles away. With this wind I could reach that island in less than four hours. Navigating while steering at the same time would be tricky, but as long as it does not snow, it's hard to miss Nantucket altogether.

I decide not to. I have rational reasons, research calls I must make, and the boat hauler awaits. But I'm also conscious of being nervous, affected by the hangover of fear that lies at the heart of what I'm investigating. I remember the lacy complexity of what Maguire studies and wonder if people's brains are structured differently, if perhaps there is some subsection of the hippocampal formation that, built one way, makes person

A less fearful of getting lost than person B: something that regulates spatial intrepidity, a navigational rheostat of sorts.

Twenty-odd minutes after leaving harbor I adjust the foresail and steer northward, sailing close-hauled for Cotuit Harbor. The wind steadily strengthens. Clouds now cover the entire sky.

THE DAY AFTER *ODYSSEY* is hauled out snow sugars the landscape and forms little islands of icing on the blue tarp with which I covered the boat where she now sits in the driveway, a sea thing beached. A boat in the water is alive, always dancing to the lilt of water and wind, and she dies a little when propped on jack stands near the garage. But a boat in the water also generates a constant hum of background worry for her owner because she is always at the mercy of a sudden nor'easter, a worn mooring line.

I cease watching *Odyssey*'s whitened bulk, visible from the room where I work, and turn back to the computer. I have been writing e-mails to my aunt Imelda, who lives in Portland, Maine, as well as to the Norwegian relatives with whom my mother was still in contact when she died, asking for any letters or information they might have on Halvor Michelsen and his ship. So far, only Imelda and Reidar Bornholdt, a cousin who lives in New York, have responded. Imelda sent a rough family tree written in longhand by some unidentified ancestor. It includes the following information from which, though I know very little Norwegian, I have managed to pick out the relevant bits: "*Stavanger Paquet;* wrecked in storm;

Halvor, who went back for the ship's papers, died at age 31. . . . married to Dorothea Thorsen Eeg."

Reidar sends me a brief family history written by his mother:

> *Your great grandfather, Halvor Michelsen, was a sea captain in command of the* Stavanger Paquet. *He was married to Dorothea Eeg. She was from Sognefjord.*
>
> *She was said to have been very beautiful and they were said to be an unusually happy couple. He worshipped her and as they say in Norway: 'Han bar hende på hendene'[He held her lovingly in his hands] . . . The* Paquet *was a busy ship but now and then things were quiet. This was the case in 18?? . . . [illegible] . . . Halvor was asked to move a load of herring from one place to another on the coast. A terrible storm broke . . . the cargo shifted. The ship went down with all men. That was the end of the* Paquet.

No mention is made of getting lost in the storm. And the part about the ship disappearing with all hands clashes with what my mother told me. But family stories are like dead reckoning: the farther away you get from the last known landmark, from the most recent facts, the vaguer and more unreliable your own position.

Queries to Norwegian maritime sources have proved only slightly more productive. The Oslo Maritime Museum possesses few records for that period. Its librarian, Arne Sørli, e-mails, "We are having some problems finding any information about this ship. What we know is that a steamship named '*Stavanger*' (without '*Paquet*') was wrecked March 1st 1886, in Kvaasefjorden near the city of Kristiansand."

This clearly is not the same ship. But Arne adds, "Also, a sloop named '*Stavanger Paket*' [sic] . . . might have sunk in 1847. The captain of this ship was Knud Helliesen." He suggests getting in touch with the Sjøfartsmuseum, the maritime museum in Stavanger.

Arne's year and ship type seem right; the captain's name obviously does not square with my mother's stories. I wonder now if perhaps Halvor wasn't master of his ship after all. Maybe he was only a mate, the same job I held once, working on cargo ships in the North Sea. Of course, as mate, he could still have been responsible for faulty navigation.

The name Helliesen rings a bell. I look back over the family documents and in the family tree find that Halvor's father was the stepson of "Ole Helliesen."

I send an e-mail to the Stavanger Sjøfartsmuseum, and the next day I receive a response. It's from Gry Bang-Andersen, the curator.

"We do have some information about a ship called *Stavanger Paquet,* a sloop built in 1834," Bang-Andersen writes. "The ship was referred to as the '*Paketten*' by the sailors . . . the sloop had a captain named Halvor Michelsen from 1841–44."

My pulse speeds up as I read this, for now I have the first objective confirmation that family legend was true. Bang-Andersen says her information comes mostly from a book by M. L. Michaelsen on the history of Stavanger shipping. She continues: "The vessel mainly went with freight between Stavanger and Hamburg, Germany. In February 1844 it was on its way to Stavanger with a freight of herring, it was caught in a snowstorm and sunk by Espevær, on the Norwegian West coast. Michelsen, the captain, went down with his ship."

I click into Google Earth. Espevaer, Bømlo, Norway pops up in the index box. The app, in a dizzying replication of Skoyles's index/associations—cascade model of human memory, zooms down to the southwestern corner of Norway, a savagely chopped-up stretch of inlets, fjords, and islands, all the way to a cluster of islands off the Bømlo peninsula of which Espevaer is the largest. It's shaped like a mutated butterfly with wings stretching wide northwest to southeast. A dozen or so smaller islands hang off its southern, northern, and western edges. Farther to the northwest lies another freckling of miniature islands.

Google Earth doesn't show much info on terrain and none at all on maritime hazards, but on the face of it this looks like a nasty piece of water. The island is not high and therefore must be hard to spot in poor visibility. And those islets, so tight and jagged, must be rock, which means each is probably surrounded, like a local demonstration of fractal geometry, by a miniature version of itself and the larger archipelago; a secondary necklace of yet smaller reefs and lone rocks. I shudder inwardly, thinking of a ship blinded by snow, driven by storm into that hard wilderness; of water shouldered by shallows into high breakers, the breakers turned into ten-foot triphammers that smash everything around them against anvils of weed-slicked granite. Wooden hulls crushed into foam and splinters, men broken and drowned.

Espevaer, for all its dangers, lies only fifty miles from Halvor's home port of Stavanger.

Bang-Andersen goes on to write that the *Paquet* was coming back from Grøtlefjorden, in northern Norway, where she had loaded her cargo from fishing boats owned by someone named Peter Köhler. So I look next for Grøtlefjorden. It's not listed on Google Earth's index, though a Grøtfjord is, in the Tromsø region. I consult a large-scale atlas and find Grøtfjord to be a short inlet running south from the line of coast, which faces the North Pole at that point.

Grøtfjord is indeed far north, as Bang-Andersen intimated. It's two hundred miles uphill from the Arctic Circle.

I close my atlas and stare out the window. In stark contrast to the images my mind was crafting of Espevaer, Nantucket Sound looks peaceful, subdued by a hush of snow. The wind is out of the south, the temperature hovers around freezing, grass shows in patches through the white. I go back to imagining what it must have been like to take a sailing coaster north of the Arctic Circle in February, without benefit of radar to see trouble before it happens, or engine to speed you out of trouble when you see it. How bitterly ironic it must have felt to Halvor to make it all the 1,400 miles to Grøtfjord and back, only to founder fifty miles from home.

It makes my idea of sailing from Cape Cod to Maine, less than two hundred miles offshore in summer, appear ridiculous by contrast. No matter what limitations in terms of navigation I impose to mimic Halvor's passage, my trip looks too easy, too short, a pleasure cruise in humane temperatures.

A conceit, no more. And yet what choice do I have? The boat is hauled and anyway not fitted out for a winter trip. And winter cruising in New England is impossible because, except for major ports, the harbors and anchorages tend to freeze solid.

I own a sextant, which I will need to navigate à la Halvor, but it needs repair, as does my skill at using it. And I have trips scheduled over the next few months that are just as important to this project as any experimental sail.

Finding *Paquet*'s wreck after so long is going to be hard if not impossible, but if I want to try I shall probably have to charter a boat. I email a couple of dive clubs near Espevaer, figuring they can advise me on boat rentals. In Europe chartering means showing seafaring credentials, which in turn means I'll need to renew my hundred-ton Coast Guard master's license; this also will take time.

However artificial the idea of sailing to Maine, it does have a side benefit in that it forces me to consider carefully climate and currents and the vulnerability of sailing vessels. This is how navigators had to think until very recently. If you visualize the history of navigation as a calendar year, it's only in the late evening of December 31 that mariners equipped with satnav, radar, steel hulls, and powerful engines could plan trips independent of their environment, or near enough. For virtually all of human history, navigation of the kind my ancestor practiced was not just a skill but the roughest of magics: a spell cast in the face of mystery and fear against the near certainty of loss.

CHAPTER FIVE

At the Shrine of the Navigation Gods

I t's to learn more about the history of this human drive to find out where we are that I plan a trip from New York to a town named Alexandroupoli in northeast Greece. From there I'll take a ferry to Samothrace, a small island twenty-two miles offshore, equidistant from both the Greek coast and the Turkish.

The only way to reach Samothrace is by ferry. The tourist season is over, however, and no one will tell me when the ferry leaves or comes back, and I don't want to fly to Greece till I'm sure I can get to the island. I harass various tourism and ticket agencies and finally the ferry company itself. My friend Kathy Nora, who speaks Greek, even telephones the Alexandroupoli harbormaster. The ferries were due to reset to a winter schedule but no one knows if that happened or what schedule is in place. I start to wonder if some kind of conspiracy is at work. The harbormaster, clearly part of the plot, won't crack under pressure; he refuses to divulge how often the boats sail. He won't even admit they're running.

To find my travel plans thwarted by bureaucratic roadblocks pumps me tight with frustration.

NO ONE KNOWS, BY DEFINITION, by what method prehistoric humanoids found their way out of Central Africa, no one can be sure what they were thinking as they left the smoky caves and familiar hunting grounds of home, why they felt compelled to risk adventuring into the unknown. It's likely that food scarcities, changes in climate, and group rivalries all played a part.

It follows that no one knows how they navigated. Analysis of DNA among surviving populations, as well as the archeological record, suggest that our ancestors favored moving along coastlines: by the eastern rim of Africa to the Red Sea, for example; and beside the edge of ice sheets, a route possibly followed by Amerindians as they moved south and east from the land bridge or chain of islands linking eastern Siberia with Alaska in those days, then skirted a vast glacier covering what is now the Rockies.

It is tempting to speculate once again that the importance of axial lines, as determined by grid cells in our hippocampal formation, made such boundaries as coastlines, the sides of glaciers, or strings of islands more tempting and easier to follow than not, especially in the absence of known landmarks.

But all we know for sure is that our forebears made their way out of Africa to Asia between eighty thousand and sixty thousand years ago, to Australia by the forty-five-thousand-year mark, and to every other portion of the planet except Antarctica by roughly 15,000 BC. They reached the Greek islands early in the process, around 50,000 BC.

THROUGH E-MAIL I HAVE MADE a friend in the office of Saos, the Samothrace ferry company. One day she writes to give me the boats' winter schedule, which has at last been released by the ministry of transport.

A week later, in Alexandroupoli Harbor, I embark on *Saos II,* a boxy blue car ferry that like most of her kind is equal parts parking garage, pinball parlor, and Best Western lobby. Youths in cheap ski jackets, a bouzouki player, a dour, bearded priest, and blue-rinsed grannies hang tight to their thimble-cups of coffee as *Saos II* bangs and twists into swells raised by a powerful south wind. A woman retches from a leatherette couch. Standing on an upper deck, I spot from afar the island we're heading toward, steep mountains of dark blue lynched by clouds. I watch the purplish swells open into valleys flecked with jade, and am content. For this is the wine-dark sea Homer spoke of; and this wind is the sirocco, blowing out of Africa—the same wind, most likely, that caught Ulysses as he left Troy, heading westward and home to Ithaca, or so he hoped. It drove him north instead, past Samothrace to the coast we have just left, which was the heartland of the hostile Cicone people.

Riding this modern ship that labors to make its way against the wind, I get a better feel for how Ulysses, on a small, clumsy craft powered by oars and a square sail that only worked well when the ship was traveling in the same direction as the wind, must truly have felt condemned by the gods to wander helplessly wherever they decided to blow him.

I'm fond of *The Odyssey*. Its account of Ulysses' travels builds one of the best portraits of a rogue I've ever read. And quite apart from being a good story, it contains factual information about some of the earlier forms of navigation: this is part of my motivation in coming to the north Aegean in the off-season.

It's not the only motivating factor. To fully understand the history of navigation one has to visit this sea, learn its moods, realize in the gut how safe terrestrial navigation was by contrast. On land, travelers could leave trail marks or backtrack, ask locals for directions, or simply stay put and wait for help. There was no sharp need for specialized wayfinding techniques on land.

This was not the case on the vast, fickle, unmarked surfaces of a sea. Since it was so easy to get lost offshore, mariners were likely first to develop specific techniques to find position and direction, and it appears the sailors of the Aegean were among the earliest to both develop and record those techniques. But their methods did not always work and here, too, Homer's *Odyssey* serves as a guide to how badly navigation could go wrong. It was in large part due to navigational perils that sailors took out insurance of sorts by seeking initiation into the mystery cult of the Dioskuri, whose specific remit it was to protect mariners and bring them safely home.

The headquarters of the Dioskuri cult was a shrine on Samothrace. When in midafternoon *Saos II* docks at Kamariótissa, the island's sole port, I rush ashore, hoping to visit at once the shrine's ruins, which lie three miles to the east along the northern coast. Kamariótissa is not big: a hundred-odd white-washed houses with red roofs, the taller russet cupolas of an orthodox church, all smeared between a spur of ragged mountains and a harbor whose breakwater shelters a couple of coastal freighters and numerous small fishing caïques. The main industry here is tourism but the tourists have long gone, and as I hustle along what passes for a harbor promenade the islanders stare at me, once, then avoid my eyes, probably figuring that anyone who comes to this place in cold weather is too crazy to deal with. No one speaks English or French and guidebook Greek elicits shrugs or looks of panic. I try my schoolboy German, and because many northern Greeks have worked in Germany, I finally am able to communicate. A fat clerk in a flyblown office tells me a bus carrying schoolkids will leave shortly and stop in Paleopolis, where the shrine is located.

When the bus drops me off I find Paleopolis is a lonely intersection between a gravel beach and a rough slope of olive and juniper leading upward to cloud-soaked mountains. I follow signs along a path to a building guarding the shrine's entrance, where a guard tells me everything is closed for the day.

In town that evening I rent a room, right on the beach,

sterile but comfortable enough. I was hoping for moussaka, but the restaurants are closed; all that's open are *tavernas* offering grilled chicken with yogurt dressing, wrapped in unleavened bread. The wind is blowing harder, rain comes in harsh gusts, and it's gotten colder. I pick a *taverna* near the breakwater, its terrace enclosed by a plastic roof and plexiglass sides. A wood stove churns out smoke and heat in the center. "*Mehr Wind, mehr Regen,*" the *taverna* owner comments as he serves me the souvlaki and a bottle of resinated wine, "more wind, more rain." A storm is predicted. It would be too ironic, I think, if I could not enter the shrine of the sailor gods because it's closed due to stormy weather. I should have remembered, from my Saos experience, from Homer's works as well, that gods and schedules do not necessarily mix.

Ulysses might have put it even more strongly than that.

ONE OF THE EARLIEST PIECES of evidence that proves humans had invented navigational techniques at a given point in time comes from the southern portion of the sea surrounding Samothrace. Sites in Knossos, on Crete, indicate the island was colonized in the late eighth millennium BC, at a time when Crete was at least sixty miles distant from the mainland. The calculation to make here is the same as one would make for the Manx shearwater: given that people of the period did not know how to sail, and assuming a dugout cannot be paddled any faster than two miles per hour, these colonists must have had to maintain course overnight. The early Cretans found and kept direction using celestial bodies.

Carvings on stone seals from Bronze Age Crete as well as from the island of Thera depict ships carrying a single large sail and following a round celestial object. The sun's east-west course, the steady northern beacon of polar stars, the nightly run of recognizable constellations and planets rising on the eastern horizon and setting in the west, provided sufficient guidance for short voyages out of sight of land. A text in Wenamun, Egypt, written in Aramaic and detailing an Egyptian ship's voyage to the Levant in 1075 BC, mentions using stars to find a latitude that would enable the ship to avoid the "Sea Peoples," presumably one of the many groups of pirates who infested the Mediterranean then.

A passage in Homer's *Odyssey* illustrates the kind of stellar navigation current around 700 BC: "Odysseus hoisted sail and steered skillfully, taking care not to let sleep ambush his eyelids. He observed the Pleiades, and Boötes that sets later, and the Great Bear . . . which always holds its ground . . . and is the only constellation that is spared a plunge in the deep ocean. It was this constellation that the nymph Calypso advised him to keep on his left hand as he sailed." Calypso's island, to judge by the sparse clues in Homer's text, lay somewhere between Sicily and Sardinia. Thus, keeping the northern, polar stars such as the Great Bear on his left ensured Ulysses would hold an easterly course toward Ithaca, and home.

On Thera, the suite of carved images that shows ships following stars also depicts sailing vessels shadowing birds. The practice of deducing proximity of land by tracking seabirds was of long standing. A Mediterranean shearwater, for example, never flew farther than thirty to fifty miles from land while breeding and zoomed back to its nest around sunset, so any sailor spotting it at teatime knew land lay in the direction of the bird's flight. The technique was widespread: a fifth-century BC Hindu text describes how sailors on the Indian Ocean brought birds on long journeys to release later and follow home. This form of navigation is coequal to knowing enough about the aquatic environment to read certain aspects of it like signposts. It's likely that Irish monks, millennia after Noah, followed flights of geese to discover the Faeroe Islands, and Iceland after that.

Norse navigators, like the Greeks, benefited from living on high coasts. Their place cells were attuned to the higher mountains of Norway and Iceland, and they could stay on course for thirty miles on a clear day by sighting backward to a high peak they recognized. For the thousand-mile stretch between Norway and Greenland, however, they relied on other types of local knowledge. When they spotted whales and seabirds feasting in mid ocean they knew they were crossing Iceland's continental shelf, which stretches five hundred miles to the southwest of Iceland and where upwelling currents churn a rich buffet of nutrients to the surface.

In shallower waters experienced mariners could figure out where they were by the sea's depth and the rate at which that depth changed: the gradient of shallowness, in other words. They did this using one of the oldest, simplest, and most efficient maritime tools ever invented. The weighted line is so basic as barely to need explanation: a piece of rope, knotted at intervals to indicate length (usually every fathom, or six feet, equivalent to the length of a man's outstretched arms), with a hunk of rock, lead, or other metal attached at one end. Here is the entire instruction manual for what came to be known as the lead line: Throw the weight over the side, a little ahead of yourself to compensate for the ship's movement, and let the line run through your fingers. When the lead hits bottom and the line is straight up and down, note how many knots have gone out. That is the water's depth. In advanced models, the weight's bottom contained a hollow into which one could jam a wad of sticky stuff, such as pine tar or tallow. A piece of ground would adhere to the stickiness, telling the skipper if the seabed there was made of sand or gravel, seashells or mud.

This was crucial information for a navigator approaching, say, the low-lying Mediterranean coast of Egypt. He had an idea that shore was near because the polar constellation he was using—Ursa Major if he was Greek, Ursa Minor if he was Phoenician (due to millennial wobbles in the Earth's rotation, those stars at the time stood closer to true North than Polaris)— was now four hand's breadths and one finger above the horizon, compared to four hands and two fingers at his northern departure point in Attica or Asia Minor. But perhaps fog had risen and knowing roughly how to figure his latitude was not enough. So he cast the lead line, which showed twelve fathoms, growing shallower by a fathom with every turn of the hourglass. He noted that mud had stuck to the bottom of his weight and knew, because of the depth gradient and the muck, he was approaching one of the mouths of the Nile delta, and it was time to strike sail and drift till daybreak. When the sun came up he could employ another innovation, dating at least from the time of Egypt's Old Kingdom. This was the crow's nest, a platform built as high up the mast as possible, from which a lookout could spot terra firma from significantly farther out than he could from the deck of a ship.

THE NIGHT AFTER MY ARRIVAL in Samothrace I am woken by thunder and lightning so loud and bright that through my beachfront windows they seem to unpack the sky into separate components of bright light, utter darkness, huge sound, slabs of obsidian sea. If I were an ancient Greek I would definitely worry about the gods' opinion of my presence here under the loom of Fengari, the "Moon Mountain" from which Poseidon was said to observe the fall of Troy. This was the same sea god who, according to Homer, adopted Samothrace as his pet island. He sent storms and wind to confuse Ulysses' navigation, sink his ships, kill off his crewmen, and lengthen to ten years a voyage that should have taken a week.

At daybreak the wind, as predicted by my *taverna*-keeper, is blowing harder than yesterday. Though the storm still drives from the south, the visual effects seem no different from those of a northern gale that forced Ulysses to seek shelter, perhaps on Samothrace itself, after visiting the Cicones: "Zeus, who corrals the storm clouds . . . ordered the north wind to hide land and sea with thunder and storm; and from the heavens darkness drove down upon us." On the northern, lee side of the island we get more of a vortex effect, rain lashing from different directions down the neck of my canvas jacket. The sky is dark as evening. The school bus is long gone and a solitary taxi stand is empty of cabs, though the occasional hack hisses through puddles on the promenade; the drivers, when they see me waiting, immediately accelerate and disappear toward the ferry dock. Finally I spot one stopped at an intersection well down the seafront. I gallop after it and open the passenger door before the shocked driver has time to speed away.

We arrive at Paleopolis fifteen minutes later. I pay my fee at the gatehouse and make my way up an uneven path to the entrance.

The shrine of the *megaloi theoi,* the great gods, is built in a ravine that connects mountains to shore. Three streams flow down the ravine from the steep flanks of Saint George Mountain. Saint George in turn is a stepchild of Mount Fengari, shoving its head and shoulders into storm wrack to the south. The trinity of streams might have significance: an ancient Anatolian rite consists of plowing three initial furrows, mimicking the triangle of a woman's sex, to ensure fertility. This shrine's myth of origins is definitely female. Myrina, queen of the Amazons, supposedly was shipwrecked at this desolate place and declared it sacred in gratitude to the Great Mother who saved her from drowning. Whatever the truth of the Amazon legend, the Great Mother here became associated with a Phrygian fertility goddess named Axeiros, the "mother of rocks." Gods, like humans, have their pecking order, and next in line after Axeiros stood the deities who most concerned sailors: the Dioskuri twins, Dardanos and Eëtion.

I slog uphill, splashing south along steep, rock-strewn, pud-
dled paths that cross the various streams and braid their way
toward the shrine's apex. The paths follow rough walls of por-
phyry, a gray stone larded with cubes of pink mineral. Grassy
terraces bear ruins of volcanic rock and marble. The smashed
temples, shrines, and amphitheaters of the cult are separated
by olive or juniper trees, or bushes, the kind of waist-high
scrub known in France as *garrigue*. It's all half-wild, unkempt.
Five marble columns, obviously rebuilt, focus the V of valley
against mist and storm and when the clouds part a little, a
darker sheen of sea to the north. Wind and rain, like an amateur watercolorist, blur the hues of everything, rocks, olive
leaves, sea, to a silvery version of their original green, brown,
and blue-gray. Goats bleat from the hillside above and a distant shepherd, bearing a crook and a baseball cap, pretends I am
not here. In fact no one is here, no one but me and the shepherd and the rain and the gods.

I think—soaked to my foundations, still clambering and
slipping on the rocks—that if this place has power it lies in a
gathering together of everything around, clouds, streams, sea,
and what people built here by hand; as if the various forces
were meant to be part of one another, the kind of syncretism
whereby fertility became a feature of sea as the sea moves
monthly within woman.

The Dioskuri were Phrygian, as well. Dardanos and
Eëtion were associated with Saint Elmo's fire, the electrical
charge that plays ghostly on ships' rigging during thunderstorms; and also with metals, particularly magnetic rocks. If
you came here to undergo the secret rites and become an ini-

tiate, if you made the right offerings of fishhooks and seashells and other gifts, they would protect you from shipwreck, back up your navigation, and guarantee safe harbor.

I skirt one set of ruins, where the first stage of rites in the Dioskuri's mystery cult took place, and enter another: the *hieron*. Here the rites were said to culminate.

This is a rectangular temple, or what remains of it. At its southern tip is a square, sunken area, with a large flat stone on the north rim. In the middle of that stone a hole opens into a pit.

The rites of the Dioskuri, archeologists believe, were creepy as a cheap horror movie. They took place at night in the light of torches reeking, smoking, and flickering in whatever wind blew along the ravine. Those seeking help in navigation had first to undergo ritual bathing and purification. As part of the introductory process the priests dressed them in white robes, handed out lamps, and led them through the gloom to a special chamber where the cult's first secrets were divulged. The graduates of this stage were given rings of magnetized metal, probably fashioned from veins of magnetite that run through the ravine's rocky outcrops, to symbolize their passage.

The rite's next phase must have been tougher, since only a tiny percentage of people who passed the first stage went on to become second-degree initiates, or *epoptai*. Archeologists speculate that a giant torch was lit at the northern end of this temple, and in its light the candidate was harshly interrogated by masked priests and forced to confess all sins and impurities. After that he or she—for unlike other mystery cults the

Samothracian rite allowed everyone, including women, children, and slaves to participate—made a sacrifice to the gods and was led to this pit by which I stand on the southern end of the *hieron*. Back then this was a sunken grotto, a working model of hell. It was here that the climax of this ritual of catharsis and confession took place. Here, in loose earth under the pierced stone, I dig a small hole, finding a small spindle-shaped shell of the type initiates used to offer to the Dioskuri. I pocket the shell and bury my field compass in the hole as an offering to the gods of navigation.

And in this temple I make my own confession, silently explaining to the storm and stones why I am really here.

TO LEARN ABOUT THE HISTORY of ancient navigation by experiencing storm and stones at the epicenter of its one avowedly navigational cult is not the only reason I came to Samothrace. I've been hoping, as well, to find evidence for a continuation of this cult, a secret society of navigators who passed on the incunabula of their trade to other members around the Mediterranean: a guild that might even have survived into modern times.

Myriad themes in the history of Mediterranean navigation suggest a link between secrecy, occult groups, and navigational discovery. One revolves around the discovery of the magnetic compass. The Samothracian mysteries emphasized the Dioskuri's association with magnetic minerals, the wearing of magnetized rings by initiates, the related themes of metal-working and underworld. Although Homer concentrates on navigation by stars and dead reckoning, one passage in his epic hints at a lodestone used to direct navigation in the war against Phrygian Troy. If this is true, it would mean a form of compass appeared in the Mediterranean two millennia before the late 1100s, when first such a device was mentioned in Western texts. Alexandrians in the second century AD used lodestones as a form of divination, moving magnets around to attract toy ships, with iron chips attached, in basins full of water. They also employed magnets in a mystical transcription ritual associated with the original compass rose. The Chinese knew lodestones pointed north as early as the twelfth century, but no link has ever surfaced to prove this discovery made it to the Greco-Roman world. Some scholars believe the maritime compass appeared in the Mediterranean spontaneously, possibly in Amalfi.

Secrecy in related arts was necessitated by Christianity's fierce doctrinal condemnation of Greek astronomy along with other "pagan" sciences, as the religion spread to Rome and eventually stifled Europe under the mantle of its bleak, lethal prejudices during the Dark and Middle Ages. Scientific knowledge was seen as the work of Satan, the same demon who manifested himself in metals, blacksmithing, and alchemy.

And so with the ascendance of Christianity, the knowledge of the ancients went underground. Those who would not abandon such dark arts were forced to find refuge in the forbidden world of pagan sects and other apostates: heretical Nestorians (many of whom were descended from Phoenician navigators); Saracen scribes and Egyptian Muslims who translated into Arabic the works of Greek philosophers; and

Jewish scholars, persecuted in Europe but tolerated under the Muslim caliphates, who translated first-century Alexandrian texts into Arabic and Hebrew. The transmission of Greek thought from sect to cabal flashed like a sparking arc of curiosity against the shadowed crypts of Rome and her inquisitors.

It took centuries to shake the clamp of bigotry off scientific thought. Eventually, the early European Renaissance, with its renewed interest in the classics, allowed survivors of Rome's Inquisition to leave the shadows, and Hellenic science came with them. Knots of heretical scholars, in particular Jewish gnostics (some of whom nurtured links to the neo-gnostic Albigensian heresy), bobbed up like flotsam as the Islamic tide receded. Thinkers such as Abraham Zacuto tethered the sun's altitude at different times of year to specific distances from the equator and refined instruments like the astrolabe, the better to gauge the altitude of planetary bodies. This knowledge was adopted by explorers who sailed out of Spain and Portugal, allowing their ships to be guided with fair accuracy to a point along the axial line of Africa's western coast. From there they could cross the Atlantic on a given latitude by adjusting course so that the sun at noon always stayed at the same height, as indicated by their tables.

The lodestone compass came into more frequent use by the fifteenth century. Marine charts, called "portolans": the first maps to include scale, distance, and compass directions, and with them some pretense at exactitude; appeared more frequently among ships' inventories. Coastal pilots or "routiers" listing landmarks and other features likely to trigger place cells, along with lunar tables to predict tides, gradually took the place of folklore and sailors' gossip. A peculiarly hybrid figure, a navigator/astronomer/ astrologer—almost a wizard in those multiple arts—appeared on ships such as a galley described by the monk Faber that sailed from Germany to the Holy Land in the fifteenth century. Powerful men in Madrid, Lisbon, Paris, and London took note of the strategic importance of spatial skills in establishing overseas empires. They founded navigational academies, of which Amerigo Vespucci's in Seville was the first, and bribed foreign navigators to leave their homelands and reveal their secrets.

Yet despite the increased precision the Renaissance brought in its train, navigation was not to achieve significant breakthrough until the start of the Industrial Revolution. Time and its measurement posed a major problem. Time is one of the three legs on which dead reckoning stands, but a rough version suffices for most trips; navigators through the seventeenth century measured it with an hourglass, calculating speed by how long it took a chunk of wood (a "log") to travel the ship's length, and applying that number to the distance their routier told them they should travel. And one did not need to know precise time to measure the sun's altitude at midday, since our star marks its own noon by not rising any higher.

To get a precise fix, however: to liberate himself from the clumsiness of latitude sailing, a navigator needed a second bearing, another line to intersect the east-west arc. With stars and planets that had no noon but changed position day by day as Earth wheeled around the sun, one required tables that defined their altitude at an exact point in time. In the fourteenth to seventeenth centuries, as in Ptolemy's day, the theory of longitude was known, but no precise timekeeping instruments existed. Clocks were rude and inaccurate. (A method of determining time by measuring the moon's apparent distance from stars existed before the eighteenth century, but it was abstruse and inconsistent.) Ships' masters continued to rely on lead line and landmarks to a far greater extent than they did on solar altitude. For all the incremental progress in determining latitude and using compasses, navigation in the Renaissance was still based on techniques Ulysses would easily have recognized.

A good example of this is Bjarni Herjólfsson, the first European in recorded history to discover the American continent. While familiar with the concept of correlating latitude to the sun's height, Herjólfsson mostly relied on dead reckoning, landmarks, and the kind of star steering Ulysses employed in order to find his way from Iceland to his father's farm in Greenland, four centuries before Columbus. He ran into Canada by accident, the way Ulysses discovered Circe's island, after getting disoriented in fog. He was then blown off course by a type of snowstorm the sagas referred to as "white-bearded devil." He missed Greenland entirely.

Herjólfsson's experience, and the subsequent Norse colonization of Vinland, are probably typical of human colonization everywhere. When eventually he made it back to Norway, Herjólfsson told everyone a colorful, if factually thin, story of his adventures and the nine days it took to sail from this new territory back to Greenland. Leif Erikson, excited by

Herjólfsson's tale of virgin lands, tried to follow those directions and stumbled upon Newfoundland. Those five stages—
forsaking familiar territory, accidental discovery, return,
telling the story, and embarking on a new expedition—
probably represent the very archetype of human exploration,
from *Homo erectus*'s day to the present.

The novelist and storyteller in me is tempted to emulate
Herjólfsson and spin a yarn. And it's true, the association of
heretical groups with navigational science is strong. But despite many months of research I have found no solid evidence
to prove that thinkers and navigators were linked in a single
guild, much less that it lasted beyond the Middle Ages.

I LEAVE THE *HIERON*. Now I'm looking for the rock that was
the umbilicus of this shrine, the original Phrygian altar to
Axeiros. Clambering down a rain-slicked wall I slip and tumble three feet to land butt-first in a muddy puddle. If I were
not already drenched, the puddle would have finished the job.
As I pick myself, dripping, out of the water, I realize I have
found it, a reddish-black boulder the size of a small refrigera-
tor stuck in this grassy terrace just north of the *hieron*. A sign
reads, helpfully, "Rock Altar." As if that were not indication
enough, someone has raised a cairn of small stones on its crest,
an offering to the gods perhaps, a shrine within the shrine.
I stare at the cairn, wondering wildly if this means the cult
really does exist and people come here unnoticed to reconse-
crate its core. Then, carefully, I add a stone to the pile.

I stop by the museum and talk to the guards. They know nothing about the cairn or who might have put it there. They are not particularly friendly. It's possible their English is so poor that they don't understand my questions to begin with.

JUST BEFORE CLOSING TIME I leave the shrine and hitch a ride back to Kamariótissa with the school bus as it completes its homeward run. The storm is still blowing full force. A medium-sized freighter has anchored for shelter in the island's lee. Tall clouds tumble from the south, snagging their dark train on Fengari's summit. They grump in the language of thunder and toss rain around in volleys. To the northwest the waves are high and fringed with white. I wonder if the ferry will sail tomorrow.

That night I return to the *taverna* for more souvlaki. Retsina animates the shadows and stories therein. With storm slatting the terrace's sides, sucking smoke from the woodstove, with the men sitting around and muttering darkly, it does not require much effort to imagine myself tempest-bound; marooned, like Ulysses, by a pissed-off Poseidon stirring up mischief on the slopes above.

Then *Saos II* appears out of the night, from the east, her high blue hull ablaze with lights. She slows and turns to anchor in the tiny harbor, and I raise a glass to my ship out.

CHAPTER SIX

The "Exploration" Gene

When I return to the Cape, winter has clamped its Doberman jaws cruelly on the seashore. The bays are freezing up, a white drool of ice oozes from the salt marsh. As I resume my research it seems right to be in this house in winter, with a print of the *Stavanger Paquet* and my grandfather's library of books on Arctic exploration and the pictures of Norwegian polar explorers whom Pop counted among his friends.

These men catalyzed some of our legends growing up. My mother used to recount how Roald Amundsen, the first person to sail a boat through the Northwest Passage and who in 1911 was first to reach the South Pole, held her on his lap in this house to tell stories of his life and travels. He also told her that as a kid he kept all windows open in his bedroom, right through a Norwegian winter, to toughen himself for what he knew he must do later on. At one point in my own adolescence I used to keep my bedroom window open in winter and take cold showers in the morning to emulate him; a practice that clashed with the lazy, self-indulgent side of my nature and did not last long.

Amundsen's mentor, Fridjof Nansen, spent more time with my grandparents, due in part to a passion he shared with my grandfather for printmaking, an art at which both excelled. Frederic Michelsen's etchings of ice-skaters and skiers, of docks in Maine and boats swinging to anchor in a fog near those docks, are displayed throughout our house. One hangs next to Nansen's etching of *Fram,* a vessel the latter loaned, somewhat reluctantly because he had longed to find the South Pole himself, to Amundsen. That picture shows the ship trapped by ice in the Arctic, observed in the foreground by a bemused polar bear. Nansen tried to reach the North Pole first by allowing *Fram,* which was massively built to survive ice pressures, to be locked in a position from which the frozen pack, circling counterclockwise around the Arctic Sea, would carry his ship near the pole. The theory was not wrong, just inexact. The ship did not come close, so Nansen and a companion set off on skis for ninety degrees north, finding their way with sextant and chronometer.

The Arctic summer was drawing to a close by then. Running short of both daylight and supplies they turned back and skied south across the ice pack to an island off northern Russia. There both men spent the winter in a home-made stone hut, living off seal and melted snow.

These tales fill me with wonder and insecurity. I don't think I could spend a week bundled in my sleeping bag in a snow-covered hut, eating blubber and drinking snowmelt, without sinking into profound depression. And an entire winter with only a Norwegian for company? I like my Norwegian brethren but they are not renowned for their airy joie de vivre or vaudevillian sense of humor. I am sure, lacking someone with whom to goof off occasionally, the endless dark would affect me to the point where, like Robert Scott's lieutenant, Oates, I would soon tell my companion, "I am just going outside and might be some time."

Clearly I am not the stuff explorers are made of. I mentioned earlier the theory that life equals movement equals navigation. I believe now there's another facet to this equation, one that is implied in the history but which I didn't pick up on in Samothrace. Human navigation, as it developed, was based not only on understanding the environment in which we moved; the process of it required also being *unsure* of where we were. This still holds true. There is no point in navigating if you've been told where you are and where you're going, without the slightest risk of getting lost. It was this aspect of the art—getting lost and possibly losing your life in the process—that was the central narrative line of Homer's *Odyssey*. It was the associated stress that initiates to the Samothrace rites sought to palliate because they did not have the technology (which assuredly they would have welcomed) to reduce movement to touring territory every detail of which has been pinpointed by others and presented in graphically pleasing format to the traveler.

The shades of Nansen and Amundsen must have something to do with this line of thought. I hunker in the kitchen of my grandparents' house, the only room I can afford to heat to livable temperature when the mercury sinks below twenty degrees. Obsessively, I measure distances between Espevaer and Grøtfjord where, according to the Stavanger Sjøfarts-museum, Halvor picked up his cargo of fish. I make research forays into the wilderness of Internet while Fridjof's visage, strong-nosed, bearing a white walrus moustache, stares disapprovingly from an etched self-portrait as if to say, "I wouldn't have wanted you on my expedition either." Seven hundred miles from Stavanger to Grøtfjord, in winter! What if I, for psychological reasons, simply am not equipped for stressful navigation? A reference on the National Geographic Society Web site to something called "the exploration gene" deepens my self-doubt.

The "exploration gene"—DRD4-7R—is an allele, a component of the human genome. Researchers trying to trace the history of human migration by figuring out what genes ended up in which population have correlated DRD4-7R to ethnic groups that tend to travel farther, push beyond conventional boundaries, presumably on the leading edge of a migration. These groups include the Ariaal tribe in Kenya and possibly the French trappers and voyageurs who were the first Europeans to explore much of North America. In the long run-on sentence that is the human genome, or so the theory goes, it's this clause that makes those who possess it less frightened of getting lost, more apt to travel beyond the next horizon and figure out where they are once they get there.

. . .

I TELEPHONE KENNETH KIDD at Yale University, one of the trailblazers in DRD4-7R research, who assures me that the correlation is far too vague to make simplistic assumptions such as "if you have this gene you will explore unknown territory." It is mostly useful, he says, as a tracer to show what populations migrated where at a time when our planet was not wholly settled.

I understand what Professor Kidd is saying but something inside me is not convinced. Outside this house it feels like the Ice Age, when groups of hunter-gatherers trudged over the Bering Strait from Siberia, braving cold and fear to settle this continent. Snow is building, soaking up all that is not blue or white or the snot green of sea. No wind blows, the flakes tumble as straight and glum as dashed hopes. I dress in ski clothes and rubber boots and push a kayak down to the shoreline, riding it like a sleigh down a snowy slope to the beach. Once aboard only basic, instinctive navigation is required to paddle along the line of coast, westward. I am a funambulist toeing a wire between cold, dark water, white shoreline, the nacreous glint of sky. The tide is on its way out, it floats pancakes of ice from bay to ocean. When I reach the harbor breakwater and turn west the ice grows thicker, forming very thin, soft floes the size of tables through which my kayak slices with ease. In between floes the water is soupy with frozen particles that I know, from a boyhood spent browsing those tomes on Arctic exploration, are known collectively as "brash." The kayak makes a hissing sound as it moves through the brash, which changes to a soft munching when we break apart pancake floes.

As I penetrate deeper into West Bay, fighting the thrust of tide, the floes fatten and grow closer, platelets of white clotting over an indigo wound. Finally it takes too much effort to paddle and pole my way into the thickening pack. When I quit paddling the kayak stops dead, gripped by the friction of ice; it feels as if I had hit the brakes. And everything goes still, for there is no one around on land or sea: no fishing boats, yachts, airplanes, no gardeners or beach walkers, no leaf blowers, no revelers in summer houses.

It is as quiet as an empty page.

I love ice kayaking. I love the feel of being in the middle of this bay surrounded by pleasure palaces of a resort community, as isolated and alone as if I were in the deep Arctic. I'm aware that my pleasure is prismed, if only subconsciously, by the illusion of doing something akin to what men like Amundsen and Nansen, Frobisher and the voyageurs once did.

It seems logical to me that some population groups; possibly through natural selection, through some crapshoot iteration of the genetic code, certainly mediated by complex cultural factors; must possess a greater predisposition to exploring farther afield than others. And by association, since going into the unknown and surviving implies better-than-average ability to figure out where you are, they probably enjoy a greater talent for the dark art of navigation. Whether it's genetic or not, I reflect, everyone most likely possesses some version of that navigational rheostat, a gearing that correlates to appetite and aptitude and whose setting, high or low, nudges one away from or toward the event horizon of unknown space.

By such a definition, if your navigational rheostat has a high setting, you are more likely to go hiking or sailing in places that are not signposted. If it's set low, like Melville's Bartleby you'd prefer not to.

I wonder what the Michelsens' navigational rheostat looks like. What it feels like is a relatively high appetite for slightly risky navigation, for kayaking without a life jacket in a half-frozen bay. Given my ancestors' survival record—given my own mistakes—the high-ish appetite would be paired with a low-ish aptitude.

If zero is nil aptitude and ten the highest, were appetite to be measured on the same scale, I'd guess the Michelsens would rate maybe three in aptitude and six or seven in appetite, with a combined rheostat setting of four to five.

AFTER RETURNING FROM THE KAYAK ride I light a fire in the Viking fireplace to warm up. I am still thinking along the lines of low rheostat settings and what they might imply. And so the *Tower Helen* comes to mind.

She was a five hundred–ton coastal freighter of the Tower Shipping company of London, England. The *Helen* sailed short-handed with a crew of four: her captain was Rick Parcell. I was mate, aged twenty-one, a year out of university; I had lied about my sea time to score a job as officer.

We were traveling south along the east coast of England

with a cargo of zinc ingots. Everyone else was asleep below. I was on watch, navigating visually, using as reference points only the buoys and lighthouses dotting the coast, taking compass bearings to figure out where I was and what course I should plot to complete our run to the Thames. Cocky and sure of my abilities, I had switched off the ship's Decca position-finding system, a local forerunner of GPS. But somewhere in the process of navigating I mistook one lighthouse for another and drew in our position using the wrong landmark. Half an hour after making the initial mistake, I realized a buoy had not showed up when it should have. I went back to the chart and checked my dead reckoning. It indicated, if I ignored the dubious landmark, that we had traveled farther south than I had thought. When I looked at the radar screen the outline of coast had altered in a way that made no sense. I realized I had no idea where I was. My stomach turned, my breath grew short; for a few seconds my mind seemed to freeze. The *Tower Helen,* her crew of four, and her zinc ingots were barreling at eleven knots into the unknown.

Then my shock subsided, and I switched on the Decca. The cross-bearing it gave proved I had badly overshot the buoy I was aiming for: *Tower Helen* was a mile and change away from Goodwin Sands, which is an English version of Nantucket Shoals. I turned the ship, plotted a new course, and eventually piloted us back to where we should be. The skipper never realized what had happened. But I never forgot the mistake I made then. The memory of the panic I felt, when I realized the ship and crew for which I was responsible were lost, never

entirely left me and must have informed the fear I felt in a
similar situation off Martha's Vineyard.

The fire dies down. Blue thoughts tend to summon their
like, and here is another. A guy like Halvor, with a regulator
setting of four or five, might have preferred sticking to the
coast as opposed to running much riskier voyages well offshore. But Halvor nevertheless managed a 1,400-mile round-
trip to Grøtfjord, well north of the Arctic Circle, in the heart
of winter.

I open the laptop and consult Google Earth, enjoying as I
always do the dizzying virtual zoom into the planet's topography. Seven hundred miles in a northerly direction from Cape
Cod would put me off the south coast of Newfoundland, an
area which, while poetically appropriate for a descendant of
the first Europeans to find it, is not the coziest place to sail
in this season. Icebergs calving off the Greenland coast, for
example, might be an issue.

When I reenter *Paquet*'s loading port on Google Earth,
however, the program spits up a different "Grøt" in its index
box. This one, "Grøtle," is much, much closer to Halvor's
home: only forty-odd miles to the east of Espevaer, in the sheltered waters of Vikafjord. The name is slightly different, of
course, from the one Bang-Andersen at the Stavanger seafaring museum sent me. And the dour Norwegian side of me is
inclined to doubt such felicitous revision.

An Internet search turns up nothing about this second
"Grøt" except for one, quite relevant document: a clipping
from *Fisketsgang,* a fishing industry journal from the early

twentieth century, listing landings from herring boats in a series of south Norwegian coastal ports grouped by proximity. "Grøtlefjorden," presumably the fjord next to Grøtle, is included in the same paragraph as Haugesund, which lies just south of Espevaer. Landings from Espevaer itself are described a couple of lines lower.

This new, very suggestive fact changes everything. It certainly seems to make more sense: whether or not the northern "Grøtfjord" is free of ice in February, it's unlikely on the face of it that a herring fishery would be in full swing there in the near-permanent night of an Arctic winter. If Halvor Michelsen picked up a cargo of herring from local boats, on the other hand, he'd only have needed to travel forty miles to get out of Grøtle and Vikafjord, plus another forty to Stavanger. The Stavanger museum apparently had no information about the cargo's destination but if *Paquet* was traveling her usual route to Germany, Halvor would have sailed west at first to clear the fjord then turned south for Hamburg—or for Stavanger, which from Vikafjord lies in the same direction.

I shut down the laptop. It's cowardly, I know, but a wash of relief floods me. If the Grøtle scenario checks out, to duplicate Halvor's voyage between his loading port and Stavanger means I'd only have to sail eighty miles. Cape Cod to southern Maine, for example, is roughly 70 miles; to Isle au Haut and the Midcoast, 120. Of course 120 or even 70 miles can be risky if a storm blows up, if I get lost. Even if I brush up on my stellar navigation techniques I will be at the mercy of fog, of enduring overcast, which would render navigation by celestial objects impossible.

And if I fuck up, if the wind blows hard, I will have as lee shore the coast of Maine, which is just as rich in rocks as Espevaer.

For now though, with darkness drawing winding sheets of purple across the windows and snow still piling up outside, with the thermometer dropping further, and an easterly wind starting to hum corny folk songs of loneliness in the frozen eaves, I am not unhappy to contemplate a shorter voyage. I stoke the fire, observed by the portrait of old Fridjof, who as usual seems thoroughly unamused.

CHAPTER SEVEN

Adventures in the GPS Trade

My next few days are spent planning the trip I might take on *Odyssey* to mimic the final voyage of Halvor. I base those plans partly on this new information, the proximity of Grøtle and Vikafjord to the island where the *Paquet* sank. I go back and forth between Google Earth and my old, tomato-hued edition of the *Times Atlas of the World*. Each has advantages and disadvantages. Google allows me to zoom down on the fractal coastline, though when I pull away, as if riding a rocket launched from Norway, it greatly loses definition. When I click to open the filter, the screen clots with icons full of irrelevant information and snapshots of indifferent quality.

The atlas cannot zoom down or provide such large scale, but it does offer a clearer, broader, and more visually attractive overview of the region. The trade-off between interactive immediacy and a cartographic tradition that over centuries has subtly balanced detail and context seems significant in ways I don't fully understand.

I wish I had maritime charts of the south Norwegian coast, but the nearest place I could easily consult such charts is King's Point, the federal merchant marine academy in New York. Still, between atlas maps and Google Earth's distance finder, I can deduce that for part of the trip, in decent weather at least, Halvor would have been sailing through fjords or close enough to a coastline to identify landmarks. And I remember the importance, in Viking navigation, of back-bearings on the mountainous terrain those sea raiders came from.

One aspect of this navigational puzzle remains confusing. Espevaer's archipelago lies roughly three miles to the north of the entrance to Vikafjord, in the opposite direction from Stavanger or Hamburg. This discrepancy might be explained if the storm blew from the south and *Paquet* got into trouble, her cargo shifting, perhaps, as family lore indicates, and was pushed northward. It's also possible that Halvor, in order to avoid Espevaer and its attendant rocks, as well as a mess of islets to the south of Vikafjord, might have headed straight out to sea. Maybe he noticed the storm clouds too late, when he was not within easy reach of a safe harbor on the mainland in which to anchor. If that was the case, as a prudent navigator his next course of action would have been to gain sea room: steer well offshore and avoid the narrow, rock-strewn passage between islands and mainland and other hazards against which wind and waves might throw him.

Such a dogleg could have lengthened his trip and brought

him out of sight of land until the snowstorm, perhaps the same "white-bearded devil" of a gale that blew Bjarni Herjólfsson off course, slammed down over *Paquet* and finally pushed him toward Espevaer. That kind of storm, most likely, would have veiled the sky and made it impossible to check his position by measuring the altitude of sun or stars with a sextant.

Midway through this process of plotting and imagining I receive another e-mail from Gry Bang-Andersen at the Stavanger Maritime Museum. After warning me that she is taking maternity leave, and I should refer further queries to Harald Hamre, the museum's chief historian, Gry writes: "I agree that as the ship sank by Espevær . . . it sounds likely that it has been going to Grøtle (near Vikafjord). Grøtlefjorden might have been an older name/other name of the fjord, no longer in use." I smile as I read Gry's message, for it seems to confirm me in my navigational cowardice: I will not have to sail into Arctic waters to model Halvor's trip.

Given this new information, an offshore passage from Cape Cod to Midcoast Maine will likely take quite a bit longer and lead me farther from land than Halvor's last voyage from Grøtle to Espevaer. But I decide to stick to that idea. By completing an offshore trip of some 120 miles, I will mimic the kind of longer voyage my ancestor routinely made from southern Norway to Germany. I figure the higher risk of going well offshore might compensate to some extent for the lesser peril involved in sailing in spring or summer as opposed to the bleak and cold of February.

I will need charts for the Maine trip. Those at least should be available locally. I drive to a marine supply supermarket in the nearest town. It's a quiet time of year in the nautical trades, in Hyannis generally. Three salesmen strain to look busy. A bespectacled, officious young man hurries to greet me as I walk in. "I'm looking for a sailing chart of the Gulf of Maine," I tell him, and he leads me to a section of the store bearing multiple electronic screens. "We've got C-Map, Navionics, you can buy the entire US or just regional—"

"No, no," I interrupt, "I'm looking for *paper* charts." He stares at me incredulously, the first shoots of a patronizing smile sprouting from the loamy valley of his lips. I cringe, half expecting him to summon the idle salespeople, yelling, "Hey Jack! Maureen! You'll never believe this, I got a guy here wants a *paper* chart!" He spares me that humiliation, but the patronizing look deepens as he says, with forced tolerance, "Of course it's safer to have a paper chart aboard as backup, but no one uses those much anymore; it's all electronic, all GPS. You can order them," he continues in a tone one might use to suggest that farriers and crossbow repairmen still ply their trade somewhere, his eyes now shifting to the store's entrance from which a profitable client might yet emerge, "but we don't carry what you're looking for."

Once home, an Internet search reveals that the National Oceanic and Atmospheric Administration, which used to print maritime charts, no longer does so. A depressing number of Web sites, such as frazzleberries.com and nauticaldecorstore .com, offer disused NOAA charts for decorating the den. However other online outfits do print up-to-date NOAA material, and I order the Gulf of Maine chart and a separate book of charts covering coastal waters from Block Island to the Canadian border. All are listed as providing GPS-specific data and waypoints, reinforcing the Pleistocene feeling I got earlier while talking to the marine store guy. And part of me, perhaps the navigationally timid Michelsen side, asks, why insist on using such obsolete tools? Why not just do the damn trip with GPS and tablet like everyone else, tracking my way across the gulf with ease and a precision such that I could, if I wanted, phone in my GPS coordinates and get a pizza airdropped into the boat's cockpit, were Domino's delivering pie by drone?

IT'S CERTAINLY TRUE THAT, in the two decades since they became readily available, global positioning satellite systems have transformed our lives to the point where most people find it inconceivable that one might reject them for any reason. I used to argue about GPS with my brother, who was my most constant sailing companion on *Odyssey*'s trips around Nantucket Sound. Louis loved gadgets and viewed my fixation on honing older navigational skills with a loving tolerance, as one might humor a relative who is a fanatical War of 1812 reenactor. I own a handheld GPS, but I bought it to check the accuracy of my compass or verify speed as I sailed; I never use it for position. Louis, on the other hand, had not one but two late-model GPS receivers in his car. And in the evening of the day I was humiliated in the marine store, realizing that at some point I'll have to forsake my navigational purism and examine more closely how this technology functions, I start searching for his devices.

There is no moon, the sky is overcast. I walk unhesitatingly through darkness from the main house toward the garage where Louis kept automobile equipment, recognizing the textures of this land under my feet: grass, dirt driveway, broken clamshells, dead leaves. Skirting a trio of hollies, a small vegetable garden, I pass the great pale shadow of *Odyssey* where she looms next to the garage. A bird in the hollies, disturbed by my passage, emits an irritated squawk. I find an Ikea tote bag filled with bottles of oil and brake fluid, but my recall has slipped; Louis did not store GPS units there.

Back in the house, I climb the stairs to his room—in darkness also, because to lower expenses, I keep lights off everywhere except in the kitchen and whatever bedrooms are in use. I search through his desk, also to no avail. I am fighting not to think too much about my brother right now because it is late and I am tired, which means some of my emotional levees have cracked and the fact that less than a year ago he was still alive feels like a big river rising past flood stage in my chest. To distract myself as I walk through the black hallways toward a storage closet where he might have stashed the device, I imagine how I navigate this house in the dark, using what experts in perception call my cognitive map.

The term *cognitive map* is somewhat misleading. I don't see a map in my head, or at least not the kind the *Times Atlas* is full of, what the word *map* conjures. For psychologists, the idea of cognitive map covers the same conceptual territory as sense of direction, spatial orientation, even dumb avoidance of obstacles: like remembering to watch out for that step at the entrance to the living room. But if I think of my spatial sense as a fluid, three-dimensional, semi-coded, partly image-based, and overall pretty hazy awareness of where I stand in relation to my people and worlds both near and far—something that I can imagine consciously but that also perdures, like creases in a folded paper which remain visible when the paper's unfolded, even when I'm not thinking about it or when I'm asleep—that "hazy awareness" resonates more with how I feel as I move from room to room in my family's house.

Those same psychologists think of this map as a picture of what we see and also of what we cannot see but know is there. The picture is made possible by two distinct systems: an immediate "direction" frame that organizes the world based on where our eyes are pointing and where our bodies sense they are going at a given instant; and a more abstract "sketch" or dead-reckoning system that focuses on landmarks, visible or not, with which to track where we've been moving, in what direction, and at what speed.

Both systems, researchers say, rely on the use of gradients—a sense of the changing frequency of cues, like that light-to-dark progression of morphogens by which fruit fly cells figure out where to go. They also, of course, use explicit cues, such as a familiar tree or the "south" mark on a compass. All are constantly updated by our senses as we move about. Both make use of place cells as building blocks to construct the cognitive map.

Scientists make a further distinction between active maps—conscious ideas of a world we can describe—and passive maps that include landmarks we only recognize when we catch sight of them. Following this model, we might advise a visitor to

New York to bang a left at a bagel shop we know is on Ninety-Eighth and thus is actively mapped, by us at least. This turns out to be advice she doesn't need because her passive-mapping function suddenly kicked in when she saw a barbecue joint she once frequented on Ninety-Seventh and Broadway, reminding her of where she was.

These notions feel soft to me when I think about them, a wash flowing back and forth in my mind, a tide of brain activity that includes plankton of place and boundary, memories cued by direction and color and vaguer emotions that might be triggered also by place but whose deeper, affective source and destinations are clouded.

I'm not particularly good at this cognitive map stuff. I can make mistakes even walking around my family house, where every salient detail is stained forever into the synaptic quilt of my brain: the banister on the main stairs behind which our mom, as a little girl, spied on her parents' cocktail parties during Prohibition, and where Louis and I sat when, as an older woman, she performed recitals of Chopin and Debussy in the living room; the melodeon we played with when we were kids, and which now doesn't work, that signals I'm halfway down the second-floor hall; the door to my father's room, where my son swears he saw his grandmother appear, dressed in white, years after her death. Even surrounded by these details, which fit the navigational model by which the hippocampus summons a cascade of associations based on details of place, I have to float my hands along the second-floor banister to stay on track, hold my arm stiff in front of me in case I miss the third-floor doorway in the dark. At times I misjudge and stub a toe against a corner that is nearer than my cognitive map said it was or bang my forehead on a dormer I forgot about till pain abruptly updates my spatial memory banks.

WE ALL KNOW OUR SPATIAL map is foggy and far from perfect and that it varies greatly with the individual. Some people are equipped with good directional sense, able to keep heading northeast even among the twisted alleys of an old city like London. Others don't have the haziest notion of north or south, right or left even. Tests suggest that those with good directional ability are expert at updating, consciously or no, their roster of landmarks. Various experiments show that while the average person is able mentally to "map" new environments, she or he tends to balk at revising old ones. This explains the ticket I got at the intersection of Oak Street and Race Lane, which was a "merge" instead of a "stop" all my life until about five years ago and which even today I tend to cruise through, looking for traffic but thinking of something else and ignoring the new red sign.

Folklore, and male stereotypes, insist that men have a better sense of direction than women, but the truth as always is more subtle, and more interesting, than clichés or sexist quips. It's long been established that males on average enjoy marginally better spatial coordination skills than females, while women, perhaps to compensate, are a shade more skilled at the linguistic side of things. And some studies indicate that men have a slightly better sense of direction, but whether this is due to differences in brain physiology or to a culturally self-fulfilling prophecy that insists women are less adept at finding their way around is unclear. Certainly both bias and physiological difference could account, each on its own, for a primal division of labor that assigned homebound child-rearing roles to the mother, which in turn meant the father had to cruise the wilderness searching for mammoth cutlets to feed his family, a task that of necessity involved directional skills.

If that's the case, however, why is the female hippocampus, by most accounts, of proportionately the same size as or slightly larger than the male's? Why does a recent study suggest memory, which as we have seen is largely controlled by the same center as navigation, works more efficiently in women than in men? Research that focuses on specific navigational skills tends to find that genders do not navigate better or worse but differently, as men are more apt to use orientation—cardinal points such as west and east—whereas women prefer sequential routes based on a succession of landmarks. ("I turn left at the Prêt à Manger," Eleanor Maguire told me, "while a man might head 'north' to Southampton Row.") Almost every study on the subject finds that males are measurably more confident about their navigational skills than females but here, too, a culture that assumes men are better navigators than females is guaranteed to generate such a result. In my own experience, those who have an excellent sense of direction, as compared to the general population, are rare and just as likely to be female as male.

What's more interesting to me is the fact, often noted by search-and-rescue experts, that lost hikers who do not hew to the standard advice to stay put until they are found—people, more often men than women (probably because of the self-confidence factor), who fool themselves they can find a way out of wilderness on their own by following this stream, that ridge—tend to walk in a circle, ending up near the place where they first got lost. Sweden, a paternalist society, attributes this trope to an evil female spirit named Skogsnuva, who likes to divert men from the straight and narrow. Amerindians invoke an instinctive need to head home. Various studies have cast doubt on the more prosaic explanation, which is that the human stride marginally favors one leg over the other, resulting in a trajectory that trends left or right.

The gender difference pales compared to cultural variations in navigational ability, for some peoples still navigate as part of daily life the proverbial trackless wastes of sea or desert, managing to orient themselves using what we crudely describe as a sense of direction based on wind, waves, dune and snow patterns, and other natural clues. Individuals from the Saharan Adari tribe, studied by Victor Cornetz, traveled for days across sandscapes that a European would find utterly indistinguishable from each other. Yet the tribesmen knew always where they were and exactly how many days' walk in which direction lay a given oasis.

SUCH SKILLS CLEARLY WILL NOT be honed by using GPS. I keep searching for Louis' devices anyway, in part because of that consciousness I had, even before this quest started, of the importance global positioning satellite systems have acquired in the days of Americans, in the lives of most people in the developed world. And each hour seems to gather new evidence of how pervasive, how crucial, how expeditious a tool this system has become. We use GPS to find our way down city alleys and blue highways across the continent, we rely on it to locate chain stores and espresso joints even in towns that are familiar to us. CIA pilots sitting in Nevada, navigating drones by GPS, fire GPS-guided Hellfire missiles into the cars of jihadis in Yemen. The satellite system guides combine harvesters so perfectly down earthen furrows as they reap corn in Iowa that the machines no longer require an operator. Supertankers cue all systems, navigational and otherwise, to GPS-based programs: so do US power and communications utilities. Global positioning satellites steered the fully automated Google car as it traveled one hundred thousand miles of the western United States without a driver.

The Federal Aviation Administration, which until 2013 guided the eighty-seven thousand flights crisscrossing America daily by bouncing radar waves against their carapace, currently is switching to a system that harvests position data from the plane's GPS transponder and feeds that to a computer system which then generates a 3-D map, far more precise than radar input, of where each aircraft is at any given second. This allows more tightly layered flight paths, quicker landing/takeoff rhythms, and fatter profits for the airline industry.

Eventually, many days after starting my search, in a wooden escritoire in which I throw stuff I don't want to deal with and then (being male) forget about, I finally locate one of Louis'

GPS units. It's a thin rectangle of silvery metal with a screen on one side, manufactured by the Garmin Corporation of Olathe, Kansas.

The next day I hook up the GPS to a twelve-volt outlet in my ancient Jeep Cherokee and start driving around Cape Cod. I do this with the sense of loss that comes from a memory of something gone, someone missed, because the last time I used a GPS it was this one, this little silver box that Louis fastened to a plastic perch on his dashboard, and programmed so that prompts were uttered by a toffee-nosed British female voice he named, with mixed fondness and sarcasm, Imogen. I rode with my brother often in the last four years of his life, on our way to and from the hospitals in Boston and Hyannis where he was being treated; and those rides, in which our affection for and trust in each other were accented by urgency, were flavored in turn by Imogen's stilted diction, her Received Pronunciation of "In tew hundred yawds turn LIHFT on Frunt Street. Preou-ceed one hawf mile tew the round-AY-bout."

For this first GPS trip without my brother I am only traveling seven miles to Hyannis, and Imogen and I immediately clash. She advises, "Left on Pah-*keur* Rewd," whereas I know the village Parker Road leads to will be clogged with work traffic at this hour; an oversight that is not Imo's fault since I don't consult the traffic function, which in any event probably wouldn't pick up on the microlevel tie-up that happens around 9:00 A.M. at the intersection on Main by the post office. When I continue along Seaview Avenue she pauses and then states, "Re-CAL-culating," in a tone of voice I can only describe as huffy. Imo then advises me to turn left onto a road so narrow it becomes a single lane in places, wending its way around golf course, woods, and plot houses to rejoin Seaview farther on. Still avoiding busier roads I steer due east, while Imo now counsels me at every intersection to head north to the state road, where the trip would take much longer because Route 28 is staggered with traffic lights.

Her traffic function, tapped on at the filter menu, doesn't seem to consider Hyannis traffic much of an obstacle, and I suppose she's not wrong about that. But I'd bet good money that I can reach Hyannis faster using the routes I know; just as Derek O'Reilly, when the *Daily Telegraph* staged a race across London between him and a reporter equipped with the latest GPS, beat the satellite-enabled journo by forty minutes on a trip between Regents Park and London Bridge.

On subsequent journeys I start to gain a feel for how Imo's mind works, or rather how Garmin put together its route-finding algorithm. The two guiding principles seem to be, first, a preference for the most direct route as reckoned by distance only; and second, for main roads as opposed to lesser lanes, although obviously the least-distance imperative at times trumps the main-road compulsion. All of which must take the form of settings in code on the order of, $a=b \rightarrow$ no conflict, $a \neq b \rightarrow$ $a > b$; cybernetic ukhazes that feel very distant from the shaded shifts in reasoning and preference of the human mind.

GPS discussion forums list common user mistakes: forgetting to switch out of "pedestrian" mode, for example; but also suggest that the Garmin algorithm tries to avoid left turns, across traffic, in any situation and consistently underestimates driving time on city streets. Participants have suggested fixes, such as including "via" points when the Garmin makes suggestions that are clearly wrong. They counsel working with the unit to ensure it functions properly. (I e-mail and telephone Garmin on several occasions, asking for comment on these problems, but no one responds. Requests to Magellan, TomTom, and Google for information on the algorithm behind their maps software meet a similar fate.)

GPS screwups with far worse consequences than delays on Cape Cod are a staple of Internet "you gotta see this to believe it" posts and slideshows. In England, a truck driver programs "Gibraltar" into his GPS, which then directs him to the nearest south-facing beach; geographically correct but, in the absence of a roll-on roll-off ferry, of little help in practical terms. An Apple Maps glitch directs commuters onto an active runway at Fairbanks Airport in Alaska. Also in Alaska, a driver blindly obeys his version of Imogen as it orders a hard right after leaving the ferry dock and plunges his car into Prince William Sound. A Swiss motorist follows GPS instructions up a road that becomes an Alpine path so narrow and rocky he cannot go forward or backward. Closer to home, a woman in Boston, blindly following instructions from her direction-dispensing gadget, drives her van with kids aboard onto the railroad tracks in Belmont. She sensibly drags out her offspring and abandons the vehicle just before the 9:01 Fitchburg Local converts it to scrap metal.

It's clear that while some GPS mistakes are due to factors built into the technology—high buildings, for example, will mask or distort the satellite signal—most start with glitches in a mapping program that depends, after all, on the fallible humans who plug in its underlying data.

My ongoing road test of Imogen duplicates the problems of the British truck driver. A few weeks later, as I drive from Cape Cod to JFK Airport in New York to pick up my daughter, who is arriving on a flight from France, I switch on Imogen in Fairfield County, Connecticut. She immediately and persistently urges me to follow the most direct route south from Westport to Queens, off Interstate 95 to a local road. Presumably, since no one in his or her right mind would choose Route 1 over I-95 when the latter is free of traffic, she's expecting my Jeep to float across Long Island Sound to the airline terminal. I refuse indignantly, feeling smart and superior—and get my karmic comeuppance a half hour later as traffic clogs on Bruckner Boulevard, and I brake, whereupon a terrible sound emerges from the Jeep's hindquarters, as if someone had emptied a trash bag of shrapnel into each of the car's rear bearings. I pull off at the nearest exit, somewhere in the Bronx. Liz, who has never shared my weakness for old cars, glares at me. Before she can say anything, I cleverly forestall criticism by proclaiming in a loud voice, "That's *it*! We're abandoning this car *here*! We are buying a *new car*! One with a *warranty*!"

Half an hour later I have parked the Cherokee in her final resting place, a street festooned with Puerto Rican flags near Woodlawn Cemetery. Liz and I wait there for forty minutes, trying to find a cab; desperate to reach Manhattan before our daughter arrives at our apartment, for which she has no key, an effort in which we are unsuccessful.

CHAPTER EIGHT

Stellar Screwup

In planning the Halvorian trip I took for granted the part about navigating the way my ancestor did. I've been studying marine navigation in its various forms since I was a kid and always assumed I was adept at its techniques. What geometry I have, I learned in order to accomplish piloting, which requires the fixing of position by taking bearings on known landmarks or measuring angles between.

I also practiced celestial navigation when I was in my twenties on a two-masted yacht belonging to my uncle's company, which made marine hardware. That sailboat—I am struck by this belatedly, a function of how deeply ingrained such stories are in us, that we don't immediately remark such crystalline connections—was named *Paquet III, Paquet II* being his previous boat.

The first *Paquet* was Halvor's ship.

While on the Cape, I assembled books I collected over the years on the subject of celestial navigation. Now in New York, I spread them on top of my mother's old piano and start to reread the theory.

I might be overly influenced by family background, yet I find navigating by sun and moon, planets and stars, an art of abiding elegance. The idea of riding this planet as it zooms, spinning, around the sun, and at the same time being able to find out where we are on the planet's surface by tracing its dance with other celestial objects: the moon orbiting our Earth; the sun, the stars that shift in our sky in relation to both spin and zoom; all reinforce for me the idea of a harmony, a kind of tango in the way our universe works and how we fit into it.

Such harmony and the ability to use it to pinpoint one's position might imply a tiresome predictability. But for me at least, the depth and variety of astronomical knowledge and calculations reinforce the notion that the cosmos is an immensely complex, fascinating, and ever-changing place. Being able, however roughly, to perform stellar navigation when I sailed on *Paquet III* made me feel as if I was for the first time, through being able to read the sheet music, a participant in that cosmic dance.

As I reread the texts, I find the theory of celestial navigation not hard to understand in poetic fashion; it's a theory, as I learned from studying the history, with which the ancients were familiar, in rudimentary form at least. At any point in time, a celestial body will stand at a precise altitude over the horizon for observers located on a discrete arc across Earth's surface. By taking the altitude of another body at the same time and seeing where the two arcs cross, you obtain a point that is your exact position.

This of course is a grade-school explanation. Position on Earth is a cross defined by one's longitude (a line drawn from pole to pole) and one's latitude (a circle parallel to the equator). Ptolemy and others measured the sun's noon altitude as it changed with the seasons then worked those data into tables in which Drake or Vasco da Gama could look up the day, line it up with the sun's altitude for that date, and see how far north of the equator—on what latitude—he stood.

The Greeks, as noted earlier, also figured out the theory of longitude but were stymied by lack of a reliable clock. The calculations needed to solve longitude are abstruse. They require correlating a line that runs from sun, star, or planet to the Earth's center; its angle to two other lines running, respectively, from Earth's center to both "zero" longitude (established by convention in Greenwich, England) and to what the observer thinks is his position at the time the sight is taken. Finally one must use trigonometry to solve the spherical triangle defined by those lines to calculate the theoretical altitude and direction of the celestial body, and from that the arc it defines on Earth.

What all this means in practice is a threefold discipline: First, using a sextant to measure the altitude of, say, the sun, at a precise time; second, correcting that "sight" for the observer's height above sea level and other local distortions. Third, one must compute the difference between measured and theoretical altitudes, using tables compiled by the US and British naval observatories, to find the true "line of position" one's vessel floated upon at the time of shooting.

This last part is by far the most complicated. It's also—and this is no coincidence since I am by nature indolent—the part I have not bothered practicing in a very long time. I study the books I consulted a quarter century ago when I was on *Paquet III*. My memory of the practice is much bound up in a trip from Denmark to an island off Africa on my uncle's ketch, and I remember the discipline seemed straightforward at the time. This was in part due to being mentored by the boat's hired skipper, a South African nicknamed AC, a hereditary peer with a seat in Britain's House of Lords who had thrown over his posh roots to become a hard-drinking, blue-swearing charter captain in the British Virgin Islands. Celestial navigation as taught by AC required great attention to detail and checking and rechecking calculations but otherwise seemed parsecs away from rocket science.

I have drunk many bottles of beer and rum since then, and perhaps my brain has rotted, which would account for the difficulty I now experience in picking up the thread of this forgotten art—an art, at any rate, forgotten by me, and on its way to being forgotten by everyone else. The US Naval Academy, by way of example, eliminated its stellar navigation curriculum in the late 1990s, only to revive a basic course in the subject in 2015; but it is taught as a mere backup in case an enemy should jam satellite systems in wartime. Navy ships—like everything else, it seems—run exclusively on time and space coordinates defined by GPS.

I reread the instructions in my textbooks, growing ever more confused. What principle determines whether or not you subtract the "hour angle" from 360 before computing a line of position? What the hell *is* an hour angle? Why should I draw this sketch all books insist I should attempt that shows, within a circle representing Earth's circumference, the different angles the sun forms to the observer's meridian? I hunch over online astronomical tables, cross out my failed attempts with strokes of black ink that grow thicker and more jagged, and obsessively drag back my hair which, given my balding state, constitutes a terrible habit. I pound the top of my mother's beloved Steinway. My son peeks in to ask if I'm OK.

I search for advice online. Despite the obsolete nature of this pursuit, a number of Web sites exist to coach people through its complexities. Most recommend I download an app that will take the raw numbers of my eventual sextant sight and figure my position with perfect accuracy in less than a second.

I am tempted to do this, of course. And again I ask myself, why shouldn't I perform the "pretend-I'm-Halvor" voyage using GPS? The navigational unknowns of this kind of trip are far less grave than those inherent in taking a small boat out of sight of land. Only the image of my ancestor, clutching his sextant when the sun winked for a moment out of storm wrack, keeps me from giving up: that and the desire to get to the bottom of this discipline we both followed, and through it to the sump of insecurity and panic into which I am dunked when I fail at position finding.

I turn to housekeeping details to take time off from the pitfalls of celestial navigation, as well as to avoid further depleting my hair cover. My sextant is old, a Hezzanith model manufactured by the Heath Company of New Eltham, London, sometime around World War I. It's a beautiful object, a four-pound triangle roughly eight inches wide, made of black-enameled bronze with a movable measuring arc, a sighting telescope, and a battery of mirrors. But the mirrors, which are supposed to swing a celestial object's image to the horizon, measuring its angle to Earth's surface and thus its altitude, are corroded. The only sextant-repair outfit left in the area is the Eldridge White Company of Medfield, near Boston. The owner, Ridge White, says he can get my mirrors resilvered within three weeks.

I order the navigational tables I'll need to work out sextant sights. They come in two volumes published by the US Navy, the *Nautical Almanac* and *Sight Reduction Tables for Air Navigation,* the latter being a tad simpler than the marine version, and of sufficient accuracy for small boats. The navy is out of stock, but commercial firms offer the same texts, photocopied, at half the price.

My time on Samothrace, in retrospect, was powerful: the discipline of imagining how the ancients navigated, in a place where that skill was most revered, has got me thinking about contemporary cultures whose mariners sail the same way. I recall, from talking to Seth Rolbein, an old friend and comrade in the journalism game, who has been traveling to Haiti for decades, that most Haitian sailors navigate without GPS. Indeed, they mostly use sloops similar to Halvor's for island cargo traffic and own no technology but sun and stars. Seth gives me the Internet address of Marco Pierre, a friend in Port-au-Prince. I send Marco an e-mail and receive no reply.

I recently learned that, despite my long history of attending antigovernment rallies, I passed the security check that clears the way for renewal of my Coast Guard license and, eventually, for renting a boat with which to find the grave site of *Stavanger Paquet*. While I'm at it I apply to the air force for the security clearance required to visit Schriever Air Force Base, the control center for America's GPS system. My experience using Louis' Garmin has made me aware of a paradox: although the power, influence, and attraction of GPS are so great and growing so fast, no one I talk to has any real idea of how the system works or of how these satellites that navigate us are themselves navigated in space.

Sex and Navigation

Losing my Jeep hurts. I loved that car, the high and wide of its front seat, the roar and power, if not the mileage, of its V8; the smell of old jalopies, which tend to hang on to flavors of lube oil and mold, of stale beer and teenage sex, of all the long, lazy miles of this country. From now on, the sight and sound of the Bruckner Expressway will always bring back my old Cherokee and our final trip together.

More serious hurts and stronger emotions are triggered by different locations in New York over the week following my wonky reintroduction to stellar navigation. I ride the subway down to Saint Mark's Place in the East Village to pick up a sandwich for lunch. It was to Saint Mark's, number sixty-five, a shabby former tenement between First and Second Avenues, that Liz and I brought our first baby home from

Beth Israel hospital, a few blocks north up Second. Every time I see that stoop and its creaky iron gate, the smog-chewed brick façade, the French jazz joint in its basement, I reexperience the profound happiness I felt buying secondhand furniture in which to store diapers and baby clothes before Emilie was born; carrying her, a tiny disgruntled bundle, with that over-the-top care of new parents up the steps to her first home. I wonder if there is not an addictive quality to nostalgia, or rather to the strong emotions memory summons. Is it the need to experience more nostalgia, or curiosity as to its nature, that leads me farther downtown to First Street and the building where, three years before Emi came along, I moved into Liz's studio?

More recently, after my brother took over that apartment, I used to visit Louis here. This was before he developed lung cancer and moved back to the Cape. I saw him here as well during the year and a half following surgery and chemotherapy when, believing he was cured, he took up his New York life again.

That memory, of course, is bittersweet. Due to its force—because of how it makes me feel like a bowl emptied of my usual broth of obsessions and grudges and then refilled with the boiling, flavor-soaked, bouillabaisse of what I felt and still feel for my brother, even though he is physically gone; what I feel for my family who are very much here; filled in this way with energy that seems neutral only in that it drives both sadness and joy, I am a hundred times more alive within memory and in the places associated with these people than when soaking in the dull issues of day-to-day life.

Because of that soupy image perhaps, I slope into Lucien's

on the ground floor of our old building at First and First. After talking to Lucien and his son, Zach, I pick my way through the dimly lit restaurant, thirty feet east to a table in back. There I try to organize my thoughts as well as the feelings these surroundings bring forth. Zach pours me Brouilly and, while drinking the wine, I stare at walls hung mostly with photographs of Lucien arm in arm with the famous and semifamous, a few of which were shot by Louis; and these notions shuffle into some kind of order.

If I wasn't already sure of it in theory, how I feel in Lucien's would prove once and for all that places trigger memories, as memories spark emotions. This causal proximity is hardly surprising in physiological terms given what I learned in London: the key memory-control center of the brain is also our primary navigation center; the important bits of our memory are spatially based.

Serial images link up in my head, stitching together location and recall, memory and emotion. I remember Queen Square in relation to Maguire and Lucien's in relation to Louis. I experience the weird recursive sensation of thinking about the very process that supports thought itself. Pondering the proximity factor leads me to consider the intimate wiring that links the hippocampal formation to the amygdalae as well as to other parts of the emotion centers. Might it not follow, I wonder, that emotions also are vitally dependent on how we track, plan, and recall our movements in space; and that how we perceive the territory, in turn, is colored and changed by emotion, the way a smooth-looking ocean is twisted and complicated by the strong currents in its depths?

The social psychologist Robert Sommer outlines four geographical/emotional zones to which we navigate, most often unconsciously, according to their perceived level of safety and alliance: the "public," where encounters with strangers are allowed and encouraged; the "social" zone, in which groups of people who know each other meet and interact, in alliance or hostility; "home," a place with clear boundaries that a person or group claims as his or her own, and access to which is strictly controlled; and finally the body, that ultimate private territory, the locus where transgression is most evident and sharpened to the knife-point question: who is allowed to touch me, and when?

I examine the rest of Lucien's, trying to understand how this classification might work here; whether the emotional needs and offerings of its inhabitants are subtly reflected in how people navigate its tables. Watching customers come in, I notice their eyes flick around the restaurant; almost by definition, they are drawing a subset of their cognitive map to decide where on that territory they will place themselves, whether in protected isolation or in a position from which they can spot those they're supposed to meet, while remaining shielded from unwanted contact. Lucien's is a watering hole for models, actors, and galleristas for whom being seen, even while meeting friends for dinner, is part of the business model. Members of this group alter course left or right immediately after coming through the door to sit near the restaurant's windows.

Singles keep tracking eastward to the bar, a more fluid,

"public" zone where one can venture beyond the boundaries of the personal and protected to meet new people: potential business contacts, sex partners. My brother liked to sit at the counter before he met Juliet, waiting to talk to one of the scores of pretty women who drifted through and who often waitressed here till Lucien's strict discipline drove them off.

After Juliet became part of his life, they tended to hold at a corner table between windows and bar, a "social" zone where they could establish their own small satrapy of talk or converse with others if they felt like it. Or else they walked all the way east, where I'm sitting now, where intimate parties, courting couples, and those who wish to remain solitary prefer dining. These shadowy corners, protected like Leonidas' Spartans by a narrow defile (in this case between bar and wall), constitute a home area, a place of relative privacy. Today the back is empty save for a table in the southwest corner where a man in an Italian jacket talks in a low voice to a much younger woman who sobs and tries to hide her tears and blow her nose at the same time and then, maybe from embarrassment at her failure, at how disheveled she looks, sobs harder. "Somethin' Stupid" by Nancy Sinatra and Lee Hazlewood plays on the sound system, adding—for music works easily on the amygdalae—to the atmosphere of wistfulness. For both of these people, I'm certain, the sadness of whatever they're discussing will always be marinated in an idea of this corner, its crowded photos, waft of roasting lamb, hubbub of diners in front; of their table set parallel to the aisle, sheltered by the bar's inside edge. And if later they stumble across one of those sense images: a guitar riff from "Somethin' Stupid," perhaps; it will forever after trigger desolation and a memory of that restaurant on First Avenue in New York.

A STRONG EMOTIONAL SYMBOLISM PERMEATES the places of which our world is composed. It's a symbolism we navigate without being aware, using affective maps that overlay our more prosaic physical chart of streets, landmarks, frontiers. Concepts of personal territory and alien kingdoms, of free or closed access and boundaries, of fear and refuge, are built into how we move through city and country, around bedroom and kitchen. Some of these symbolic matrices are old as human consciousness, such as the integration of cardinal points with our body structure: north with head, south with feet, east and west with extended arms, in European cultures at least.

These notions also surface in myths, children's stories, nightmares, since all are heavily freighted with emotion. Woodlands, for example, evoke both fear and excitement. Such forests as Robin Hood's Sherwood or Morgan le Fey's Brocéliande feel like places through which we must navigate swiftly and accurately because they are wild and also full of the potential for change represented by the outlaws and witches inhabiting them. The sea plays a similar role as icon of peril, protector of mysteries, and zone of freedom, and summons the same navigational reflexes, as does its other inland equivalent, the desert.

A big city's red-light district, with its massage parlors,

dive bars, porn shops, and hot-sheet motels, corresponds to our darker drives and pleasures, all the lusts and repressions glopping volcanically from the id. Islands—and here I think of Circe's Aeaea and Calypso's retreat, not to mention Samothrace—are places to long for and sometimes hide in, or else, once confined there, escape. Red-light districts and islands have this in common: people find their way there, very often, for privacy. Behind the bulwark of a peep show's curtain or the restricted landing places of Vinalhaven they find a refuge of sorts. Islands tend to be isolated, out of time, both refuge and trap. Having lived on islands before, I can testify to their ability to evoke all those archetypes at once.

I know from experience that New Yorkers work the hell out of their grid cells. They hold very strong maps in their heads showing the boundaries of areas they visit in work or play, of zones seen as risky, of streets that define their neighborhoods. That idea of neighborhood is a powerful one, connoting safety or at least the possibility of protection within its borders. At its core lies the apartment, a haven of relief from the disorienting rush and stress around. Gothamites are often reluctant to venture into neighborhoods not their own and tend to visualize navigation in the form of voyages undertaken away from and back to home ground. I lived part of my childhood on East Ninety-Sixth Street, Manhattan, which at the time represented a scary frontier to the white middle class. South of Ninety-Sixth was safe, "civilized," white, whereas north of that boundary was the dangerous, dark, alien territory of black and Spanish Harlem. I remember, inexcusably if unconsciously accepting this prejudice. When I looked from my bedroom south I saw quiet bourgeois apartment buildings full of Caucasian therapists and magazine editors, while through the back bathroom window, from Ninety-Seventh north, pulsed drumbeats and the thrilling, exotic rhythms of salsa. My father sometimes walked his family up to 125th Street—he believed, rightly, that we should see what the city was like outside the white enclaves—but to me it always felt like an expedition to foreign, even risky territory. When I planned travel I invariably went south, down avenues leading to Midtown or the Village. The return trips stopped dead at the east-west boundary of Ninety-Sixth. I don't think it would be an exaggeration to say that, in the '70s and '80s, the whole racist dynamic separating a middle-class white majority from poorer people of color was played out across the axial line of Ninety-Sixth Street.

The island of Manhattan is symbolic in other ways. Seen from afar, it meets some criteria of Cythera or the enchanted isles of Celtic myths. For Connecticut clubbers on Metro North, as for Guatemalan migrants making their way across the Sonoran desert, the idea of "New York, New York," shines neon bright, a place of mythical hope where the density of opportunity surely must palliate the misery, or boredom, of home. As a result, when people build cognitive maps of this hemisphere, the Big Apple often serves as a navigational nexus toward which they chart an emotional course.

I once stood outside an employment agency on Forsythe Street in Chinatown, watching through the plate-glass window as a job tout pointed with a broken car antenna to various spots on a wall map of New York and environs, yelling directions in Cantonese to a crowd of men, all freshly arrived by the look of their clothes. And I marveled as I watched at the ability of humans to assimilate new maps and lines of direction for a place utterly foreign in its language and systems. Despite the fear surely attendant upon entering such an alien world, these men would all somehow navigate to a place where they could start anew.

FROM LUCIEN'S I GO TO the NYU library and work till evening, then walk west to the subway. It's past sundown, and Washington Square is almost deserted, poorly illuminated by streetlights and a quarter moon; on the blank slate of shadows my memory sketches the gallows that once stood here, the thousands buried underfoot when the square was a mass grave. But in spite of such lurid associations, my mind keeps drifting back to Lucien's, trying to imagine what sort of cognitive chart those in the restaurant are dealing with now. Because humans are spatial beings, their navigation must include the usual: landmarks, obstacles, axial lines; all memorized in the mental atlas. Onto that, however, they graft another dimension of power and insecurity, friendship and threat, desire and terror. It's a mix so potent it must overshadow all other geospatial charts, the way a loud talk show running on TV will dominate a room filled with dusty books.

But as I take the subway home, I realize that I'm no longer much concerned with the psychological map, of sex and power algorithmed by place, that underlies so much of our daily navigational practice. I suppose, because I'm neither hunter nor prey tonight, courses based on id and ego do not exercise me as once they might have.

What does preoccupy me is the cognitive emotional land-scape I am navigating as I pole dance on the racketing roaring 1 train uptown. This layer of my own cognitive map, I'm be-ginning to see, has been torn, splotched and confused by loss. When earlier I walked to Saint Mark's Place for a sandwich (which I then forgot to buy), I was attracted not only by the myriad delis in the East Village but also by the great emotional intensity the area kindles in me, mostly because of loss; it was the landmarks of loss that I was navigating here from the first. Those early days of parenthood on Saint Mark's—though they have been replaced by joys, just as deep if more complex, of being father to teenagers—are time and strong sensations deeply missed, and missing was what drew my footsteps there. One kind of loss, like a single chorister singing part of a round, seems to call another to join in, swell the music to a level we somehow crave where it will take over, imbue our lives with power and direction. I kept walking to Lucien's because of it.

The same factors work on me in the subway. How many times did I ride this line north or south to get off at Lincoln Center and visit my mother at Juilliard; change to the M66 bus eastward to visit my father crosstown when he was ill, in their apartment on the East Side? Louis has not been long gone from my life, but how many times since he died have I rocked and swayed to the Broadway rhythm of this train, wishing it would rattle through time as it does through space, that this map might change—that I might again disembark at Times Square, hop the N train to Eighth Street, walk from there southeast, back to the East Village where he would be alive and waiting for me outside Lucien's, a glass of Brouilly in one hand, a Camel Light in the other. "*Hola,* man!" he'd growl with that half-snarky smile of welcome, and as usual suggest dinner at the Swiss-Nepalese fondue joint up First Street.

If all deeply felt anxieties and hopes, dreads and imaginings of life convert to space-based maps: the soft power of family at home, sex and territory in Lucien's, a more officious game of power and conquest at work; then the cognitive territory of love and memory for people I've lost is the one I navigate most often, and not only in New York. My family, our house and boat, the streets, shops, and cafés we frequent, build a dense landscape of what I have, the enormous psychic riches I enjoy now. I plan my routes around the physical world in large part based on what touches my life today and the emotional weight each course or landmark evokes. But those places of the present are balanced, overbalanced even, by the mass of blue coordinates, the sacred places where I lived with those who are gone. It feels sometimes as if two planes of navigation are involved here, one for the living, another for those I can no longer see. For the latter, the only navigation I may use is emotional, confused by fog. It is less precise, which means I must think about it harder.

And that is not bad, I tell myself, getting off the train at my stop; it's not even sad. This map of the lost and the places we were together keeps them alive inside. It's an overlay that provides reference points to a million other place-memories of my life as son, brother, lover, husband, father. These are rich memories, places that *are* me.

But I'm beginning to wonder if the dominance of loss on my map does not, in ways I cannot consciously perceive, tremendously sap my attention to and confidence in more prosaic chart work, the nuts-and-bolts recognizing of where in the world we are.

I think back to that episode when I woke up on Route 195 and did not know where I was. I'm sure I would have been shocked anyway, given how basic is our need to situate ourselves, but would I have panicked as I did absent this ongoing emotional erosion? Was my panic amplified by insecurity stemming from the tricky nature of landmarks linked to people who are gone and therefore stored only in memory, no longer updated: the abode of ghosts, and the street-level shrines of mourning?

CHAPTER TEN

Bad Latitude

There is good news on Cape Cod on the boat repair front. Laura Richardson, a friend who runs a marine canvas repair business, has agreed to fix *Odyssey*'s dodger; she has so much work she usually refuses nonregular customers but I apply pressure by simply showing up at her workshop in Chatham bearing the bundle of torn blue cloth, and she laughs and says OK. I feel guilty about pressing her; I feel worse because her hands are chronically aching and clenched from all the sewing and canvas handling she has to do, and repairing my dodger will make the problem worse. But I don't feel so bad that I change my mind.

During a dry spell in the weather, Ned and his chief carpenter went back to *Odyssey* bearing a GRP-33 moisture meter marketed by the J. R. Overseas Co. of Prospect, Kentucky, to check whether portions of her fiberglass shell have been compromised by seawater. The rudder: a slab of hollow fiberglass attached to a stainless steel post that runs vertically through the stern (or back) of the sloop to her steering mechanism; is as waterlogged as pound cake left in strawberry syrup overnight. But the rest of the hull is sound, and the carpenter tells me the rudder looks strong enough. All I need do is drill a hole to let out humidity, and patch it later.

The carpenter is less sanguine about the corroded steel structure that supports my mast. The space under the mast step is so tight he sees no way, short of cutting through the hull, to get inside there and weld in more steel. But he reckons enough metal is left that, as long as I'm not offshore for too long, I won't encounter serious problems. I accept this verdict with a mental gulp, trying not to imagine the usual: sudden squall, knockdown, the crazy strain such events would put on the cup holding my mast at its base. Ned and I discuss sneaking a small steel supporting plate under the step and bolting it into place, something I might be able to do using the three fingers I can fit in that gap. He is skeptical. All this work around the mast step reminds me that the steaming light at the pole's top hasn't worked right for years. Here is another job for my disappearing marine electrician, who has now been AWOL for at least eight months.

RIDGE WHITE SENDS ME MY resilvered sextant. The mirrors are clean as spring rain. A few days later the *Nautical Almanac* and sight reduction tables show up via UPS. On the next fair morning I hurry to a south-facing beach to try a test sight of the sun. And the sextant works beautifully, measuring an angle of forty-eight degrees, ten minutes, and some damn number of seconds it takes hours to figure out on the instrument's antiquated vernier—a microscale that reads off fractions of a minute. In the course of casting about online to understand the scale, however, I have come upon a Web site that holds my virtual hand. It advises me to forget about longitude at first and start, as did everyone from the ancient Egyptians on, with measuring the sun's height at noon to find my latitude.

A federal Web site informs me that the time of celestial noon, when the sun reaches its zenith locally, is 12:37, and I make my way to the beach ten minutes earlier to track the sun's rise, feeling both odd and cool, for there sure as hell is no one else on a Cape Cod beach in winter measuring the sun with a century-old sextant. The seagulls jeer while I try to measure with fingers on cold metal how this planet spins fifteen degrees or 1,040 miles an hour (at the equator) against the beacon of our star. Fine adjustments to the sextant's mirrors can be made by turning a gear to hold the sun's lower edge on the horizon, and it feels as if in doing so I touch a digit to the pulse of the universe, gauging its steady beat. And the sun follows the rules, it rises through 12:37, then slows, hovers— and after a pause that seems impossibly long, and triggers the first symptoms of disorientation panic, because I am convinced somewhere I'm doing this wrong; or else my equipment, as usual, is deficient—begins its descent toward night. I read the vernier scale with a magnifying glass, the gradations are that tiny: sixty-seven degrees, forty-eight minutes, zero seconds.

The formula to find noon latitude is, indeed, simple. Go to the almanac, pick out the sun's theoretical altitude (or declination) for your area at roughly the time it stopped climbing. Subtract your sextant angle from that, subtract the result from ninety. As the chef on TV says, *Bam!* That result is your latitude.

With pounding heart I write down the numbers, subtract as instructed, find the corresponding latitude on a chart. Forty-one degrees, zero minutes, thirty-five seconds. And the disorientation panic fires up again. The number I have computed puts me on the same latitude as Sag Harbor, Long Island, a good ninety miles southwest of the beach where I shot the sun's altitude.

I check my figures. My subtraction was off. Forty-one degrees, thirty-seven minutes, twenty-six seconds latitude. I return to the chart. Relief floods my gut. This time, while I'm not on the precise latitude of my beach, I am not far off; only one minute, a paltry nautical mile farther north.

I lay my instrument back in its case. Though I'm no closer to solving the longitude enigma than I was before, it feels as if my navigational rheostat, thanks to improvement in the latitude department, has shot up at least half a point.

MARCO PIERRE HAS BEEN IN bad shape recently, Seth tells me. Our Haitian contact might be hard to get hold of for a while. We're standing in Seth and Ellen's kitchen in Wellfleet. A parrot shrieks from the living room, then flutters in and lands on my head; a sequined doll representing Ezili Dantor, a powerful *lwa,* or divinity of vodun, eyes us in frozen skepticism. In Haiti, where neocolonialism, corruption, disease, and natural disaster are often interpreted through allegories of witchcraft, "bad shape" can mean a lot of different things. Woodmyha and Hernitte, Seth and Ellen's Haitian godchildren, examine me with curious, intelligent eyes. "Why do you have no hair?" one of them asks me.

Outside the sun sets over Chipman's Cove, where once I joined a team trying to free twenty-seven pilot whales whose navigation, for reasons no one has ever conclusively explained, went so badly wrong they left deep ocean and blundered into Wellfleet Harbor. There they ran aground and started to die. We basted them with water and heaved them seaward with canvas slings. That pod was lucky: twenty-five survived, and when high tide floated them again, found their way back to sea.

I'd like to think that the *lwa,* via her sequined effigy, heard us talking and approved. However it happens, only two days later, Marco resurfaces in virtual form. He will be free in two weeks, he writes, and can find fishermen who use the stars to navigate. "They are used to organizing boat people to go to the States . . . They don't need compasses to sail . . . they don't believe in it," his e-mail concludes. I start searching for cheap fares to Port-au-Prince.

I AM WORRYING HARD NOW about the electrical work that requires doing before I can go offshore. On my own traditional sailing craft I will want radio for emergencies, I will require that masthead light for night sailing. It's clear my disappearing electrician must have died or, more likely on Cape Cod, checked into rehab. Online, I find another who lives not too far away and leave a message on his voice mail. While awaiting a reply I measure and carve a wooden matrix to the trapezoid space between *Odyssey*'s keel plate and the beam supporting her mast step. I will get the Finnish welding shop near the town dump to cut me a steel version that I'll bolt to the existing plate to shore it up. Though the days are lengthening it's still cool out, and my fingers stiffen and ache as I work, but I don't mind. I spend so much time sending queries online, consulting Web sites, waiting for e-mails, I am beginning to suspect my cognitive map, as well as being emotionally scrunched, has become too virtual: my extended mind laying, over the more standard chart of people and places both here and gone, its own thin topography based on relative download speeds, time zones, the turnaround gap between online order and parcel delivery.

So it feels good to do something that cracks me back into the purely physical world, where I measure Earth's flight with the twist of finger and thumb; a world where the right move warms muscles and the wrong causes pain, that basic signal of "something is not right here"—a primal give-and-take that will be very much my reality on an offshore sail. . . . I don't dwell on that last thought. Let my rheostat enjoy being relatively high for once, let me feel pretty much content.

But the next notch of movement in the Halvor quest comes electronically a week after Marco's message in the form of two e-mails. The first, from a Norwegian government archive where I'd requested information on the *Stavanger Paquet,* conveys no new information about the ship but mentions that the sloop's previous skipper, Knud Helliesen, was the son of Ole Helliesen, the ship's owner. I remember now that Ole Helliesen was listed in the family files as stepfather to Halvor's dad. It seems likely, for what it's worth, that Halvor got his job through a family connection.

The message also answers a question I'd asked about government investigations into *Paquet*'s sinking and newspapers that might have reported on it. No record of investigations exists, the archivist says. A local newspaper, the *Amstidende og Adresseavis,* was published in 1844; I should be able to find it on microfilm at the Stavanger library.

The second e-mail is a reply to a query I sent to the Haugesund dive club. Apparently using information from the M. L. Michaelsen book, Erik Bakkevig writes: "The *Stavanger Paquet . . .* foundered in a snowstorm with a cargo of herring off Espevær in February 1844. Water depth estimated to 80 fathoms (about 150 meters). 'Off Espevær' can mean anywhere around these islands. She did not run aground, but sank in deep water. Exact position cannot be established." The Michaelsen information includes a fact I was not previously aware of: after the cargo shifted, the main hatch failed. Presumably, the ship sank quickly after that.

I write Erik back, asking if he knows where I can find further information on the wreck that might pinpoint its location. He replies promptly, saying no further data are available but adding, "The islands of Espevaer [are] a charming and exotic place, and weather permitting, I can take you there in my dive-boat *Risøygutt,* equipped with depthsounder and chart-plotter. The trip from Haugesund to Espevaer will take one and a half hours."

He adds: "Our chances of finding traces of *Stavanger Paquet* are like nil. . . . and no diver can search in such water depths. In our waters all wood would long ago been consumed by sea worms, leaving only a few iron fittings." He appends a list of books he wrote about the wrecks of Norway.

I am happy about Erik's offer to take me to Espevaer. Though it means I went through the Coast Guard license hassle in vain, I won't have to worry about renting a boat. Nor am I unduly upset by Erik's pessimism. I am friends with several wreck divers in the United States, and I know they're an opinionated bunch, in part because they do things under-water no one else does, take risks no one else takes, and there-fore, quite reasonably, prize their experience over others'. They are also willing to undertake projects that appear impossible to normal people.

A picture of the *Risøygutt* shows a tubby, seaworthy-looking trawler-yacht with a red hull, pounding through moderate swells. She will be laid up now for the cold season, like *Odyssey.* Looking over pitch pines, yellowed grass, land held down to the hard gray rule of sea horizon, I get the feeling our boats are like the land, asleep for a reason, slowly storing energy for a day when the sun's warmth finally unlocks the world and they can venture out once more.

CHAPTER ELEVEN

Colorado: The Dark Heart of GPS

My request to visit the GPS base at Schriever has been approved. Ten days later I fly to Denver, rent a car, and drive to Colorado Springs. When I arrive in early evening at the airport motel where I booked a room, the temperature is minus six degrees Fahrenheit and dropping. The next morning it's minus eleven. I walk outside and cold sucks warmth from the semisober clothes I wear for interviews. I hurriedly change to long underwear, jeans, and sweaters before setting off.

Three industries thrive in Colorado Springs: higher education, mall religion, and the military. The metro area encompasses four large air force installations, including NORAD's Cheyenne Mountain bunker/city and the Air Force Academy. Of these Schriever AFB is the farthest east, on the road to

Kansas, in the badlands of El Paso County. Past city limits, the Great Plains are scuffed like a cheap motel rug into shallow undulations of snow, yellow corn stubble, black dribble of fences, tan gash of an arroyo. The road's monotony—it is straight as my security clearance—is occasionally relieved by junkyards and signs for gun shows. The temperature rockets up to minus six. My rented Ford is warm. Not for the first time, I think with guilty pleasure of how easy we have it in these early years of the twenty-first century. Jetted from New York to Denver in three hours, coddled in the warm cocoon of my Detroit ride on a smooth tarmac road while winter hammers everything around me flat and dead, I wonder how they navigated their way across this vast land, those Irish, German, English, French pioneers of 150 years ago. Standard road maps were not available until the 1930s, when automobile ownership became widespread. Before that, civilian travelers relied on rough maps based on information from earlier travelers, or word of mouth; landmark by landmark declination of the roads and pathways to follow. This method was similar to how the *US Coast Pilot* works, to the routiers that Renaissance mariners compiled, both being sequential lists of prominent features and hazards.

The first pioneers apparently followed preexisting Native American trails and relied on guides such as Sacajawea, but before that? Little is known of how the original inhabitants of this land found their way around. The very dearth of information on the subject points to what was probably the case: the Arapaho who lived in this area were so much a part of their landscape that navigation was near instinctive, the prairie and its buffalo migration routes as familiar from childhood as the layout of their home tepees.

Traveling these plains in weather that will kill, I think of how important is boundless space to the idea Americans have of themselves. Perhaps it's no coincidence that the first president of the United States was a surveyor by trade; so many of our myths and folk songs since Columbus are built around the mapping of unknown geographies. "From California, to the New York island . . ." What does it mean, then, to our idea of ourselves as Americans, if we all come to resemble the tourists I saw following GPS directions in Washington Square and lose the skill to find our own way around? What will it mean to a people who pride themselves on freedom, independence, and the ability to move on and start again if we end up dependent for guidance on machines of whose workings and protocols we know absolutely naught?

The warmth and comfort of my little rental compact provide a clue: ease is what these complex systems provide. Convenience, and the near-elimination of risk, is what we enjoy in exchange for losing the ability to find our own way.

SCHRIEVER AIR FORCE BASE IS a chessboard of manicured drives and huge, low-slung buildings, most of them of the same dun color as the plains, surrounded by razor wire and signposted threats. Various white antenna domes bulge over the horizon, like Titleist balls teed up for some giants' game of golf. My public affairs contact, a bright and courteous Missourian named Jennifer Thibault, picks me up at the visitors' center. As we pass the first security checkpoint a huge digital sign flashes THREAT CONDITION ALPHA, goes black, then lights up with an apparently unrelated message: WELCOME MR. FOY.

Schriever is one of the air force's smaller bases, Thibault tells me, since it has no runways or hangars, but it includes one of the biggest restricted areas, a square roughly three-quarters of a mile long on each side, entirely surrounded by a double fence: 356 acres in total, with twelve miles of razor wire fencing. Near the center stands a building of tan cement the size of a city block. More signs speak of dogs and advise that only one car may enter at a time. Red-and-white-striped antitank barriers slide underground and we enter the death zone between two walls of chain-link. While MPs check our credentials Thibault warns, "I have to tell you, stay next to me at all times; you don't want to be chased by eighteen-year-olds with guns."

The headquarters of the USAF's Fiftieth Space Wing/ Second Space Operations Squadron—2SOPS, for short—looks like any other big office building inside: long sterile hallways, pastel walls, fake wood, awards cabinets, carpets in neutral tones. A succession of tech officers walk into a conference room, shake my hand, flash PowerPoints, explain the skeleton of America's Global Positioning System, which consists of thirty-one operational satellites and eight backup craft, all orbiting Earth in different positions at an altitude of roughly twenty thousand kilometers, all launched elsewhere but controlled from Schriever. The officers pile on acronyms and information about command structure and how the Fiftieth Space Wing's budget has been slashed and how their award-winning canteen is open to all, which is unusual for the air force, and eventually we get to what I'm here for, which is how all these satellites pinging away in space, all these radomes and saluting captains, how they all work together for the sleepy salesman relying on GPS to find his way to a late-night dry cleaner in Wichita. As it turns out, everything comes down to what I do on my boat; what I was doing on *Odyssey* that saved my ass when I was sailing under small-craft warnings on Nantucket Sound; which is to say, dead reckoning.

Dead reckoning, again, is based on the simple equation: distance equals time divided by speed—speed itself being the amount of ground covered in a given number of hours, minutes, seconds. A GPS satellite is essentially a radio station in space, broadcasting a signal that is received by the TomTom, Magellan, or Garmin device stuck on your dashboard. What your device does is take the precise time the signal was sent and subtract that readout from the time it arrives to figure out how long the signal took to travel from spacecraft to car. Divide that number by the signal's speed (a.k.a. the speed of light through atmosphere) and you get the exact distance between that satellite and your car where it sits at a red light on Station Street in Wichita.

There's more to it, of course, than this simplistic formula, but DR is at the heart of it, and so are some of the concepts of celestial navigation I've been wrestling with. Knowing the exact distance between satellite and car gives you the same sort of information as shooting the sun does: a series of dots running in a continuous arc along the globe's surface, each of which stands at exactly same distance from the satellite. The "line of position" in celestial navigation is just that, a line, whereas in the absence of a defining horizon the GPS result gives you a sphere of points equidistant from the spacecraft. Just as you need at least two sextant-based lines of position to cross each other and define a specific place, the GPS unit on your dashboard requires at least two more satellites, and the sphere of equidistant points their signals define, to cross each other before narrowing down to that single common intersection and your car in Kansas.

I TAKE NOTES FURIOUSLY AS the brass explain, looping long ink circles back to stuff I'm not sure I get. For example, the time factor: it's the trickiest part for me. Trying to hold my boat on course in twenty-five-knot winds off Hedge Fence shoal made it hard to link a particular hour and minute with a given landmark in order to judge later how far I'd traveled, and this was a key factor in my ensuing fear; but a GPS measurement depends on a whole other dimension of time-keeping, each signal tied to seconds diced down to their tiniest feasible components, nanoseconds (one billionth of a second), picoseconds (one trillionth) even; measurements made possible only by using a clock that counts the rapid, immutable ticking of atoms as they decay from a chunk of cesium. The little silver box that holds Imogen surely does not have an atomic clock built in, so how does it figure out in nanoseconds the benchmark time against which to measure the signal's departure?

I ask this question of Lieutenant Colonel Matthew Brandt, the officer sent by Central Casting at the end of my initial briefing: by this I mean Brandt seems the Hollywood image of an American military officer, tall, solidly built, his face a cross between Ed Harris and that kid next door who won the middle school science fair prize; a self-described Ohio farm boy who is open, friendly, and full-on devoted to his mission. He explains that the signals from three satellites include, in code, the time the signals were sent, while a fourth provides Earth time, the benchmark against which Imogen measures the interval. Every satellite, Brandt says, contains three to four atomic clocks, of which two at least are active while one remains on standby. Each is automatically corrected to compensate for the shortening of time that relativity theory predicts will happen at orbital speeds.

The colonel leads me to the next floor up, down more long hallways with signs warning "Use of Deadly Force Authorized" and finally to a metal door protected by a peephole and two code boxes. I am shuffled around outside, for the door won't open if more than two people are standing nearby, a visitor must hover close to the officer guarding him while the latter talks to a security guy within. Finally Brandt keys the box, the door clicks open, we walk down another passageway, through another armored door. And my heart starts beating faster, because this is the holy of holies, the exact grid reference on our planet that guides the thirty-nine GPS satellites circling Earth in high orbit—and through them performing navigation for everyone or close enough: salesmen in Wichita, carrier-group admirals in the Indian Ocean, Imogen on Cape Cod—all the people and outfits who depend on GPS to work and travel and generally know for sure where they are.

Everyone stands to attention as we walk in. "Cover your name badges," Brandt orders, adding that all classified screens must be shut down.

Many screens shine in here, they are the focus of all eyes in this moderately dim space of gray walls and dun carpeting. The Mission Control Section is smaller than a Holiday Inn function room, divided into two smaller rectangles containing multiple cubicles, one area raised a foot higher than the other. Every cubicle contains a couple of seated airmen and airwomen, each with at least three medium-sized flat-screens lined up on a desk in front of her or him. A larger screen on the wall displays a map of the planet, with arcs showing satellite trajectory in relation to ground station coverage. The model of a satellite hangs shining in its golden foil in one corner, a large American flag is pinned against another wall, a dozen smaller Stars and Stripes poke up from partition boards.

I've been conditioned by scores of sci-fi epics to expect a stadium-sized atrium overshadowed by a screen a hundred feet wide showing an entire galactic system, at which grim-faced space warriors stare as they bank their craft at warp speed, shooting photon torpedoes; but this room, counterintuitively perhaps, is more exciting, because instead of the cinematic war-room display, everyone is working in cubicles shabbier than the one I labored in when I was a magazine editor, tapping at off-the-shelf PCs, guiding spacecraft as casually and easily as we would search the Internet or play video games on our Dells. And it all feels as if maybe I could do that too if I just plugged in my own laptop and downloaded the Schriever app.

Which is rubbish. These people might look casual but what they do is not simple. The two sections contain over a dozen stations, each of which is capable of tracking and redirecting every aspect of a satellite's travels. A serious-looking ponytailed young woman on the raised section is in overall control of navigating satellite *SVN-69,* whose position is currently being reviewed. Another noncom, through magnetic "torquers" on the spacecraft's frame, adjusts the details of motion—roll, pitch, yaw—by typing commands on his keyboard. The screens I'm allowed to see show a profusion of spike graphs, columns of numbers, dials. "Talking" to the satellite involves checking its time function, its "ephemeris," or positional data, and its "almanac." This last is the info it shares with other satellites so that every GPS satellite knows where every other satellite is, which in turn enables Imogen to know which spacecraft will be within range to help her establish a fix.

Brandt, describing the different roles his subordinates play, sounds as excited as the science fair winner explaining his tadpole experiment. He says he has not lost the enthusiasm he had when he first worked on the GPS system as a young lieutenant. One of his crew asked him then why he got so excited over his job and he replied, "Have you ever flown a remote-control plane? Well, here we do the same thing through (one of the satellite-control radomes in) Kwajalein, and then twelve thousand miles out into space! That's so cool!" To which the airman replied, "You're weird, sir!" "Take a second look,

Airman Jones," Brandt advises later, speaking to one of the workstation rocket jocks, "someone somewhere is relying on you to get home."

As the satellite "talks" to Schriever through one of sixteen monitor stations spaced around the planet, the different flight officers call and respond across the MCS in a dialect hedge-clipped by a military jargon stuffed with numbers and acronyms, very few of which I understand. Every satellite has its "personality," Brandt says, and the operators know which is likelier to cause trouble; Brandt listens for malfunction even as he talks to me. If it comes, he says, it will be in the form of numbers that seem a little off, tiny indications of skew in systems tuned to picoseconds, microjoules.

I have many more questions about how all this works but in the midst of this intricate action movie, in the cool/intense atmosphere of MCS, I cannot go through the list. Colonel Brandt, leading me out of the control section, pivots and in a parade-ground voice says to his crew, "Thank you for keeping America free and strong!" with only a slight smile on his lips. If I had a yaw-pitch-torque gauge handy to measure the quantity of irony in the colonel's exhortation, I think it would read less than 2 percent; it might even register zero.

I feel regret as I leave the MCS. In only twenty minutes I too have been seduced by the coolness factor Brandt mentioned. Is that because of the movies with *Star* in their titles, the training kids get in books and video games to escape the surly bonds of Earth, of school, of parents, and fly through those dark spaces filled only with starlight and possibility, to Mars, to anywhere—narratives inevitably crushed by the realities of adulthood in that same safe life of strip malls and 401(k) plans that GPS in some measure makes possible? The fact that the men and women in MCS don't actually work on board a spacecraft is merely a detail; and I remember the extended-mind thesis proposed by Chalmers and Clark, which posits that our senses must be considered now to include data from electronic instruments, whose data register in our minds almost as strongly as if the instruments were directly wired to our body.

THE AIR FORCE IS GENEROUS with its time and personnel. I eat lunch in the award-winning canteen. The turkey wrap is good. I spend a solid hour and a half in the office of Lieutenant Colonel Thomas Sainte-Marie, in overall command of 2SOPS. Sainte-Marie is a friendly, articulate Massachusetts native who displays a grasp of the scientific intricacies of satellite flight that I find scary. He answers my questions in a flood of details and precision that despite their rhetorical clarity I can apprehend only vaguely, grasping at concepts of some mathematical elegance—the decay rate of rubidium, pseudo-random error—like a kid trying to catch lightning bugs with a spoon.

But I catch enough lightning bug ideas to answer the biggest question I had coming here, which was, how does Schriever navigate the actual spacecraft? For the time-speed-distance calculation to work, it is axiomatic that one must know the satellite's exact position in space. So how do Sainte-Marie and Brandt and their people know where the satellites are, where they're flying to? What, finally, is the art and practice of navigating the ships of the "final frontier"?

Two processes, it turns out, are most important in navigating a craft in space. The first, before and during launch, is figuring out trajectory, the arc of a rocket fired from Vandenberg AFB or Cape Canaveral. From that you calculate, as you would the flight of a cannon shell, where it will end up: either in a given orbit within Earth's gravitational field or, in the case of NASA craft moving farther out, the gravitational matrices of other planets and the sun. These calculations obviously are highly complex and light-years beyond my ability to replicate. Factors as tricky as deviation due to pressure from cosmic winds must be included, but overall, the calculations rely on basic rules of astronomy. "Kepler," as Sainte-Marie notes, referring to the sixteenth-century astronomer who first worked out the physics of planetary motion, "is Kepler."

But the main technique is identical to what our dashboard receivers and smartphones employ, only much higher powered and in reverse. Ground stations receive signals from a given satellite and by exactly the same computation of dead reckoning—knowing the signal's time of dispatch and time of arrival, working out that difference, and dividing it by the signal's speed—obtain an exact distance between station and spacecraft. Through this process, known as trilateration, they get a fix on the satellite itself. Far-roaming NASA probes add an elegant wrinkle to the art by comparing the trilateral position to the known location of certain quasars: extremely bright, mind-bogglingly distant stars, so far away in both space and time that they appear, from our point of view, as immovable as an earthbound lighthouse.

Refining and updating the satellite's position and flight path is a key function of 2SOPS. One way to do this is by dedicating a ground-based receiver, whose exact position is known, for use as reference point. If a GPS satellite signal takes a microsecond longer to reach the ground station than it should mathematically, then the amount of atmospheric, or "differential," interference the satellite's signals are suffering from equals one microsecond, and that correction can be applied to mobile receivers in the area. Processes such as these have increased best-case GPS precision from three meters in 1990 to an astonishing one centimeter today.

THE RATIONALE FOR REFINING SIGNAL precision, for the military at least, is brought home to me in another dimmed room on the same floor as Mission Control.

"This is '911' for military GPS users," Brandt tells me as we enter, sweeping a hand at the usual constellation of screens and desks. The operators here are all men, civilian contractors working for a Colorado Springs outfit called Apogee Engineering. They stand at attention with the ease of ex-military and show me screens displaying maps of our planet's entire surface, painted in different colors for varying degrees of GPS coverage, white being perfect and black meaning nonexistent. I am amazed to see no black at all: every inch of the globe has at least 99.9 percent coverage, meaning GPS reception is perfect in northern Alaska, the Brazilian rain forest, the middle of the South Pacific, the North Pole, and everywhere in between—although the poles, one of the techies tells me, occasionally dip to 99.8 percent because of the high level there of electromagnetic interference.

Even 100 percent coverage, however, does not guarantee GPS accuracy. Satellite signals, already weak due to the satellites' high orbit, are easily distorted by the angle a GPS antenna on an air force tanker adopts when the plane banks; by thunderstorms through which an Aegis cruiser (which runs its complex systems according to position and time references supplied by GPS) is forced to sail; and by mountains.

One of the Apogee boys leads me to a screen in one corner. Here, spike charts quantifying the proximity of Schriever's satellites are overlaid on a Google Earth view of a mountain valley in Afghanistan. Large parts of the valley, the sides of which are precipitous, read black. The blackness denotes shadow areas where, because the satellites are not directly overhead, their signals are bounced away by rock, and do not get through. It's a GPS shadow, and it's a problem.

This is what the men here do. A company commander of the 132nd Infantry calls into Schriever, saying he needs to support an assault in the next two hours by firing GPS-guided 120 mm mortar rounds into a Taliban-held ravine fifty meters away. At such close range the precision needs to be perfect so his troops won't be shredded to hamburger by "friendly" ordnance. "They'll ask, what's the status, what accuracy to expect for a strike. . . . We'll tell him when a satellite is coming over the horizon . . . we'll tell him the DOP is worst at

11:04 but best ten minutes later at 11:14." ("DOP" means *dilution of precision;* I'm starting to get the hang of their jargon.) So the commander schedules his assault for 11:14.

It's the 911 service Brandt referred to earlier: the ability to obtain updates on GPS function anywhere in the world.

"Seriously," I say, "you do this with Google Earth, the same as I use on my laptop?"

"Same one," the Apogee guy replies.

I LEAVE SCHRIEVER IN THE middle of the afternoon. The temperature has risen to ten above zero but the air doesn't feel much different and the plains seem as shell-shocked by cold as before. As I drive west, then north up I-25 to Denver, I think back to the idea of America I considered while driving in the opposite direction, about how being American was tied in some way not only to the notion of wide-open spaces in which to expand and start anew but to the skills required to navigate them. Those theories seemed to imply that the society of big tech and high ease of which the military-industrial complex is a prime mover must be castrating us in navigational terms and therefore changing at a core level the idea of what it means to be American.

I cannot square that theory with the people I met at Schriever. They were, every one of them, friendly, helpful, open— "American" in the best sense of the term. They were also, as far as I could tell in a few hours, fully invested in the country's frontier image. "Keeping America Free and Strong" was no empty slogan for them. They believed in their mission, and the fact that it involved technologies of such scale and complexity that not one of them could possibly know or understand every facet thereof did not faze them. The belief in a structure that made personal navigation obsolete did not dilute their commitment; nor, as far as I could tell, was it having much effect on their navigational rheostats, their ability to think and imagine solutions spatial and otherwise.

I am left to wonder, as Denver's suburbs dissolve the foothills of the Rockies in a solution of tacky architecture, whether close involvement in a system of navigation, even if it's technocratic to the core, substitutes for a dilution in personal skills. Or is my notion upside-down and independence in thought is not linked to the ability to find our own way?

CHAPTER TWELVE

Searching the Chart

I don't spend much time on the beach in any season; as a Cape Codder, I suppose I take our sandy fringe for granted—despise it even, at times, as the domain of tourists and the kind of narcissistic one-percenters who crowd the area in good weather. In general I prefer scrub-pine landscapes, the bogs and slag of moraines, the eelgrass marshes stalked by killer herons. But I find I like walking to the beach with my sextant every morning and shooting the sun, around 9:30 for longitude, noon for latitude—though the longitude results, even with a new, superaccurate digital wristwatch I bought at Sears for sixty dollars, remain badly inaccurate.

I must get the stellar component right to approximate Halvor's navigational skills, to complete a trip that, in technique and feel at least, parallels the kind of journey the *Stavanger Paquet* used to undertake. After that cold snap I endured on the Great Plains the weather in New England seemed balmy; then the mercury started to rise, and a few weeks later we are into spring temperatures. By implication this means that the time I have to prepare a *Paquet*-style voyage to Maine, not to mention a boat trip off Norway to find where she actually sank, is starting to get tight.

I am ready to seek help, but no one I know on-Cape has any idea of how to use a sextant. The Massachusetts Maritime Academy is nearby in Bourne; its professors are all on a training cruise. Finally, through the Hyannis maritime museum, I track down one of the few people left in southeastern Massachusetts who teaches the old skills. Larry Hall is a former electrical engineer and a professional yacht navigator who both appreciates the need for a backup system when the machines go *phut!*, and loves the combined tactile and intellectual discipline inherent in keeping track of one's own position using stars.

I meet Larry at the Beverly Yacht Club. It's in Marion, across Buzzards Bay from the Martha's Vineyard harbor of Tashmoo, where I set off on that stressful, hungover sail; two miles from the rest stop where I woke up geographically clueless. Marion is a town that heretofore I've known mostly from the mildly lewd song "Entering Marion," in which "entry" carries a sexual meaning and the singer, driving around Massachusetts, penetrates Sharon, Beverly, Lawrence, and finally Athol before returning to his first love because he's "the Marion kind." The yacht club reeks of money that, if not old exactly, certainly would qualify for Medicare. It's dense with varnished panels, model boats, silver trophies, brass clocks, and a big round table, also varnished, where Larry explains to me, and to two other weirdos who want to learn stellar navigation, what the basics are—and in my case, where I've gone wrong, which has to do with that bloody diagram I didn't bother trying to understand from the first.

Larry is in his sixties with a close-cropped white beard, a ready smile, and vast reserves of patience. He explains that I really must work out the principle behind the diagram. "You have to see it in your mind," he says, drawing the confounded circle for me again. "That's where you went wrong," he adds, pointing at the angular scrawl with which I recorded my fucked-up position. "You should have subtracted that from 360. Understand the diagram and you'll be fine, I guarantee it."

"So all I had to do was subtract from 360?" I ask, pointing at the diagram. I'm still having trouble with this sketch. "Is there another rule that sums it up?"

"Ye-e-s," he drawls, "if Greenwich Hour Angle is lesser than your assumed longitude, you subtract from 360; if it's greater, subtract as it stands. But it's better to draw the diagram." I write down the rule nonetheless, and in so doing entirely miss the point Larry is trying to make, and hew to a way of thinking that will prove dangerously skewed.

THE SKY IS OVERCAST DURING the next few days, and while anxious to test Larry's rule I am also happy to give those much-macerated calculation areas of my brain a rest. The sailing chart for the Gulf of Maine: the archaic paper chart, thirty-six inches by forty-seven; arrived a few days ago, and I unroll it on the dining room table. It's a beautiful document in itself, with multiple variations on blue ranging from deep navy to the increasingly light shades of shallows. The curves of land are painted in strong tan.

I am aware, from researching the history of maps and portolans, how deeply political a chart is. The concept of having north on top is one method by which Western Europeans imposed the worldview of their countries on the "savage" south, in a world that might just as easily have oriented itself toward humanity's birthplace in sub-Saharan Africa. The pervasive nature of north as prime reference point, among Europeans, is reflected in the French term for losing one's bearings, whether geographic or metaphorical: *perdre le nord,* or "to lose north." The verb "to orient," on the other hand, harks back to a more intensely Christian era when east—the direction toward Jerusalem from Rome—sat atop the compass rose on early maps; a "rose" whose quadrants were originally named for the individual Mediterranean winds, such as the southern sirocco I experienced on Samothrace, that blew from eight directions.

I have looked at maps of the Gulf of Maine before, but this is the first time I've examined the gulf with all maritime data included: deeps and lighthouses, shipping lanes and buoys; and while I keep my mind open to other possibilities, the shape of the gulf itself is suggestive. A clear geodesic, from the Cape's tip to the end of the most easterly run of coast off Penobscot Bay, draws my eye. Two protuberances, bottom and top, seem to call for an axial line to be drawn between Provincetown to the southwest, and to the northeast Matinicus Rock, which plays sentry to the approaches of Penobscot.

I measure the distance between Race Point, marking the end of Cape Cod, to Matinicus Rock. It's exactly 120 miles, quite a bit more than the 40 miles Halvor might have sailed from the mouth of Vikafjord to Stavanger. But sailing farther north up the Maine coast means making landfall at a more shallow angle, increasing my chances of confusing one promontory for another. I prefer aiming for this isolated landmark well out to sea, even if it is solidly backed up and reinforced, if one imagines the seacoast as a series of defenses, by revetments of rock and weed and barnacle; whole ramparts of skerry and islet just waiting to crush any tempest-toss'd sloop attempting landfall.

I even like the name: Matinicus. It sounds solid, imposing, a good name to shoot for. It bears a light tower ninety feet high, which will make it easy to spot at night. The course from P'town to Matinicus is all deep water, a straight 047 degrees, almost due northeast by magnetic compass.

PHYSICALLY CHARTING A COURSE BRINGS the offshore trip closer, makes it more real. The last time I sailed in Maine was on my uncle's *Paquet* with my mother, my brother, and a hired skipper, cruising in leisurely fashion from harbor to harbor. This was before my uncle, Fred, left his wife of thirty-odd years for a much younger woman and moved to Maine. I remember that his second wife, Imelda, inherited Halvor's sea chest when Fred died, along with a sextant and the watercolor of the original *Paquet*. I call to ask if I might examine these artifacts sometime, perhaps before I've sailed to Maine. I'm hoping she will lend me the sextant, if it truly was Halvor's, so that I can use it on my own trip.

Imelda is in her sixties now. She sounds friendly and welcoming on the phone. I am free to examine anything to do with the Michelsens, she says; then her voice clouds with doubt. "But it was Thomas Michelsen, not Halvor, who died on the *Paquet*," she adds. "That's what Fred always said. We named Tom"—the child she had with Fred—"after him. And of course [Fred's] boat was named after the *Paquet*."

I look up the family tree Imelda sent me, and while I cannot translate the Norwegian any better than I could when I first saw the document, it's clear that Halvor is listed as *skipsfører,* or skipper, of the *Paquet*, and that his son, Thomas, died much later, in 1877.

Imelda photographs the sextant with her smartphone and texts me the shot. The instrument is jet black, with a modern micrometer. It's a US Navy sextant, too slickly machined to date from Halvor's time.

Misunderstandings of this stripe make me nervous. They bring to mind another story my mother told me about World War II and my grandfather. When the Nazis invaded his country, Pop donated a lot of time and money to the Norwegian government in exile and its resistance efforts, and invited the Norwegian royal family to stay at his summer house on the Cape. And they came, with the exception of the king, who remained in London. Queen Marta, the crown prince, his siblings, various equerries and servants, and bodyguards from the Massachusetts State Police all spent a summer at our house, a stay documented by news stories and photographs of the prince (now King Harald) in my grandfather's arms. Sometime that summer, in the middle of the night, a great commotion arose; my mother's Scottish terrier, Quincy, barked madly, state troopers blundered around with flashlights blinking and guns drawn. The guards ordered my mother to stay inside. She was told later that a raiding party from a U-boat had landed in an attempt to kidnap the queen and crown prince, but the attempt was foiled by state cops and Quincy's warning. When my mother was allowed out the following morning, she found her nightwear had disappeared from the clothesline where it had been drying, stolen by German commandos in the only panty-raid on American soil attributed to the Kriegsmarine.

I believed this story for years and then, somewhere in my twenties, realized abruptly how preposterous it was. For an enemy submarine to enter the mad patchwork of currents and rips of Nantucket Sound to begin with would have been near suicidal. In any event, even surfaced, the shallowness of waters immediately to the south must have prevented it from getting within five miles of our house. And would a raiding party that somehow made it this far, paddling in rubber boats and armed with Schmeisser machine pistols, have been deterred by a handful of state cops—clearly overweight, in the pictures, and carrying only revolvers—and a barking Scottie? "It's true," my mom insisted when I challenged her, "that's what I was told," but she smiled as she said it as if to acknowledge that this, like so many other matters, fell into the category of guns and male evidence and a certain hard-edged idea of reality to which she, as a 1940s woman, as a musician, maintained only the lightest of connections.

A few years later, I interviewed one of the wreck divers I knew who worked out of the Cape. While discussing a U-boat that had been wrecked off Nantucket, on Orion Shoal, he told me that a member of his diving team had gone to Germany to research WWII naval records and discovered that a different U-boat had been dispatched to Cape Cod to kidnap members of a European royal family. Later on I found corroboration of sorts in an article about a U-boat sent on just such a mission to Cape waters. The royal family targeted in this case was said to be Dutch. My mother had died by then but, Dutch or no Dutch, I sent her a silent apology for a cynicism that had been, on some level, misguided.

The U-boat story makes me smile because of its narrative awkwardness, its switchbacks and inaccuracies; makes me smile most of all because of how it reflects my mother, in her naïveté maybe, but much more in her enthusiasm for life in all its quirkiness, and in the tales, accurate or no, that reflected her enthusiasm.

I HAVE BOOKED A FLIGHT to Haiti from New York, and as I pass through the city, I seize the opportunity to visit the US Merchant Marine Academy in King's Point. It's a WWII-era campus of brick buildings trimmed with lawns and well-swept walkways. It lies beside Long Island Sound, just east of the city, in the Gatsby-slash–Mrs. Robinson suburb of Great Neck. A football banner reads BEAT COAST GUARD! A squad of uniformed cadets marches up and down a promenade, drilled by a female noncom bellowing "left-right-*hep!*" in the classic military style that sounds like Sarge hasn't moved her bowels in three weeks. The squad reminds me that, in a nation which has let its merchant marine wither to almost nothing, King's Point is still valued as a training school for the naval reserve. In the library, after a little time spent tracking down various indexes, I slide chart 3547 from under a sheaf of its fellows.

This is the first time I've had a chance to examine closely the marine environment where *Paquet* sank and Halvor drowned, and it feels good to pull out a chart and see everything laid out before me, unconstrained by a laptop screen. But the good feeling soon dries up, for Espevaer, if you look at it with the eyes of a navigator, is even scarier with the chart data than without. Oh, sure, these carved-up islands are all little cousins of fjords, massively scoured by glaciers, and the water is deep and navigable right up close and personal to the archipelago: on an islet called Sauøya, next to Espevaer's southwest corner, you could jump off the beach and plunge into water nearly one hundred meters deep. Here the eighty-fathom mark mentioned in Michaelsen's book lies only a couple of dozen yards farther out. But no matter how deep the waters within the perimeter of islands I can find no clear ground; all those tiny islets I saw on Google Maps are shown but between them it's all cruel with small skerries and a freckle-work of rocks that though tiny would rip the bottom out of the USS

Theodore Roosevelt let alone a wooden cargo sloop driven there in a snowstorm. It reminds me of the raft of tiny islands past Matinicus and around Isle au Haut and Seal Island.

A shelf in the same room holds volumes of coastal piloting books compiled by the Department of Defense. The chapter covering this section of Norway's coast reads: "When passing west of Bømlo [the mainland] it is advisable to keep well clear of its outer dangers, for although most of them are either visible above water or are indicated by breakers, they extend some distance seaward."

The passage on Espevaer states: "Numerous above- and below-water rocks lie within and on the edge of the group. . . . Only small vessels with local knowledge can enter . . ."

I write down these words perhaps to remind myself, in case I get too wrapped up in the details of my jaunt to Maine, of what my great-great-grandfather had to cope with in the dead of winter. I am about to close the *Coast Pilot* when my eye is caught by a name on the next page.

"Grutlefjorden (59 degrees 40' N, 5 degrees 10' E) indents the west coast of Bømlo. Shoal water extends 0.2 miles from the head of the inlet."

At first I figure this must be the same as the "Grøtle" I found on Google Earth, which Gry Bang-Andersen confirmed as being in Vikafjord; but Vikafjord has its own, separate entry, two paragraphs under Espevaer. Going back to the chart I find a small inlet as advertised, almost six miles up the trend of coast from Espevaer. It runs along a southwest-northeast axis with a village, Grutle, nestled at the top.

I stand straight to ease my back. Always, in the bilge of my brain, that forty-mile run from Vikafjord to the sea bothered me; it was such a long, constricted distance for a sailing vessel. Grutle is only different by one very similar-sounding letter from Grøtle, *fjorden* simply means "the fjord." And the first half of the nineteenth century was notorious, in the rest of Europe at least, for the looseness if not outright inexistence of spelling standards.

And wouldn't there have been ice so far up Vikafjord in February? And would herring school that far from the sea? I remember when I was living on the Cape, down and out in my early twenties, waiting for the alewives (a local variety of herring) to run. My girlfriend and I wanted to catch them with a dip net in the Marstons Mills River, we were out of money for food and didn't want to bug our respective parents for yet another loan. That river is less than a mile from Nantucket Sound. Would herring not tend to school near the sea, in Norway as in New England?

If Halvor picked up his cargo in this inlet, it means I don't have to jump through hoops to explain how *Paquet* foundered farther north, off Espevaer. The Espevaer archipelago lies right across his path to Stavanger and Hamburg, southward from Grutlefjorden.

Later I will go back to my research files and check the newspaper clipping with the herring listings and find it mentions only coastal catches, suggesting that "Grøtlefjorden," like the modern "Grutlefjorden," is on the coast . . . For now I put away the chart, feeling much more confident that I have at last located the port where Halvor loaded his cargo. I sense also the emergence of other questions. Given that the run from

Grutlefjorden was so short, if Halvor saw storm clouds gather and felt the wind rise, why did he not seek shelter? If a storm was threatening, why did he leave harbor at all?

I feel a weird connection to this ancestor of mine, about whom I know next to nothing except for the basic facts of his death and an unattributed comment to the effect that he had a beautiful wife and loved her. I think the connection must rest largely on our common body of knowledge about ships and seafaring that allows mariners from Yokohama, Japan, to Yarmouth, Massachusetts, to empathize with each other on some basic level, even across the generations.

Another link, I believe, is fear. Halvor must have felt fear as a dark and paralyzing force that overpowered him when he realized he had lost his bearings and was in a bind he and his ship could not escape. This imagined dread was familiar to me from the first, because of my own experience, and it's still something I want to explain, to understand more fully.

Odysseus in Haiti

Roosters crow. From a backyard church down the hill come voices raised in song, a Kreyol hymn: lovely and powerful by opposition to, by synchresis with a world so ruined and weak. The rip of dirt bikes, roar of *tap-tap* buses, calls of women selling wares on the sidewalk populate the air, spiraling upward in a cyclone of dust, levitated by the sun's rays.

It is hot, midmorning in Haiti. I sit on a terrace drinking a fourth cup of coffee while Andrénor, the septuagenarian waiter, passes back and forth near my table like, not a ghost exactly, but someone who is deep in conversation with ghosts and prefers it to dealing with guests. I think of the *lwa* I imagined prompting Marco to summon me here. Reluctant to embrace a cheap tourist image of this place, I nevertheless will invoke anything to further my aims, cliché or religious farce, and these are everywhere, shop-front priests will pray for you, *houngans* two streets away perform rites for the right price; a statue of Baron Samedi, god of the dead, grins under a top-hat from an alcove right beneath this terrace.

But the spirits don't talk to me or help, though Marco has done his bit, coming to consult every morning, driving me to meet contacts on the waterfront, people who don't call or visit anymore. From the shade of the great cockeyed ginger-bread ramble that is the Oloffson Hotel I watch Port-au-Prince, or what's left of it after the earthquake, tumble downhill to the Caribbean in a farandole of busted breeze-blocks and color.

I am not good at waiting, yet this is what I've been doing for five days here. Waiting brings out the doubts: what am I doing in Haiti, after all? I wished to study firsthand what I started researching in Samothrace: how people still find their way around lacking the tools that wired Westerners absolutely require to tell us where we are. But I'm no closer to that goal than when I first got here.

FOUR DAYS AGO MARCO TOOK me to the city's main fish market in Carrefour. It's a long sidewalk against a red metal fence by the harbor where dozens of "Madames Sara," the tough, hard-bargaining women who are the professional middle-persons of Haiti and the spine of its real economy— the trade in products from small plot gardens and sidewalk workshops—sit in the shade of makeshift awnings, hawking pink-gray chunks of fish in plastic buckets lined up on shelves next to their scales. We visited the headquarters of a fishermen's cooperative, the Association des Marins d'Haiti pour le Développement de la Pêche, situated in an alley next-door. Two very pretty young women sat in a cinderblock reception room, the only furnishings of which were a single bare desk and a big sign reading SÉCRÉTARIAT.

In another room, equally bare but for a conference table, Marco and I broke the news to Luc Williamson François, the co-op's president, that I wanted to sail with fishermen who went out of sight of land using only traditional methods of wayfinding. I told him it was for a book, and he said yes, it should be possible, especially now when pollution from the coast extended farther out, for the quake broke what erosion controls existed and forced refugees into coastal shantytowns from which rivers of raw waste flow daily to the sea. Thus fishermen have to sail farther offshore every day to get past the shit. "They use stars, the moon, the mountains, enough to get back," he said.

François was a doughy-faced man of about thirty-five. He assured Marco he would find a boat for me, from Port-au-Prince or towns nearby like Léogâne. His words echoed hollow off the bare concrete. He hoped my book would somehow help his co-op obtain outboard motors because the fishermen now had to spend two-thirds of their time sailing to and from the fishing grounds. I heard myself agree and hated it: was I not just one more *blan* blandishing assurances he might not be able to fulfill so he could obtain what he wanted, information, insight, sugar cane, was there any difference? Yet I promised and meant it for what it was worth: if he found me a boat, I would do what I could to help.

FIVE DAYS LATER, IN THE evening, I sit at the Oloffson bar trying not to imagine I'm a character from Graham Greene, who wrote *The Comedians* here. But it's hard; the ceiling fans pivot slowly, a breeze from the sea whispers among the chandeliers, the rum drinks are strong, another crowd of whites, high on partying in an exotic land full of quaint dark people, throng the dim arcades and terraces. At a table nearby a sixty-six-year-old Frenchman who comes here to sleep with high school girls—"*Les fi-filles*," he calls them, you can see the drool welling at the corners of his mouth—conducts business on his iPhone.

Now I'm thinking that, instead of the fishing angle, what I should do is find passage on one of the sailing cargo vessels that run out of Cap-Haïtien, Port-de-Paix, or Île de la Tortue on the island's north coast: vessels fifty, seventy feet long that sail to the Bahamas, the Turks and Caicos. The latter is a clear run of 120 miles, same as the trip I'm planning from the Cape to Maine. This is the other thing about waiting, it allows room for the fears, like so many little psychic hedge-trimmers, to fire up and snip at one's equanimity, and there would be plenty of reasons to dread such a trip, many of them stemming from the very experiential qualities I am searching for; stuff that goes along with archaic wooden sailboats, the dearth of radios and life rafts.

Other fears are more a function of the type of trade some of these sailors in north Haiti conduct, which is basically smuggling people, guns, drugs; the cartels have long been a presence on this island. All make historical sense in north Haiti, for Île de la Tortue was the stronghold of a de facto pirates' and smugglers' republic in the early seventeenth century, a period when the vampire empires of France and Spain were busy sucking blood from different shores. And these guys are their descendants, smugglers still, pirates if need be, and it will be tricky to secure passage on one of their boats, to convince them I'm not an American narc, be sure they won't take my cash and then, somewhere on the run between Tortue and Providenciales, sling my ass to the sharks. Still, I am in touch with a friend of mine from New York who owns a hotel in Jacmel and put me in touch with his manager, who got me to talk to his bartender who's from Cap and knows a guy, Jadotte by name, who's buddy with the skipper of one of these boats. Daniel Morel, a Haitian photographer who lives at the Oloffson, contacted the owner of one of the many radio stations in Haiti—radio is the chief medium of news here—who knows all the boat owners in Cap. And so on. I see myself struggling in the sapphire-blue Caribbean water, watching the sloop sail away, the crewmen laughing hysterically as they tell each other, "Stupid *blan,* we took his money, got rid of a DEA informant at the same time, it's a win–win situation!" How would one say that in Kreyol? They high-five in the distance.

I order another rum drink and lock this fantasy down with the others; gaze around instead at the lofty room with its wicker furniture, the open doors overlooking palm trees and carved parrot, the soft trilling darkness shot with moon and fairground lights; thinking of how my brother would love this place just as I love it, despite my nerves and self-distilled distress, love it half guiltily because of my ongoing awareness that it represents such a European fantasy. But Louis had a casual brilliance that always saw the other side, the white exploiters living in high palaces like this one, safe and well fed as they make deals that ultimately will doom the hundreds of thousands living in coffee plantations to the north or shantytowns down the hill; the shameful romance of it too, the pale, bored wives in sheer gowns, the perfume of danger that comes from knowing, as a *blan,* whether you fuck teenagers or own a plantation or work for an NGO selling the compromised aid of IMF, you are still holding a weenie roast 'round a volcano.

The colors here, though, seem independent of politics. My brother was a photographer, a good one, and he would have shot lovely images in Haiti. I can visualize him drinking beside me, his big frame hung with tropical-weight shirts and Nikons, his mouth pursed in one-third smile, one-third joke, one-third lipping the eternal, lethal Camel Light.

I miss him fiercely all of a sudden. This place seems only a quarter as interesting without Louis to be with, or at least talk to later. I have dreamed about him often since I've been here, the kind of dream that soaks you through as if you'd been dunked in that chowder of emotion I imagined at Lucien's. In one of them he accused me of not thinking about him, of missing others more. I would like to believe Baron Samedi had a hand in bringing him closer, I mean they are both snazzy dressers. A spiritual and sartorial concordance might be at work, and if that were true it would mean ghosts existed, spirits live, and Louis could really be sitting next to me, albeit transparent, sending the odd comment or image in stray thoughts between swigs of Barbancourt.

But I don't believe this, in the end I don't feel it, although from this time when dreams and thoughts of my brother made themselves felt in this room I will not be able to think of the Oloffson bar without remembering Louis, my missing of him, my sense that he's associated with it in some weird way; which as I know now is based on how memory functions, the method of loci working via a chain of spatial associations.

The interconnection of loss and memory fascinates me still. I thought of it before as two different navigational systems, but now I see it more as different kinds of dead reckoning, with every pun intended here (though the "dead" half of the term is actually a shortened form of "deduced"). People you see every day are clear landmarks against which you continually update your position. When the woman you're in love with leaves you, when your sibling dies, both keep living just as they existed inside you, in memory circuits in the cortex, in associated retrieval systems; you continue to fix your place in the world by their last reported position. But that position grows ever more distant in space and time, and so your emotional dead reckoning grows increasingly insecure about errors in affective position that must pile up meanwhile. The million tactile and semiconscious reference points of companionship or passion, of living with and around someone, are no longer there to refresh our course. In losing a lover, the result is clinging behavior, unwanted attempts at contact. With the death of someone close, the end product is mourning. Both are attempts to reassure the lost ship of our personality that we really knew where we were at a certain point: that she really loved me, that my love for her was not based on illusion; that my father, my brother, existed in truth, which means that my identity, navigated so often in relation to them, was how and where I thought it was. I believe this is what lies behind what feels like a deep and crying need to bring the lost one back.

The theory is interesting but does not palliate the pain. Louis is not really here, he cannot return. In my regret and sadness I leave the bar, walk upstairs through the teeming darkness, across the wooden walkway to my room.

I COULD HAVE GONE ELSEWHERE. I knew that the most adept practitioners of "primitive" navigation—primitive in the imperialist sense of not using white men's tools—were the Pacific Islanders, and in particular Micronesians. Having no Marco in the Pacific Islands, I was unsuccessful in arranging contacts there. But I brought books on Micronesian navigators to Haiti, and as I wait for the fishermen I pore through that material, amazed at the spatial sophistication of people who could sail across a thousand miles of open ocean to the atoll they were aiming for without modern technology of any kind.

The Micronesians managed such feats by studying their environment, all of it, and first and foremost stars. The chief method they used was the "star path." Stars and planets rise to the east and set in the west due to the north-south axis of

Earth's rotation, their schedule varying smoothly as a function of our planet's orbit of the sun, and the Micronesians from long observation knew what specific astral bodies rose and set in which segment of the horizon at what time of year. To that dynamic chart of the heavens they welded a deep knowledge of their archipelagoes, creating a system of star-based freeways between islands. Within this system, they kept in mind that starting from Polowat Island on a given day and hour, Chuuk Atoll lay "under" or in the direction of Sirius when it first came over the eastern horizon. For every island, they could refer to a star that would guide them there. They accurately gauged time, as well, by keeping track of when the astral body rose, peaked, and set.

Such knowledge was complex and difficult to learn, and islanders who wanted to be navigators had to train intensively, memorizing star paths from age five to eighteen or so before they could hope to qualify as skipper. They were taught not only to memorize the specific islands associated with every rise and set but the routes between, based on what stars and planets signposted landfall, a process known as "island looking."

I think "island looking" is more or less how Derek O'Reilly's "knowledge point" system works. Both teach an entire world by first focusing on individual landmarks that are the junction of a multitude of routes—in Derek's case, Hyde Park Corner, Chuuk for the Micronesian navigator—and then memorizing the paths that will get them as quickly as possible from Polowat or Hyde Park to a constellation of other landmarks around. And just as a London cabbie will recognize a thousand other facets of architecture and geography to orient himself along his route, the Micronesian will recognize eight different types of swell, one from each section of horizon, and use them to find position if the skies are cloudy; he'll pick up on a slow-moving shark that lives near a certain group of islands or how distortions in wave patterns indicate land over the horizon. He knows what kinds of seaweed or drift-wood are common where.

The Micronesians are not the only people who possess an uncanny ability to know where they are through exhaustive knowledge of both sky and planets around them. The Guugu Yimithirr, an aboriginal tribe in Queensland, Australia, are so focused on the geography of their land that egocentric directions: the idea of where things lie in relation to "me," as in the person "behind *me*," the river "to *my* right"; simply do not exist in their language. Instead, they refer to every-thing according to whether it's to the north, south, east, or west of where the conversation's taking place; so that while I, as a Westerner, might introduce "Jenny on my left" or tell the doctor my right arm was broken, if I were a Guugu Yimithirr, I'd speak of "Jenny to the south" and ask the medic to examine my "western arm." Their memories, interestingly, are aligned the same way, with events strongly and permanently linked to orientation.

Other aboriginal tribes navigate by visually based tropes that Europeans call "songlines" and the tribespeople them-selves term "footprints of the ancestors." These long chants enumerate, often in reference to various spirits and deities linked to soil and air, landmarks with which they must orient

themselves to get from point A to point B. In this the songlines are no different from sea chanteys sung by eighteenth-
century British sailors to count off the landmarks between
Ushant and the Scilly Islands.

I SPEND MY MORNINGS ON the Oloffson terrace, reading my
books on how Pacific islanders get around, waiting for Marco,
who still comes by daily, a lean and friendly presence that I
welcome; but he has no news. It seems François has lost interest. Marco and I have become friends by now and he is de-
spondent on my behalf, he feels he has brought me here on
false pretenses, which is hardly true, but our disappointments
feed on each other. Jadotte, the guy in Cap, tells me his
captain *"a une certaine méfiance, il veut pas vraiment te parler"*—
he is somewhat wary and doesn't really want to talk to me,
which translated from Haitian courtesy form means "fugged-
aboudit." Anyway, Jadotte points out in the same conversation,
the long-haul cargo sloop captains make good money and
own not only compasses but GPS receivers, as well. "Now you
tell me," I think but don't say it; he was only trying to help.

Every day I spend here the air seems to grow hotter, the
air more tightly packed. Shots were fired down the hill last
night. I feel like the Martin Sheen character at the start of
Apocalypse Now, forced to wait for what is already out of control. So when the photographer, Daniel, slouches by where I
sit at my usual table on the terrace on my sixth day here, drinking coffee number three and making useless scrawls in my
notebook, and growls, "There's a demonstration happening at

the parliament, want to come?" I accept enthusiastically. At the hotel gates we hire two moto-taxis, and we're off.

The moto-taxis are my relief from despair in Port-au-Prince. They are 250 cc dirt bikes, usually Chinese made, always driven by thin teenage boys for whom death is a foreign country. You climb on back, no helmet of course, and suddenly you're zooming full speed through the crowded streets, dodging cars and tap-taps, beeping, roaring, leaping piles of earth in construction sites, speeding the wrong way down one-way alleys, landscape on each side a wash of reds, blues, yellows, browns, the culverts overflowing with plastic and filth, past ruined buildings: on one second floor, its walls popped out by earthquake, a life-sized plastic Santa Claus gazes bemused over this trashed world; roadside stands selling socks, beer, charcoal; schoolgirls in blue pinafores, Madames Sara yanking blankets full of tomatoes and bananas out from under our churning wheels, the cracked cathedral, the yells, the smiles that would be astonishing anywhere but among these people who have nothing, my *god*—the adrenaline . . . It's exciting as hell.

We get to the parliament buildings, temporary modular boxes piled up after the original was destroyed in the quake, and hang out in the sun in Parliament Square for two hours while nothing happens, just lockdown by riot cops with Galil assault rifles and Brigades Motorisées with their dirt bikes and billy clubs; by UN peacekeepers led by a Croatian officer who struts around like Robert Duvall's Airborne colonel. Crowds of Haitians who Daniel says have all been paid off by various opposition parties to show up and protest, against each other if not against the Martelly government, clot into groups, drift away. Daniel says, "Nothing's going on, want to see the local harbor, maybe we'll find you a boat there? It's all gangs," Daniel adds, "they control Wharf Jérémie, but right now I think it's OK." We find our moto-taxis, and zoom we're off again, forty miles per hour in a hot wind northward up the waterfront road, past shantytowns, roadside markets selling six-foot-high piles of mango, used clothes; left onto a track through another shantytown, really bad potholes here and stinking sewers visible through black pits that Daniel says, when it rains hard, become maelstroms down which unwary children are washed to the sea.

Wharf Jérémie is a tract of wasteland on the harbor north of the container port with a corrugated iron hangar roof for shade. Piles of gunnysacks, a fat sow towing piglets, fuming trucks. A bunch of thin youths from the Base Vampire gang, dressed in T-shirts, torn pants, and dark glasses, cluster around me, none too friendly. "*Blan!* Give me money, *blan.* What you want, *blan?*" Daniel ignores them, directs his driver to the waterfront and my driver follows: and there I see them, what I came for really, four wooden cargo sloops fifty or sixty feet in length, very broad beamed with tall masts, a curtain of rigging, mainsails extending far aft over the water on booms hewn roughly from tree trunks. The one nearest, moored directly to a steep dirt shore, bears the name *Messager de Dieu*: Messenger of God. She is loading. Men carry sacks of flour up a plank. A dozen women sit on an open-sided wooden roof built over the cargo hold, lounging in what shade they can find between baskets and barrels.

The crowd around us swells. People laugh, make comments

I can't understand, which is probably a good thing. Daniel talks to the harbormaster, a guy with one arm in a sling, reasonable French, and an insipid grin; he'll arrange anything for money. The captain's name is Fani. He is very thin and dark, wears shorts, a baseball hat with "Jamaica" stitched on the side, a running shirt. He stands to one side, observing me; smiles but says nothing. Daniel tells me if I pay harbormaster and skipper two thousand gourdes each I can travel on the *Messager de Dieu* when she leaves tomorrow for Pestel, a village at the island's southwestern tip. The sloop operates regular service to Pestel and is thus by definition a packet. She carries no running lights, no GPS, no compass, no navigating gear at all. I smile at Fani. I'll be here tomorrow, I tell him.

DANIEL AND I GO BACK to the demo, which suddenly comes alive. A crowd of protesters march toward the police barricade from the north; some men set a truck tire aflame and roll it toward the riot cops who, well trained, sortie in a Roman-legionnaire kind of formation, shields lifted and clubs held like glaives, a black armored personnel carrier in their wake. As Daniel follows them, and I follow Daniel, the crowd pelts us with stones, striking Daniel in the leg. We retreat to the barricades. The APC quenches the flames in a gout of white foam.

MESSAGER DE DIEU DOES NOT leave as scheduled. This, I realize, is part of the lesson I'm trying to learn here: without fancy diesels and electronics, even regular packet boats are servants of winds, weather, and the slower aspects of human behavior. In this case we are waiting not for wind but for gasoline to fuel the trio of small outboards mounted low on her backside that the sloop uses to get in and out of harbor. Gas is scarce in Haiti. Crewmembers are waiting in line at a service station to fill up.

WE WAIT ALL NEXT DAY. I sit on the hatch cover, watching what's going on around me, which is no different from what would have been happening in Halvor's time. On the next sloop over a sailor hammers oakum into the seams of a whaleboat, then pours in melted tar as sealant; men scrape seaweed from the bottom of a sloop careened, or canted, on her starboard side in the shallows; crewmen heave on wooden hand pumps to empty bilges, reave manila lines through rough blocks. The passengers of *Messager de Dieu,* twenty-eight in number, consist of a half dozen young men who were looking for work in Port-au-Prince. The rest are Madames Sara or the sisters, mothers, daughters who assist them. They sit next to wicker baskets filled with peppers, onions, carrots, or take refuge in the hold, shaded but hot, where they lie on the boat's cargo, which is symphonic in its variety: condensed milk, corn oil in twenty-liter cans, boxes of transistor radios, spaghetti, fifty-pound burlap sacks full of American rice (originally dumped on the Haitian market by Bill Clinton's State Department in a deal that benefited Arkansas farmers and put their Haitian equivalents out of business), motor lubricant, Diana crackers, batteries, chicken broth.

As evening draws near, I am told to leave. It is not safe for me here because of the gangs. I protest, but Fani is adamant. Come back at 10:00 tomorrow, he says; we will leave then. I get back at 9:00 the next morning, worried that Fani will have left without me, and thank the *lwas*, *Messager de Dieu* is still there, still waiting for fuel.

And I carry on waiting, with everyone else. It's not so bad, this kind of delay, because I'm on a boat that somehow, someday, must leave harbor to fulfill its own reason for being. Or maybe I absorb some of the vibes of people around me, who take delay in stride like sun, like rain. Then three crewmen show up with two fifty-gallon drums once used for chemicals but that are now filled with gasoline. Our teenage engineer washes out a fuel filter by hand, fits it back in, fires up the outboards. The harbormaster comes aboard, finds a life jacket, and thrusts it at me. "*Ça c'est sauvetage,*" he says. "This is for rescue, when the boat goes under the sailors put this on: you too." I refuse, because the *Messager de Dieu* has only twelve life jackets, hung like orange fruit in the rigging, for a total complement of thirty-six, and I'll bet some of these people can't swim, whereas I am a strong swimmer. But the harbormaster insists. "Call me when you get there," he says and adds cheerfully, "I will pray for you." I remember Daniel laughing his grim laugh, saying, "You know these boats, they sink all the time, everybody drowns."

Somehow I'm not worried. Maybe it's because, now the waiting is done, to worry further is useless. Whatever happens, I have no choice but to deal with it. Fani fits a long tree trunk into a slot in the rudder and pushes it to one side.

The outboards whine. The sloop draws away from Wharf Jérémie, and as soon as she's clear of harbor, the crew tail on to halyards, lifting the enormous canvas mainsail, which fills with an easterly wind.

THE *MESSAGER DE DIEU* is fat, pregnant with cargo and people; she is built of heavy tropical wood from the southeast peninsula, one of the few areas of Haiti not terminally deforested. But she sails well to a strong wind. The mountains are clear at first, grayish purple in the distance, and Fani steers visually down the line of coast westward. Then clouds form to the north, tripping over the Massif des Matheux, and though they don't block the mountains north and west, a haze is forming south of us that veils the coastline. I have befriended a young man named Mario, who speaks good French, and through him I ask Fani how he steers when he can't see land and the wind changes. Fani says, "I look at the waves," and I assume by this he does the same thing Norse sailors did, steering a certain course relative to the wind but checking wave direction all the time to see if the wind is changing, since the wind will alter course long before the swells have time to follow suit.

The wind dies for a while. Our sail hangs limp against the mast. A large fin cuts the oily water, disappears. Fishing dugouts with sails like moths' wings lie pinned to their own reflection. The outboards are revved up, and slowly we resume our journey westward. The crew stands by Fani as he steers with his log tiller. Everybody lights up cigarettes. I realize they are smoking over two fifty-gallon drums of raw gasoline, whose connection to the outboards is a rubber hose wedged with rags into open bungholes on top. The stench of gas is strong. The image comes to me at once, an explosion that will surely blow the back of the boat clean off, the rest of *Messager de Dieu* on fire, sinking, the passengers screaming and fighting for life jackets, that big fin circling back. . . . Catching Mario's eye, I point at the cigarettes, then the fuel barrels. He shrugs and smiles. Whatever happens, happens, and on a boat called "Messenger of God," what could happen? Everywhere in Haiti I have seen this amazing contrast between sweet invocations of Jesus and God and the devastation that visits this island with such regular cruelty. Maybe it's fatalism and the anesthetizing effects of faith, but it feels more as if these people have such reserves of goodwill and humor that they've learned to burn disaster like kerosene in order to survive the day.

Nothing blows up except the wind, an hour later, as the sun dips behind clouds toward the horizon. The water turns deep blue and then black; the sloop heels, stitching a white frill in the sea behind. A hand of haze and night reaches out and palms us. The moon rises, orange, bloated and near full, in our wake. Fani stays at the tiller, silent as ever. He possesses a calm authority, a sort of sea dignity that would make me assume he was the ship's skipper if I didn't know it already. Earlier, two of the Madames Sara started yelling at each other and everyone laughed or made jokes about them. But it went on too long, the screaming got shriller and more aggressive. When it looked as if the women would come to blows, Fani for the first time raised his voice and immediately, albeit with a lot of residual grumbling, the fighting stopped.

"How do you navigate now?" I ask Fani, again through Mario. And the skipper answers, pointing at the stars, "*Gen un qui tombe, gen un qui remonte, chaque étoile qui change, une autre remplace;*" and even I can understand that, or maybe Fani is using French for once instead of Kreyol: "One star sets, one rises, every star that changes, another replaces it"—which, as far as I can tell, is a neat summary of Micronesian "star path" practice. I have more trouble deciphering what he names the individual stars. The evening star, probably Venus, Fani calls "Soupé," which I don't get for a while, then understand as corresponding to *souper,* the French term and etymological root for the English "supper." Orion, appearing now high and behind us, he calls *la faucille,* the scythe. The moonlight fades a lot of lesser stars to black. Near midnight Fani calls my attention to a star he names "Abat jour" (literally "bring down the day") and Mario explains that in this season it will serve as guide till daybreak. Later, the skipper points out two stars set vertically one above the other. "Pestel," he says, pointing at the stars, then at the horizon where our destination lies.

Well after midnight I ask Fani if I can steer and, somewhat reluctantly, he agrees. It's not easy. The *Messager de Dieu* has a strong weather helm, or tendency to head into the wind. The combination of tree-trunk tiller, a rudder the size of a large door, a deep hull and a big sail means she stubbornly resists course corrections. I start to get the hang of it after fifteen minutes or so and keep the Pestel stars in our port shrouds as

Fani indicated; relishing, just as I do with *Odyssey,* the job of balancing hull and wind, sail and sea.

The wind strengthens, Fani takes the tiller back. It's getting less warm. Water sprays aboard and occasionally lays a chill on the skin when our sloop slides into a swell taller than most. I lie on the roof with a bushel bag of corn flour as a pillow, trembling, for I am wearing only a T-shirt and cotton slacks. I watch Orion climb to its zenith then fall. I make out the Great Bear and Polaris, remembering Homer's words: "Odysseus . . . observed the Pleiades, and Boötes that sets later, and the Great Bear . . . which always holds its ground . . . and is the only constellation that is spared a plunge in the deep ocean. It was this constellation that the nymph Calypso advised him to keep on his left hand as he sailed." But Ulysses was headed east to Ithaca, whereas we are going west, so the Bear is on our right-hand side, holding steady as per job description to the north.

I think, in all my years of navigating I have never bothered to find my way like this, using only stars, but on *Messager de Dieu* it seems easy, normal. I get the sense as well that navigating in such a fashion, even more than when using sextant and almanac, lessens the distance that custom, cities, light pollution, and our overweening sense of human importance stretch between us and this amazing, deep-wheeling opera of fire and night. It returns our sloop and all her people to the collectivity of cosmic cycles, a company that I know, while it feels benign right now under this kind breeze on a seaworthy craft, would turn mighty cold and uncaring in bad weather. Yet this does not change what I feel. Ultimately it's a Greek-myth kind of sensation; the stars are gods who will fuck you up just as happily as they'll help, yet they are never indifferent because all are part of the same saga and maybe, if you can get past the tragedies that happen—boats like *Messager* that all too often vanish with all hands—the story is the point.

So I lie there, philosophizing and shivering until one of the younger Madames Sara comes over, lies down next to me, and throws her blanket over both of us. *"Je veux couvrir mon* blan" (I want to cover my white man) she tells her boyfriend, who does not seem to see the point of that; but she cuddles closer. People wake up around me, talk softly, and their Kreyol feels warm as the blanket. The water-like rill of vowels, the words rich in As and Ls: I recognize none of them, it's an African language being spoken here, the roots are French but those are not important when weighed against the rhythm, the run, the quotient of music and underlying chuckle; all those are Yoruba, Ashanti, language spoken wherever these people's ancestors were stolen from four hundred years ago.

Warmed by my sleeping companion, rocked by waves, soothed by the talk of neighbors, I manage for a while to sleep.

CHAPTER FOURTEEN

The Launch

I have found epiphany among astronomical data, on a wooden table by a window overlooking a ragged Japanese cherry tree. Many weeks after I first reopened my books on stellar navigation, I have at last worked out four longitude sights in a row, each resulting in a line of position that runs within a mile and a half of the beach where I measure the sun's altitude. My chest is near to busting with a dubious pride.

Larry Hall is the man responsible for this relative success. I had to visit him again in Marion, sit in his living room, and draw the cursed diagram over and over. Larry continued to be astonishingly patient, though ultimately he must have realized he was dealing with someone who was intellectually lazy, who would not force his flabby brain into going ten rounds with this problem. Because I'd been cheating, basically, using the rote rule I'd pressured Larry to set, getting it backward to boot. But as he worked with me I eventually understood the diagram: *got,* both visually and in the seat of my brain, how the hour angle drawn from my morning position west of the sun has to keep traveling westward, mathematically speaking, all the way around the globe before it can be calculated against the sun's position; whereas the afternoon angle, drawn from a position now *east* of the sun, does not.

I understood also—and this truly worked against my nature, which cuts corners, is happy with the good enough, wants easy and immediate results in all sectors barring only the most elemental drive I have, which is to write—how vital it is to be anal-retentive about every picayune detail in a navigational problem. Finally I accepted that I must reread three times those tiny numbers, check everything else over and over, figure the calculations three times too.

I have invented a worksheet that leads me through every step and marks the parts to which I need to pay most attention, and it works, it works! I whoop and holler every time I get the line of position right. My children, who, now their respective school-years are done, are staying on the Cape, look at each other with the doubtful regard that says, "He's crazy, of course, but at least it's happy-crazy."

"Hard to explain the joy . . . at being able to find my position w/ sextant, except w/ reference to panic I felt when lost," I write in my notes the day after the four successful longitude sights. I take that scrawl as indirect confirmation of the power of Halvor's myth in my life and that of my family, of its effect on our collective navigational rheostat. The more I think about that effect, the more I realize how much the loss of his father and grandfather must have sculpted the nature of my mother's dad, whom I feel I am discovering for the first time.

RUMMAGING THROUGH THE THIRD-FLOOR STOREROOM, I come across an oil painting Pop bought in the 1920s. It shows a group of people in nineteenth-century dress clustered by a rocky breakwater, leaned into a furious wind. Most of them are women, scarves and dresses kiting, clutching toddlers so the young won't blow away. Only one man is present. He wears oilskins and carries a large coil of rope in one arm while the other is thrown around the shoulders of a teenage boy. Everyone peers out to sea, clearly waiting for a ship or fishing vessel to return to this harbor and its rocky shelter, to the circled arms of family. But those waves are huge, they are pitiless, the tops blown clean off as happens only in forty- or fifty-knot winds. No boat or ship could live in such a wilderness, and something in the stance of those people says they know it, they are only doing what humans do, which is to hope even when hope is gone forever.

I used to avoid that picture, superstitiously I guess, when I fished for a living. Maybe it dragged my rheostat even lower. My mother disliked it as well. "Gloomy" was her word for it, gloomy being second only to "a damn bore" in her list of censures; she banished it to that third-floor closet. But if the picture depressed everyone why did Pop, who had lost all the men in his family to such waves, buy it to begin with?

He died when I was three so I have only the dimmest memory of him: a strange, if not unfriendly grown-up with a thread-thin white mustache holding me on his knees by the Viking hearth. Our stories paint the picture of a man who on one side seemed the quintessential American success story, who hauled himself out of the huddled masses to become a self-taught engineer and inventor. He dreamed up train air-brake gizmos for George Westinghouse and then founded a firm to manufacture his own inventions. Pop was, as I've already suggested, a polymath: gifted printmaker, amateur flutist, a serious reader in French and English as well as Norwegian: all that made up one side of him.

The other was less typical of immigrants and full-throttle subscribers to the American dream, which typically discarded dreams from elsewhere. It was built on a foundation of Norse identity at a time when this was not much of an advantage, when signs in some Chicago restaurants barred Norwegian clients. Pop changed his last name from *Michelsen* to the German-sounding *Schaefer* because this was before WWI and he thought Germans were accepted in a way Scandinavians were not. But he gave his son *Michelsen* as middle name, he brought his family back to Stavanger for visits, he taught my mother his native language, and endowed a room at Carnegie Mellon University with friezes, carvings, and books from Norway. His factory was in Ohio, but he missed the ocean, and after buying this house on the Cape, built a boathouse next door that he commissioned Norwegian artists to decorate. I still remember one of them, Ole Krosvik, a jack-of-all-trades who had worked all over the world. He had a beard like Father Christmas, lived in a shack on a pond nearby, and sped around the skating rink in Hyannis on Hans Brinker–style wooden skates he'd carved himself. I looked up to Ole, as boys will, as some sort of hero.

I wonder now if something was going on with Pop beyond the usual *mal du pays;* if the double gut punch of losing his father and having a mother who turned away from the sea and forced her kids to do the same did not somehow cause an equal and opposite reaction in Pop against his mother's influence. Why else buy a house on Nantucket Sound and hang out with sailor/explorers like Amundsen? Why serially cruise to Maine on his best friend's boat? Was it all because he had *not* gone to sea? His daughter used to claim he was not much of a sailor. Was Pop forever insecure about his navigational rheostat?

A FEW WEEKS AGO, the Norwegian state archivist e-mailed a link to an article in the online records of a Swedish newspaper, which I have asked Ola Myrvold, a distant cousin in Norway, to translate. Ola sends me the following:

"One must assume that [herring] seining is over for this season, because of the heavy storm last week. A horrible accident at sea has . . . happened: Sloop *Stavanger Paquet* which for many years has sailed to Hamburg, capsized as it was sailing from Grøttefjord with load. The crew was rescued, except the captain, Captain Mikkelsen [sic], who became a prey to the waves. His death is deeply regrettable, as the deceased was one of the city's finest sailors." The notice concludes with the words, "It is strange that, under the strong northeast winds, snow showers have been fiercer and the cold harsher and more poignant on Scandinavia's West Coast than on the East Coast."

STEVE WOBECKY, THE MARINE ELECTRICIAN to whom I recently addressed a voice mail, called me back promptly and on the agreed day shows up on time. He looks like Kris Kringle's younger brother, cheerful, white bearded. The Santa resemblance reminds me of Ole Krosvik, and perhaps that's why, in addition to the reliability factor, I harbor positive feelings about him. But the feelings turn out to be justified. In one morning Steve runs new wiring from my VHF radio to the masthead antenna and fixes my uppermost navigation light. All this mast-top work, which can only be safely accomplished ashore, was the last obstacle to launching *Odyssey,* and on a cool, overcast day in early summer the smell of cheap Chinese food invades our driveway; the boat hauler, John Peck, runs his hydraulic truck on discarded fryer oil. Peck drags her to a nearby cove and drops the sloop into her natural medium. As always that first lilt of deck as she starts to float, the slight drift to one side as the wind nudges her hull, fill my chest with a thrill that I would file, vaguely, under the memory index for "freedom." It comes, I think, out of an abdominal knowledge that from this moment forth, in potential at least, she and I can leave anytime, go anywhere the ocean goes on this blue earth, and that without permission or help.

Except, of course, we can't. I must still tune the rig, buy supplies. More importantly, I have to secure a crew. For the next couple of weeks, however, I'm happy to wait and take pleasure in my immediate family being together. The Big House is rented for the summer and the four of us live in three rooms over and beside the garage. Emilie, my eldest, moons back and forth to the beach, carrying art books, memorizing kanji, clad in a long black gown like a vision from Dante Gabriel Rossetti, her long hair snapping in the wind. Alexandre, in between growth spurts that are so energetic as to be almost visible, bikes off to play basketball with friends. Liz spends hours, happily I think, caring for plants in the tiny vegetable garden. We come together at dinner, are lassoed up in debates about anything: anime characters, Harry Potter, French arrogance, Emi's feminist film theories; that usually careen off into verbal brawls similar to the thunder squalls that drift briefly over Nantucket Sound and are as quickly gone.

I watch my family, happy and fulfilled in the moment even as we bicker. But my thoughts soon stiffen with the approach of fear. What if I go offshore and don't come back and Liz and the kids wind up, metaphorically at least, standing by the nearest breakwater, praying I am still alive? What if *Odyssey* hits a container come adrift from one of the big cargo ships that run in and out of Boston and Port Newark, that lie invisible as wartime mines and deadly in the waves? What if a gale blows out of nowhere and the mast step cracks, what if, what if?

What if fog arises when I'm out there? The Gulf of Maine is famous for fog. When warm air moves over colder sea, fog, like vaporous gray shit, happens. I've been e-mailing my friend Dan Burke, a Vineyarder who sailed so frequently in Maine waters that he ended up moving Downeast, and he writes back, "Keep in mind that there is fog and there is *FOG*. In fog you can see far enough ahead to turn the boat away from the sound of surf crashing on rocks or heavy diesels . . . but in FOG yer a free body in space and you can't say for sure which way is up, even." The *Cruising Guide to the Maine Coast* states, "Fog is . . . frequent around the outlying islands of Matinicus and Monhegan."

I feel serious self-contempt for suffering this kind of nervousness about a short trip offshore. I think of the octogenarian mariner who taught the lifeboat course at a maritime training school I attended in London. He had been torpedoed three times north of the Arctic Circle on the Murmansk run. Each time his ship sank within minutes, but he managed to make it into a lifeboat. The death rate for British and American merchant seamen in WWII was far higher than in any of the armed services. What if I had been a sailor in those days and had to say good-bye to my family, knowing a U-boat was waiting for me out there in the bitter ocean, its skipper searching for my ship through a periscope?

Self-contempt does not stop me from reflecting that my old fiberglass dinghy, which sits low to the water in a calm bay and will sink when swamped, is not up to lifeboat duty. I exhaust my budget on a brand-new inflatable dinghy with three separate flotation cells that will keep it buoyant no matter what.

ODYSSEY IS READY TO LEAVE. I have bought supplies. My celestial skills, I think and pray, are up to snuff. Despite or because of navigational panic I am aching to get started, but two last elements must now come together before I set out.

The first, as mentioned earlier, is a crew. My wild sail home from Tashmoo made it clear I can't both navigate and steer for long stretches. I need an automatic pilot, a device that holds the boat along a given compass course or wind direction, but autopilots cost thousands of dollars. The only way out is to find someone to steer while I navigate.

The second element is weather. I want some kind of southerly or westerly breeze to sail northeast to Matinicus. It would take too long to fight contrary winds, and gales, though historically accurate given what happened to Halvor, are not on my wish list. I seek to emulate Halvor's navigational techniques, not his demise. Also I really do not want fog, let alone *FOG,* for reasons already noted. And I'll need reasonably clear weather to see the sky, in order to use my sextant.

Once the sloop is ready we get a run of good weather. The prevailing wind is southwesterly, and this is good except that warm southwest winds tend to kick up fog in cooler Maine waters. But I have no crew.

Frustrated, I look up the Norwegian Meteorological Institute and send their press officer a message asking for information about nineteenth-century storm patterns on the coast of Hordaland Province, which includes Espevaer. If I can't make the weather fit my sailing plans in New England, I'll at least learn more about what Halvor was facing in the North Sea in February.

. . .

DURING THIS PERIOD OF WAITING a scientist I've been seeking to visit in Montreal contacts me, and I drive to Canada to interview her. Shortly after I return from Montreal, the *Knorr,* Woods Hole Oceanographic's veteran research ship, steams into home port. Her chief mate, Deirdre Emrich, has agreed to let me check out the ship's navigation systems.

On a sunny morning, therefore, I drive west to Woods Hole, on the Cape's southwestern corner, and meet Deirdre at the dockside security gate. It turns out we've met before, in another life; a typical peninsular life wherein, during the months of freezing drizzle and no jobs, people who are lonely and broke gravitate to the kitchen tables of friends' families— typically Irish and matriarchal—who will put up with the needs of those skint and alone. We both spent a lot of time in the warm kitchen of an Irish-Hispanic family in Centerville, drinking, talking, listening to music late into the night, reluctant to venture back into the whip of cold, to our solitary rooms.

Knorr is a blue-hulled ship with her superstructure shoved forward far enough to allow deck room for handling submersibles. As soon as we board and negotiate the coamings and companionways leading up to the bridge, I am—I want to say assaulted or wrestled down, the effect is so immediate and concrete—strongly touched, anyway, by the smell of ship, the mix of porthole grease, diesel fuel, coffee, soup, floor wax, all of which proximately reminds me of *Tower Helen* and the other small freighters I worked on in my twenties. But deeper still it brings back the ocean liners on which I traveled as a child, when my father's company paid for our summer trips to

France; ships like the *Queen Mary, United States, Leonardo da Vinci,* the SS *France.* These were trips stuffed with magic, for a boy: five days and nights (nine on the Italian Line) of unlimited food, free movies, pinball games, swimming pool, fancy hat contests, new friends, all set to the disco of waves and the rule of sea horizon, and flavored by this smell of ship.

Most strongly of all the smell brings back my father, who loved those old passenger liners with a passion that matched almost anything else he cared for in his life. He had joined the French Line after university and worked on the *Normandie,* the fastest and most elegant liner of them all. He saw those ships, anachronistic already in the 1970s, as the epitome of everything that was best, and most threatened, in European culture: a fragile grace represented in streamlined hull design, art deco fittings, fine food and wine, and civilized conversation. Long after he became a journalist, covering the UN for the French wire service, AFP, he used his press pass to ride the pilot boat, boarding the ships as they entered New York Harbor. I see him clearly in the screening room of my head, dressed in a threadbare suit and the torn trench coat he wore even as a senior White House correspondent, his sharp, forbidding features stretching suddenly into a smile that would warm the coldest part of you. The pleasure of olfactory recall mingles with the sadness of not being able to update my father memory. Once again I am made aware of the importance of mourning as an expression of this overriding mental reality: in our map of the world, memory takes up far more space and wields more power than the signposts and cues of day-to-day existence.

Knorr's bridge is the typical low, wide expanse set behind a line of windows. Several big consoles are crammed with monitors and associated controls, many devoted to Electronic Chart Display computers, or ECDIS. Modern ships and many yachts are now in most essential ways controlled by ECDIS, which correlates GPS position with a digital map, a matrix of radar targets overlaid on that chart, and the craft's autopiloting system. Thanks to ECDIS, the navigator navigates by reading an easily digested, multicolored, image-based story that tells him exactly what this vessel is doing in relation to deep channels, shallow water, buoys, land. Her own course and speed and the vectors of other ships (based on that radar overlay) are also part of the tale. Any ship of three hundred gross tons or more must carry, by law, a transponder, or Automatic Identification System, that pings out to other vessels the ship's name, nationality, speed, and course. "It makes collision avoidance so much easier," Deirdre says, clicking on the icon for a nearby research ship, the *Tioga,* which apparently is steering 204 degrees at 0.2 knots, though she is moored, immobile, on the quay opposite. "It's good for call-up, it reduces confusion in a collision situation." What this means is, instead of radioing "Large ship forty miles southeast of Nantucket" to warn the unknown navigator he is on a collision course with *Knorr,* she can call "Yo, *Texaco King,* wake up!" and *Texaco King*'s watch officer will know she's talking to him. It's a radio version of switching from allocentric to egocentric.

I mention to Deirdre that fully automated cargo vessels are in the advanced planning stage, ships that have no need for crew but would be programmed to make an entire voyage automatically, waypoint to GPS waypoint, avoiding other ships thanks to radar and visual sensors and collision-avoidance software. They would steer around bad weather on the most fuel-efficient course with the help of satellite imagery and meteorological models. In close quarters or emergencies the vessels could be guided remotely by operators in a command post half the world away, as drones are flown around the Hindu Kush by pilots sitting comfortably at Creech AFB in Nevada; as the Google car can be shifted to manual mode if the passenger inside chooses to interfere. These vessels of the future will be far cheaper to build and staff, since they'll need virtually no crew or associated amenities: only the lonely equivalent of a city apartment to accommodate the two living technicians, probably poorly paid South Asians, on call to perform systems maintenance.

Again, none of these technologies, based on feedback and servo systems, are new. What is novel is the massively augmented computer power involved in their operation, as well as worldwide coverage afforded by communications and navigational satellites. In this case, cybernetic quantity has brought about a paradigm shift in quality. There is no question that such systems will become ever speedier and more powerful, and that fully robotic ships, and trucks, and jets, will soon be navigating themselves around the world's commercial routes.

One might argue Deirdre has a professional prejudice against a trend that will make deck officers largely redundant. Yet she remains wary of this scenario for practical reasons. "I've seen enough hiccups in these," she says, pointing at the bridge terminals, "that I would not be comfortable with [that kind of automation]." *Knorr,* like most other large ships, incorporates redundancy in propulsion and power sources as well as GPS. But the ship's power plants have been known occasionally to fail, and for a ship run on computers the complications that arise from such a failure are myriad. "Watch standing is a whole lot easier [with these systems]," Deirdre says, "but if you interpret something wrong, or something is wrong with the inputs, things can deteriorate in a hurry." It has happened on *Knorr* that the generator has "dropped off. . . . Luckily when that happens [we are warned by] a distinct clicking on the relays." She grins and, while touching the controls with one hand, stares at the water in front of her ship, unconsciously keeping lookout the way every mariner has done since Ulysses and before.

As I leave *Knorr,* in the companionway leading down from the bridge, I pass a reminder of what can happen when humans believe too hard in their technology. It's a deck plan of the liner *Titanic,* whose position was lost when she went down off Newfoundland in 1912; whose wreck *Knorr* discovered, using some of the instruments I just examined on her bridge, in 1985.

CHAPTER FIFTEEN

The Downside of Cybernav

The drive home from Woods Hole is not long normally, but with summer traffic slowing me down, it gives me time to reflect that I am perhaps setting excessive store by Deirdre's doubts, and inflating in my head the risks of devolving navigation to machines. Ships across the world's oceans depend on cybersystems identical to those *Knorr* uses and despite the occasional bug and accident those systems, in daily use, vastly trim the dangers of seafaring. I keep reminding myself that, had Halvor been equipped with the equipment your average weekend cabin cruiser carries now, he would have seen the Internet weather reports, observed a storm approaching on satellite scans, and never left port. And if he did put to sea, with GPS, radar, and ECDIS hard at work, he would have known exactly where he was and steered clear of the storm;

even blinded by blizzard he could have turned around or otherwise avoided whatever fate lay in wait for him on Espevaer.

And yet that deck plan of the *Titanic* continues to bug me, as the White Star liner's demise has bothered people for over a century, and for similar reasons. We know, from the book by Walter Lord as well as from James Cameron's film, that the ship was moving too fast for safety in iceberg waters. What is less recognized is this: her collision was a quintessentially navigational issue. *Titanic* was not lost but dealing with hazards the existence of which was known but whose positions were not. If one imagines a chart with the ship's position fixed in a seascape filled with unlocated, invisible hazards, it is exactly the same for a watch officer as not knowing where he is on a chart full of perils whose positions are mapped.

Titanic was a case of unhappily staggered scientific discoveries. By 1912, breakthroughs in shipbuilding and propulsion had enabled great increases in speed and size, whereas the navigational arts, as we saw earlier, for two centuries had remained virtually unchanged. The last great leap forward in position finding had been the development of a working chronometer, and the resultant ability to calculate longitude, in 1735. *Titanic* was one of the first ships equipped with a radio transceiver, but what she really needed to avoid big icebergs in 1912 was radar, a technology that would not become practicable until the late 1930s and was unavailable to merchant shipping till the 1950s.

I don't use Imogen as I drive across three townships home. I know these roads by heart and love the fact that I can navigate them easily, it enhances my personal cognitive map in ways that make me feel more complex and more competent; or is this just a different way of saying that knowledge of its geography feels part of the idea of home? I suppose these thoughts sway my feelings. Yet I also believe the issue here is not how good the technology is—because, while it's conceived of and created by humans and thus will always contain human flaws, modern navigational technology is very, very good.

Rather, what we need to question is our relationship to the technology and the assumptions we make about it; why we choose to put our lives in the silicon grip of machines whose operation we know causes effects, both good and bad, dramatic and subtle, that we don't fully understand and cannot always predict.

ON JUNE 9, 1995, THE *Royal Majesty,* a "state of the art," thirty-two-thousand-ton cruise ship—one of those floating wedding cakes piled high with restaurants, bars, spas, and casinos, that specialize in taking retirees on leisurely swings under the tropic sun—sailed from Saint George, Bermuda, bound for Boston. The *Royal Majesty*'s officers could count on a rich bazaar of electronic navigational aids, including a computerized autopiloting system that guided and corrected the ship's course based on her GPS position. What the officers didn't know was that, one hour and ten minutes after leaving Bermuda, a poor connection broke the GPS feed to their autopilot. That fault registered on a terminal in the form of two sets of LED initials, "SOL" and "DR." The acronyms indicated satellite positioning had failed and the computer had automatically switched to dead-reckoning mode. But the initials were small, and no one noticed them.

DR, as we have seen, is a process that by definition cannot check itself against real landmarks and thus, given a dynamic environment such as the ocean, must produce increasingly skewed results as time ticks on and currents, wind, and other poorly quantifiable factors play against the ship. By the time *Royal Majesty* had traveled 550 miles to arrive at her next waypoint, a buoy marking the southern end of the Boston shipping lanes, she was 14.5 miles to the west of the position indicated on her GPS readout as well as on an electronic chart included in the radar display.

Her officers were not fools. The captain had ordered the mate on duty to look out for a "BA" buoy marking the entrance to Boston's shipping lanes. At approximately the right time, 6:45 P.M. on June 10, a big buoy showed up on radar in roughly the anticipated place. Because the chart on the radar screen was now locked into dead-reckoning data, both the mate and the system's algorithm assumed that blip was the same BA buoy they'd been aiming for. They were wrong. This marker, which bore the initials "AR," was the Asia Rip buoy anchored at the southernmost tip of Nantucket Shoals, the most treacherous stretch of water between Maine and Cape Hatteras.

But the mate did not look at the buoy, and *Royal Majesty* continued on her course. Three hours and fifteen minutes later a sailor reported white-green water ahead, a clear sign of shoals. The mate, trusting his GPS, ignored the warning. Minutes later the cruise ship, her keel twenty feet deep, ran aground on the three-foot shallows of a sandbar called Rose and Crown.

A National Transportation Safety Board review commented drily on the grounding: "Bridge automation has . . . changed the role of the watch officer on the ship. . . . The watch officer, who previously was active in obtaining information about the environment and used this information for controlling the ship, is now 'out of the control loop.' [He] is relegated to passively monitoring the status and performance of the automated systems. As a result of passive monitoring, the crewmembers of the *Royal Majesty* missed numerous opportunities to recognize that . . . the ship had deviated from its intended track."

The *Royal Majesty* incident happened twenty years ago, but the underlying issues have not faded away since. In April 2008 the General Lighthouse Authorities of the British Isles staged a test to determine what would happen if a modern vessel's GPS systems were brought down by jamming. The *Pole Star*, a late-model, 1,100-ton buoy tender, was ordered to run a course near Flamborough Head, off the northeast coast of England. Her crew knew what they were getting into, which was a good thing. According to the Authority's report, as soon as *Pole Star* entered the jamming zone her systems crashed. "Numerous alarms sounded on the bridge. . . . These alarms were all linked to the failure of different functions to acquire and calculate their GPS position, which included: the vessel's [GPS] receivers, the AIS [ship identification] transponder." The vessel's electronic chart system went south, as well.

The report goes on to warn that this kind of shutdown can

lead to "extremely hazardous consequences," especially in areas close to shore. It ends: "There are several questions raised by this trial, such as the ability of a vessel's crew to quickly revert to traditional means of navigation and also the extent to which they are able to navigate with these means. . . . Given the greater reliance on satellite navigation, in particular GPS, these skills are not being used daily and are no longer second nature."

THROUGH THE WINDSHIELD OF MY car I watch jets draw white surgical scars across the blue belly of sky. Tens of thousands of aircraft are daily guided around this continent by a GPS-based position-tracking system. Once again I remind myself to maintain a sense of perspective in all this. Dozens of drivers around me are finding their way safely to destination thanks to their personal Imogens.

But I saw earlier how the vulnerability to malfunction of computerized navigation systems affects automobiles; it can cause problems for aircraft, as well. In late 2009 the Federal Aviation Administration's air traffic control center at Newark Liberty International Airport began shutting down unexpectedly for short periods every day. Newark was one of the first airports to adopt the new, GPS-based control system to direct planes in one of the nation's busiest flight corridors. It took two months for investigators to find the culprit, a trucker who had installed a cheap jamming device to prevent supervisors from tracking his rig. He drove by the airport daily on the New Jersey Turnpike, his jammer knocking the GPS feed offline as he passed by. (A near–identical incident took out the Newark system in 2012.)

"From a security point of view, if you look at GPS's current status, [it's] more or less equivalent to operating computers without firewalls, with no basic checks," a GPS expert told *Wired* magazine in 2012. A "white hat" hacker who works for European spy agencies told me recently that cyberwarfare units in China and elsewhere are capable today of paralyzing any nation's power and communications systems simply by hacking its GPS component. The current availability online of "spoofers," devices that can transmit false but plausible position data to GPS receivers in cars, planes, and FAA centers suggests that more incidents of the Newark type are inevitable.

THE TROUBLE NOTED ABOVE WAS caused either by clear malfunction or direct human interference. Two further examples, however: the strange incident of Northwest Airlines Flight 188, and the loss of the *Team Vestas Wind;* shift the spotlight from this binary human–machine pathology to the questions that bothered me after I saw that deck plan of the *Titanic*—namely, what ought to be our day-by-day relationship to this technology? How should we reset "normal" behavior, given the potential for trouble, not to say disaster, that the vulnerability, ubiquity, and power of our devices imply?

NWA 188 was an Airbus A320 jet bound from San Diego to Minneapolis–Saint Paul on October 21, 2009. Half an hour after scheduled arrival time the pilots still had not announced preparations for landing, and a flight attendant, noticing they were late, called the cockpit. The pilot and copilot, according to subsequent testimony, had been obsessing over a crew-scheduling program on their laptop computers and until then did not notice that the plane—guided by a computer-driven flight-management system, or FMS, which accurately navigated them to destination—had overshot the Minneapolis airport and cruised on at four hundred miles per hour 150 miles eastward while they played with their screens.

If one converts this mishap into navigational facts, what really happened was this: the GPS-based program worked as it was supposed to, but the pilots were busy dealing with a different program. At that point the personal dead-reckoning system of a flight attendant, based on a pattern of grid cells correlating time and position in her brain, kicked in and alerted the crew to what was going on. . . .

Team Vestas Wind was a sixty-five-foot sloop, racing in the Volvo 'round-the-world race that in November 2014 smashed into the Cargados Carajos reef off East Africa, apparently due to the near-invisibility of that hazard on her electronic chart system. A competing skipper, Charles Caudrelier, commented: "To see [the reef] on our electronic charts, you have to zoom right in on top of it. But how and why would you zoom into it if you don't know it's there in the first place?" His words remind me of the abrupt shift in perspective I felt switching between Google Earth and the *Times Atlas,* when I first searched for Espevaer.

Both Flight 188 and *Team Vestas Wind,* not to mention the multitudinous examples of GPS mistakes mentioned earlier, highlight an issue largely ignored in our information society. It's an issue that has serious implications for all of us who live therein. To what extent are quality of life and physical safety affected by everyday changes that our systems-saturated, information-drenched routines bring about? And how much have our native navigational faculties been altered, even degraded, by the kind of lifestyle such a society forces us to adopt?

STILL RUMINATING ON ALL THIS after I get home, I dig up a stack of files holding research material I collected as *Odyssey* and I waited to depart. I dump these on my desk next to the garden window. This material consists mostly of data found on the Internet about the effects of living as we do, in the middle of a flooding Amazon of digital information. To read these articles, knowing their origin, feels a little like a scientist peering through his microscope to uncover the true nature of microscopes. Nevertheless, what I found was the following:

The sheer volume of data people in a wired society must ceaselessly deal with exceeds the ability of our minds to analyze and use. Our short-term memory can hold and consciously process only three to nine bits of information at a given time, after which it must convert what it's seeing to medium- or long-term memory or junk it wholesale. Saving data burns time and energy. The average text message contains hundreds of bits of information, not to mention the memories, places, and associations its information triggers. Multiply that by everything else going on around you—e-mails, TV, print ads, Twitter feeds, work data, Facebook, games, LinkedIn, talk, music—and it's no wonder we have trouble keeping track. We use different terms to tag the problem: information overload, cognitive buffering, data smog; but the names don't point to a solution.

Angelika Dimoka of Temple University studied the brains of decision makers assembling a stock portfolio. Those using several sources of information made substantially more objective mistakes than those using only one. Sheena Iyengar of Columbia found that shoppers considering twenty-four options were five times more inhibited in choosing than those dealing with six. Faced with more than a handful of pieces of information, it seems, our prefrontal cortex slows, runs roughly, even switches off.

Most of us deny such problems in daily life. This is especially true of young people brought up in the wired world. We tell ourselves, "That's fine, I can multitask," but as Sherry Turkle demonstrates in *Alone Together,* people who "multitask" simply switch from focusing well on one or two jobs to fulfilling five or six tasks poorly. Instead of concentrating, we are shallowing our attention and skimping on response. The effects of such shallowing and skimping on navigational tasks are numerous and sometimes scary. A 1998 NASA report examined thirty-seven airplane accidents and found thirteen involved "multitasking" pilots, a finding since corroborated by similar studies.

Another effect of information overdose that is well established scientifically is a deterioration in the wired individual's sense of time. Turkle says, "Our networked devices encourage a new notion of time because they promise that one can layer more activities onto it." A study by the Indian Academy of Applied Psychology backs up earlier research in stating drily, "Prospective time estimates [by test subjects] decreased as cognitive load increased." Our sense of time is twisted by an overload of information.

I cannot see Martha's Vineyard from where I sit reading; the island and intervening sound are obscured by trees and houses; but Tashmoo and Hedge Fence shoal are strongly highlighted on my mental map when I consider these issues. I understand that, even on that hungover sail from the Vineyard, my brain worked efficiently enough to keep track of time and realize that I had not been sailing on one course long enough to be where I thought I was from the look of the coast. What would have happened, then, if I'd been tweeting "#odyssey on boat big wind omg crazy!" and sending text messages to boot? Would I, like the pilots of NWA 188, have lost track of time passed and courted more serious trouble?

And what of memory in all this? Even now, several years after the fact, how I registered a perceived dissonance in time off Hedge Fence seems identical in quality to the nuts and bolts of remembering. If, as Dr. Maguire and others have demonstrated, the processes of memory are identical to our navigational faculties, does it not follow that a degradation in our temporal sense and attendant grid-cell functions will change our memory and thus who we are and how we live?

At Sea

O n a sun-drunk noon in full summer, I ease *Odyssey* into Nantucket Sound and set a course southwest for Succonesset Point. I have checked weather sites obsessively, watching online radar chase the green wraiths of thunderstorms across central Mass. The forecast for this three-day stretch is OK, not perfect, and it's supposed to go downhill the evening of the third day, but I know that if I wait for the ideal forecast I shall still be waiting next year.

The wind is light, northerly. Past Succonesset I hoist the mainsail, unroll the big foresail (or genoa), and the boat leans and starts to move more in concord with the waves rather than the way she does when butting against them with engine only. The new inflatable dinghy, which Liz has nicknamed "Circe," follows obediently and straight behind. I have timed the tide right and the current pops us like wet soap squeezed in a fist through the narrows of Woods Hole and into Buzzards Bay. *Knorr*'s berth, I notice in passing, is empty. Deirdre said she had a full research schedule, mostly in waters off Greenland.

By nightfall, I am moored in a harbor I've never been in before, just south of the Cape Cod Canal. It's called Wings Cove and while the boat rocks and creaks a fair amount due to wake raised by canal traffic, it is otherwise quiet; no sound emanates from the surrounding woods and marsh or from the half dozen houses built on lawns that subside into eelgrass and water.

The next morning I am under way by 7:30 to catch the last of the tide north and east through the canal. The current runs at five knots; with the boat under power we make close to twelve and it feels like a sleigh ride. The bridges loom, then drench the sloop in shade. I admire their New Deal grid work, so massive, gray, and rivet-ridden it makes the spans resemble a Thomas Hart Benton mural with a title like "Modern Man Builds a New World." I feel that light sense of occasion I think most Cape Codders experience when negotiating the bridges from whatever angle, because they are so central to our psychology: they define the peninsula while making us, technically, an island, with all this implies of safety and isolation both.

Bridges define, also, our individual identities. I know people who have not dared "go over the bridge" in years. I have friends who live beside this canal who are quite at home in Truro, an hour's drive away on the Cape's other end, because it's still "the Cape"; but if they cross the bridge and travel five miles to Plymouth they feel vulnerable and unsure because that's the mainland, a bit strange, subtly hostile ground. (This effect is multiplied on Martha's Vineyard and Nantucket.) Looking at the Sagamore Bridge rise above the masthead antenna, I remember all the times I crossed by car for reasons big and small, good and terrible; meeting Liz in Stonington, Connecticut, when we reconciled after a breakup; crossing the canal at 3:00 A.M. in a driving blizzard to be with Louis in his final days; chasing an ambulance to Boston Children's Hospital when my oldest son got sick; so many times coming home from all those other places that were not. The lines from Eliot's "Little Gidding" run through my head:

> *We shall not cease from exploration*
> *And the end of all our exploring*
> *Will be to arrive where we started*
> *And know the place for the first time*

At the canal's northeastern end I call Sandwich Marina on the VHF radio to check procedures for docking. There is no response. I tie up at the fuel dock anyway, to top up the main tank and pick up my crew.

MY CREW IS MARTIN OLIVE, known as Martini. His contradictions, and this he has in common with most of us, define him best. He is a farmer's kid from the heart of Iowa and a man who has spent much of his life hanging around the snootiest suburban areas of the East Coast. One of the wittiest people I know, he lost a brother as I did and continues, with great care and seriousness, to look after chronically ill family members in the Midwest. Contractor, Democratic Party activist, Harvard graduate, Deadhead, cornfield anarchist; a close friend of Louis' and now of mine. Martini is a man who works as hard as anyone I've ever met, who knows next to nothing about boats, and has freed up a week of his life to be my crew.

He's a good-looking guy of fifty-odd summers with a squarish face, blondish hair, an expression that veers between quizzical when worried and abstract the rest of the time. He satisfies all four criteria for crewing on *Odyssey*: good company, impervious to seasickness, able to steer, and available.

THE WIND HAS FRESHENED AS we quit the canal and head for Provincetown. The plan is to spend the night in harbor at the Cape's tip. The National Weather Service marine forecast calls for variable southerly winds tomorrow, freshening to ten to fifteen knots later. Today the wind is still northerly around ten. It's a perfect sailing day, and *Odyssey* moves well with the wind off her port bow. A pod of pilot whales travels ahead of us, northward, sounding and surfacing silver against the dark swells in a synchronous rhythm that appears choreographed and seems also to include a component of joy, of taking pleasure in the swim; although this must of course be speculation, a form of John Ruskin's pathetic fallacy, of ascribing human qualities to nature. What is not fallacious is the shimmer of joy both Martin and I experience in watching them.

By evening we are moored in Provincetown Harbor. Music thumps from a disco tea party on the waterfront. I have been trying to call the harbormaster, the marina, anybody on my main VHF radio, and get no more response than I got from Sandwich. Clearly my radio, to put it in technical terms, is fucked. I have a handheld VHF but it only carries a mile or two, which would be near-useless in an emergency offshore. The NWS weather station comes in fine on the handheld, however, and the forecast is stable. The wind is supposed to stay favorable, south or southeast five to ten tomorrow, strengthening toward night, holding southerly the next day. There is a possibility of more thunderstorms. Fog is forecast for Cape Ann, a third of the way up the coast, but no mention is made of fog Downeast.

I'm a little worried about the main VHF not working. With it, thanks to the antenna Santa Claus's brother fixed, which sits forty-odd feet above the waterline, if we got into trouble fifty miles offshore our signal would have reached any ship or fishing boat in a twenty-five-mile radius, which is a lot of sea. The handheld set, weak and low, barely reaches two miles. Now, as in Haiti, as in the methods of navigation I will use, we'll truly be sailing without backup, as Halvor did.

WE LEAVE P-TOWN AROUND 10:30 the next morning, diesel thudding and bow carving into seas that are glossy and calm. I am sick enough of waiting by this point that, however untraditional this way of sailing, I am prepared to motor all the way to Maine if we must; the spare tanks contain enough fuel to make it. But an hour later, past Race Point, the wind picks up from the southwest and I hoist the sails and switch off the engine. The pounding of internal combustion is replaced by the kiss of wake, the crunch of our bow breaking into deepening swells, the whisper of breeze in the sails, the squeak of rigging.

I planned to take a latitude sight at noon but the Cape's tip is still visible to the south, compromising the horizon against which I'd need to measure the sun's height. A couple of hours after that, with the wind steady at ten knots, the low land has disappeared. As Martini steers I fetch the sextant and shoot a series of longitude sights that work out well, each within a mile of the others. They draw lines of position running near-perpendicular to our course of forty-seven degrees magnetic: by that reckoning we are twenty-two miles northeast of Race Point and making good time, at an average speed of almost seven knots. At this rate we should reach Matinicus Rock early tomorrow morning.

A large cargo ship slides down the Boston shipping lanes five miles astern and vanishes to the east.

I check the time of twilight and note it in *Odyssey*'s logbook. I want to shoot three separate stars at dusk, when the sun has just gone down and stars start to come out but the horizon is still visible to measure against. With three stars at sufficient angles from each other I will be able to pinpoint our exact position before nightfall. I take the wheel as Martini prepares something to eat. Looking around, I see nothing but flat, shining horizon.

I feel good; more than good. Now that the waiting is over,

now we are committed to crossing the Gulf of Maine, to dealing with whatever sea and weather throw at us, my nervousness has vanished. I still don't like the fact that we have no good radio. To sail without working equipment cuts across the grain of how I was trained.

The feel of being free from land more than makes up for that. Partly it has to do with that wee thrill of freedom I experience every time I launch the boat or even drop the mooring warp. Another part has to do with being, for better or for worse, however episodic my sea time, a mariner; and as such I am aware in the fibers of bone and tendon that land is far more dangerous than open ocean. The vast majority of shipwrecks happen close to shore, for land is rocks, land is cliffs that distort wind, currents skewed by the curves of shore, shallows that raise waves to twice their usual height, reefs onto which a storm will drive your craft. It makes perfect sense to me that Halvor's ship foundered "off Espevaer," even if she sank in eighty fathoms, as M. L. Michaelsen stated, which would imply that she was not driven onto rocks—or if she did ground, was driven off afterward, as sometimes happens. But the twists in peril the coast throws at a mariner are too numerous to list, with regard to Halvor, without visiting Norway; too dark to keep in mind while knowing we must make landfall on another rock-strewn coastline tomorrow. For now I am happy to live in this moment with a good boat cantering happily (and to hell with the pathetic fallacy) across open sea. To the west a humpback whale combs a fan of vapor into the sky, and minutes later a black wedge on the sleek top of what is probably a finback describes an arc that touches the horizon. This is no Norway-to-Greenland journey but I am happy enough to use the same tools the Norsemen used to correlate life-forms in the marine environment with a portion of the continental shelf and confirm our position thereby: we're sailing near the northern edge of Stellwagen Bank, where whales gather to feed. This is what it means to navigate truly, I realize: to switch off everything that *tells* us what we're seeing and where we're going. To open our eyes and see for ourselves.

I think back to the Ancient Greeks and the difference between *pelagia* and *thalassa,* their two terms for salt water. *Pelagia* meant shallow, coastal seas such as Nantucket Sound, water that defines itself by land.

Thalassa was something else. *Thalassa* was the dark, dark blue of deep water. *Thalassa* included in its very sound and name the mythical notions associated with wild places: of mystery, danger, escape from servitude.

Thalassa is ocean, like this.

THE WIND VEERS TO THE southwest and now blows from right behind us. It's a tricky point of sail for two reasons: the mainsail, which the wind hits first, screens the big genoa foresail so that half the time, confused, the foresail slaps back and forth and does not fill. The mainsail has to be let almost all the way out to catch the wind, at near-right angles to our course. This means, if the sail is set far to the right and we allow the boat to slew even a few degrees in the same direction, the wind will catch the sail's back surface and blast it unceremoniously to the boat's other side: a jibe. You truly do not want your head in the way when a fifteen-foot metal boom swoops scythe-like across the boat.

Martin and I therefore steer with concentration as the wind continues to blow from the southwest and then, around 5:30 P.M., starts blowing harder. I am happy at first, since *Odyssey* needs a strong wind to sail her best, but the wind continues to increase. The black-white wings of stormy petrels jink between the rising swells in front of us. Low clouds, glowing orange as the sun sinks, scud from the west and speed over-head. The sky to the northeast darkens to the hue of lapis. Now the wind is spanking wave tops white and flinging them as foam before us. The sloop rides the growing peaks and valleys with grace, but regularly now her bow smacks harder into a wave and sends a slice of water foaming back toward the cockpit.

By 7:00 P.M. I reckon the wind must be blowing twenty and strengthening. The boat is moving more violently. I roll down the genny to the size of a big tablecloth and tell Martini I am concerned. If the wind keeps rising it will be necessary to shorten the mainsail. This will be harder to achieve in the dark, in seas that have grown rougher with a stronger wind.

"I'm going to put a reef in now, just in case," I tell him. A "reef" means making the sail smaller. He nods. His jaw is set to "grim," and he cleans spray off his glasses to read the com-pass better. Earlier Martini told me he belonged to the Alfred E. Neuman school of seafaring, the motto of which is "What, *me* worry?" Now he says, very firmly, "Just remember, George,

I know nothing about all this. Just tell me exactly what to do and I'll do it. But don't *not* tell me what to do 'cause then I won't know what to do."

I start the engine, put it in gear, and tell him to bring the boat slowly left, into the wind, reeling in the mainsheet, the line that leashes the mainsail, as we turn. I strap on my home-made harness—it's a rope looped around my abdomen with a carabiner at one end—and clip that to a safety line rigged up and down the boat's length. Then I edge forward to the mast. As Martini brings *Odyssey* across the wind she starts to roll and then, as we head into the waves, begins to pitch, bow rising high then crashing deep, and water comes green and white over the bow, soaking my feet. Martini holds her right on course, the sail smacking and banging about. Then the boom swings hard and fast and pushes me off balance onto the port deck. My sneakers slip on slick fiberglass. I'm attached to the safety line but fear surges nonetheless, a pressured shadow swelling from gut to throat, tightening breath and tongue. Now I'm dangling half over the side and my reptile brain is yelling at me, "You're six inches from falling overboard and if your homemade harness comes off you're in the water and it's twilight and the seas are four feet high and though you gave Martini the man-overboard drill, what are the chances he'll turn the boat in time and find you in this?"

My left hand finds a support cable to grab and, pushing myself against the wire, I scramble ingloriously back onto the cabin roof. The sail still snaps and bangs but comes down read-ily enough when I ease the line holding it up. I gather the surging sailcloth in my arms, tie its lower portion into a bundle, winch the shortened sail back up the mast, edge along the safety line to the cockpit, and we turn back on our old course.

As soon as the reefed sail fills the boat sails much easier and almost as fast as before. "Good job, Mr. Christian," I tell Martin, and he answers with a mock salute and shouts, "Aye, aye, Captain Bligh, sir!"—a joke that was corny when it started and has now simply become how Martini and I interact, 98 percent fooling around and 2 percent the reality of my asking him to do something ridiculous and he doing it.

I go below to the chart table and update our dead reckoning. Estimated position puts us well clear of the Boston shipping lanes. Getting past those lanes in daytime was one reason I chose to leave before noon, even though it meant a landfall early in the morning, usually the worst time for fog. I climb back to the cockpit to see if stars are visible. The North Star, Polaris, is easy to locate, and from practice on the Cape I have no trouble recognizing Altair to the east. I check the dinghy, out of habit. I've been observing it periodically as the seas rose. It is sturdily built with twin rings forward to attach a towing bridle. Maybe I haven't checked in a while, but when I look now I realize its motion has radically changed. Circe, from towing obediently and straight, is suddenly doing everything it should not, like a horse that just won't be led, pulling left then right, holding back on the far slope of one wave, surging forward on the near slope of the next, which slackens the towline and allows the inflatable to veer off course to one side or the other till yanked back into line by the on-charging sloop. Circe's movements are so violent that I am quite sure those rings, which are secured by rubber squares glued—strongly but still only glued—to the dinghy's forward cell, will tear off, and sooner rather than later.

I was scared on the cabin roof but it was sudden and over quickly. The concern I have now is of a different nature. It's that fear I imagined last fall when I thought of the infernal chain reaction that might be triggered by too much pressure on the mast step—the knowledge of how bad stuff occurs, one little thing going wrong then the malfunction putting more stress on a different part that is not built to take it and something bigger breaking and all of a sudden—

I think it likely a similar infernal chain must have happened in Halvor's case. Even the stories about his death, somewhat contradictory as they are, throw up so many different perils: storm, snow, getting lost, rocky islands, shifting cargo, broken hatch, ship's papers; that it feels likely no single event sank him but rather two or three, storm leading to snow leading to lost position hooking onto rocks tied to evasive maneuvers shackled to cargo shifting and then listing too far to one side . . .

Still, Halvor's fate is only a minute darkening of worry against the in-your-face realities of tonight as I stare at Circe. I've only had the dinghy a few weeks but already I've grown fond of it, mostly I suppose because it doesn't leak and under normal circumstances tows well. Something else is inlaid here too. A deeper part of me has been involved in dinghies, in the John Donne sense, since I was old enough to row. I had an old skiff, named *Hornet* for some reason, that I used to row all over West Bay imagining scenarios piratical and otherwise; it was *Hornet* I tried to save in the aftermath of our ill-fated amphibious strike against the neighbor's kids. One day when I was maybe seven, while out rowing, I lost an oar in the main channel and the ebbing tide dragged me out the cut. I tried paddling with my remaining oar but got nowhere, and *Hornet* was swept into Nantucket Sound. I sat on the thwart and cried, convinced that I would be lost forever, would never see Louis or my parents again. Then a white launch appeared, heading in my direction. It belonged to a man named MacColl, who lived near the cut and had seen what happened. He towed me and my skiff back to the dock. I did not think of this, or not consciously at least, while looking at Circe try to tear itself loose and get lost forever; but I am sure the reassurance of having a dinghy, and the associated fear of losing it, informed what happened next.

"We're going to have to get the dinghy aboard," I tell Martini.

"How are you going to do that?" he says.

"Not sure," I answer. The wind is stronger than ever. The swells in the growing dark seem eight feet tall, though they are probably less than five.

Once more I clip my harness to the lifeline. I haul the dinghy by its towrope to *Odyssey*'s backside and try lifting it aboard. This model has a plywood floor, making it heavier than most inflatables its size, and all I can do is lift Circe's front end to deck level. The rest will not come. I tell Martin to turn into the wind a bit, letting air spill out of the reefed sail, which reduces speed and drag on the dinghy. I try pulling Circe up *Odyssey*'s stern again, with similar result.

Martini and I confer, shouting against the wind; we decide to haul the dinghy sideways, pulling on a handline that runs along Circe's side. I collapse the stanchions that support *Odyssey*'s wire railing on the starboard side so we can haul the dinghy straight to the deck. While Martini steers I drag Circe forward by its bridle line, parallel to *Odyssey,* but I cannot lean far enough out to exert good longitudinal pull because of the harness. So I unclip the safety harness and lean well out, bringing the inflatable a third of the way up the boat's length. I switch my grip to the handline and haul as hard as I can and that's when it happens; a seventh wave or at any rate a high swell I was not expecting dips the sloop out of rhythm, deep to starboard, and I overbalance for the second time in half an hour and start to topple over the side, one leg gone now and my center of gravity shifting from boat to water, and heart and breath feel stopped in fear and shock.

My mind, which until then was sorting different options, seems to narrow down to one image-memory-place-thought which is *Jesus-fuck find something anything to hold on to!* I drop the handline, flail wildly. Water from the next wave sluices the deck. After seconds that feel like minutes my left hand encounters the Laura-repaired dodger, that canvas shelter over the cabin hatch, which I pull at desperately, tearing the canvas again but it holds. I drag my center of gravity back toward the boat's, banging my butt hard and thankfully on the cockpit coaming.

Heart and lungs slow to normal. I lengthen the safety harness, clip it back on, and try again. Martin leaves the wheel to help. Having two people to pull works. Together we haul the dinghy clumsily sideways into the cockpit and shove it forward onto the cabin roof, where I lash it down tight; and for a few minutes we observe what we've done, with a certain pride in getting that problem solved.

The pride doesn't last. The infernal chain is still happening, I realize. The dinghy, which flares upward in front, protrudes almost three feet over the cabin roof. We are back to running before the wind, crashing along fast over swells that look like little hills; it would be small-craft advisories here if they posted such warnings this far out. The mainsail is still set far to the right, to starboard, and if we turn right the wind will flip sail and boom to the other side; they will slam into Circe on the way, popping our life raft's flotation cells or yanking it off its lashings or both.

For the first time, though, I'm conscious of the start of an angelic chain reaction, a positive sequence; or perhaps all chains of events are random at heart, and what we should think about is more the constellation of neutral opportunities, good and bad, that each separate event generates? But this one is positive because earlier I lowered the sail to shorten it, which means I have space on the mast's upper extremity to lift the shortened sail, together with the attached boom, the foot or two needed to clear the dinghy if we jibe. I explain the problem to Martini. My crewmate's face in the compass light is red. His jaw is still set, he seems a bit tense and does not lift his eyes from the compass card as he says, "I told you, just tell me what to do. It's when you don't tell me that I get nervous."

So I explain, check the harness, make my way along the safety line to the mast. Hanging on to the mast with one hand, even with wind and water plucking at me, I don't feel in danger. I winch sail and boom to the required height, tie off the lifting halyard, and make my way back to the cockpit, where I take over the wheel.

It's almost full dark now. The stars I planned to shoot with my sextant burn into the surrounding night. The horizon, from the dark but defined 360-degree line it was only half an hour ago, has become a process, a fuzzy continuum where darkness of ocean blends into a lesser dark of sky. In reefing the sail and securing the dinghy, I have lost, with twilight, the window of time I needed to obtain a star fix.

I suppose this is a good thing in terms of re-creating the circumstances of Halvor's doomed voyage. More than likely, my great-great-grandfather would have loved to fix his position to dodge the storm. But even if he managed to claw offshore and away from Espevaer, snow would have prevented a sight. And if the cargo started to shift he would have run out of time for fancy calculations as well. What he and I have left, once again, is dead reckoning. I ask my long-suffering crew to take the wheel again, and go below to work out our approximate position. It puts us forty-seven miles offshore, on a latitude of forty-two degrees, forty-three minutes: seventy-three miles from Matinicus.

Darkness hesitates. Now the moon oozes up, large and bloated, and washes everything in mercury. *Odyssey* crashes onward through the night.

CHAPTER SEVENTEEN

Navigate or Die?

The moon was only a quarter full a week before the sail but it shone clear in a blue sky over the Saint Lawrence River as I drove our new, fully warrantied Jetta from a street near my rented room in Montreal's Mile End neighborhood to the suburb of Verdun.

An hour later, as I sat watching in the Douglas Mental Health University Institute on LaSalle Boulevard, Yolande X. was plunked in the middle of a cityscape that was both Canadian and nothing, a place strange to her, and told to find her way.

Yolande was a middle-aged Québécoise with dark hair and glasses. She sat at a computer terminal playing a modified first-person-shooter video game called *Unreal Tournament*. A black-haired graduate student named Shoshanah tracked Yolande's movements through the CGI city, tracing her route on a paper map held upon her knees.

It was a classic video game, everything seen from the operator's point of view: click left arrow and it was as if you had turned your eyes and body leftward, click up arrow and you moved toward what you faced. The landmarks in this unreal city were clearly marked; what was tough was finding them once you started to negotiate these streets in which the detail-fudging proclivities of game coders seemed to reinforce the humanity-bending instincts of mall developers to arrive at a city that could have been any regional hub in our so-called developed world. A municipal swimming pool, a store, an Esso station called, painfully, "Past Gas" . . . Between these landmarks lay many tangled streets of concrete office blocks, brick projects, Jersey barriers. Shoshanah told me that while all game characters had been expunged from the algorithm underlying this virtual world, a few artifacts subsist. Once in a while an armored über–ninja warrior will leap out from behind a corner, lasers blazing, and scare the crap out of volunteers.

"OK?" Shoshanah said in French. "You're standing in front of the church. Now find the post office. Speed is not important, what's important is to find the shortest route." For half an hour Yolande wandered, searching for different landmarks, choosing streets at random. Finally, she dropped her hands and looked at Shoshanah in despair. "I have no idea," she said, "I don't have the map in my head."

. . .

ONE MILE NORTHEAST FROM THE Douglas Institute, across an arm of the Saint Lawrence, a modern, cream-colored, balcony-scored complex of apartment blocks stood amid golf links and fake antique lampposts. Inside, a half dozen people sat near a plush lobby, unaware of where they were, how they got there, or even where they'd been ten minutes earlier.

This was Résidence Symphonie, a planned community for the elderly. Symphonie's Moments Neighborhood, a specialized assisted-living area, caters to people suffering from dementia and Alzheimer's disease. Yolande was not a victim of either pathology but she had something in common with Alzheimer's and dementia patients. Victims of these diseases, from all over Canada, participated in experiments conducted by a Douglas research team headed by Véronique Bohbot, whose work I'd been hearing about for months.

I could have described Dr. Bohbot in terms of height, weight, age, and missed the part that was important, which was her energy. "I feel like I'm in a race, too much research to do before I retire, too many new things I see that I have to do," she told me. The physical geography of Bohbot—low altitude, eyes very focused in attention and direction, black shoulder-length hair, an expressive mouth, forty-ish—seemed to me deliberately underplayed in favor of her work, which consumes sixty to seventy hours of her week and is by any measure important.

In a series of controlled experiments, Bohbot has demonstrated that people who consistently employ stimulus-response behavior in navigation—the type of behavior that typifies GPS users—suffer a measurable loss of gray matter in the hippocampus; and this atrophy significantly boosts their chances of contracting the diseases of memory from which the Moments Neighborhood inmates were suffering. It's the opposite effect from what happens to London taxi drivers after learning the Knowledge. Similar studies by research teams led by Tom Hartley at UCL in London and by Denise Head at Washington University in Saint Louis have reinforced Bohbot's findings. Ongoing studies focused exclusively on heavy GPS users are expected to reach parallel conclusions. The research performed by Bohbot and her colleagues, therefore, points strongly to a single, frightening conclusion: our addiction to advanced navigational technologies is physically harming our brains.

Bohbot put it even more succinctly, in speaking of the hippocampal formation. "Use it or lose it," she said.

She explained to me that the developed world faces a health crisis that is both gigantic and, in part, unexpected. The cost of caring for Alzheimer's patients alone in the United States currently exceeds $216 billion per annum, more than for any other disease; the Alzheimer's Foundation predicts it will shoot up to $1.1 trillion by 2050. The research being performed at Douglas and elsewhere proves these trends are in significant part due to our addiction to GPS and other technologies that do our navigating for us. Given the exponentially increasing presence of such technologies in our lives, it seems likely that the addiction, and its price tag, will soar beyond even these estimates.

"We are looking at a new model for aging," Bohbot said. "The effects on cognition, such as Alzheimer's, may have nothing to do with deterioration of the brain, but [they happen instead] because we don't use the brain in a healthy way."

While I was with her, Bohbot spent a lot of time on computer and smartphone, juggling child-care and research commitments. She is a single mother with a teenage son, travels frequently for work, and uses GPS at times, conscious of the apparent contradiction, which she resolves by advising that we turn off the technology once it's been used to find where we're going. "What I say to people is that we can use GPS to explore the environment, but don't become dependent on it. [Developing] a cognitive map may take longer, but it's worth the investment," she told journalists when results of her hippocampus study were first announced. . . .

My interview with Bohbot went longer than scheduled. I was aware that she had put off other appointments for my benefit; aware, also, that I needed to drive back to Massachusetts that evening, a four-hundred-mile journey, to continue readying the boat so I could leave promptly when Martini showed up. But I kept on taking notes, hunched in a plastic office chair, asking further questions, for what this woman was trying to do seemed to carve right down to the heart of what I wished to find out by sailing and by learning more about my own navigational rheostat.

Global positioning devices are only one aspect of the danger, Bohbot continued. The hippocampal formation seems to function as part of a binary system of which the other half is the caudate nucleus, a formation also located in the brain's center, not far from the hippocampus. Activation of one part seems to induce relative dormancy in the other. The caudate

nucleus switches on with linear, stimulus/response-type behavior, such as rote learning and reaction to various forms of
electronic media. When we respond to GPS directions and
computer programs—as was the case with the pilots of NWA
188 and the officers of the *Royal Majesty*—the caudate nucleus
jumps on its neural bike and starts to sprint, while the hippocampus slows down.

Conversely, the hippocampal formation fires while we are
actively seeking to figure out where we are, with our associa-
tive and memory functions furiously engaged. It runs hard also
when performing relatively creative tasks, stuff we have to
imagine and formulate conceptually to apprehend, problems
we must sketch out and belabor to solve. This is the mode
wherein we scan around us, take in everything we can from
a given environment, and stitch those data together with associated memories to craft ideas: the navigation mode. It strikes
me now that this mode, paradoxically, is what Colonel Sainte-
Marie and his people inhabit as they think about the trajecto-
ries and space environment of those very satellites that allow
the rest of us to shun navigating on a semipermanent basis.

OUTSIDE THE WINDOWS OF THE Douglas Institute it was
late summer. Inside, framed photos scattered around Bohbot's
office showed the treeless snowscapes of Nunavut, in the
Canadian Arctic. Bohbot pointed to a picture of herself standing among a group of smiling Inuit.

"What is startling about the Inuit," Bohbot said, "is that
only fifty years ago, they used 100 percent traditional meth-

ods, and it's all been lost in a couple of generations." Bohbot worked for several weeks in Nunavut testing the Inuits' navigational functions. She spent many hours with Théo Ikumak, an old man now, who was born in an igloo and still navigates the traditional way across tundra and ice pack: no desert to the traditional Inuit but the interface with an abundance of life. In general, the older Inuit she tested used active navigational areas in the brain 85 percent of the time, whereas subjects thirty and under used them 50 percent or less. For a multiplicity of reasons, not least the misguided policies of assimilation sponsored by Ottawa, younger Inuit have almost entirely given up traditional ways, of navigation as of everything else, for the warm, easy suburban lifestyle of the rest of Canada. "They have [regular] homes, TV, video games, they all use GPS; Facebook is on 24-7," Bohbot said.

We both were aware of the hypocrisies that can arise among ourselves and our peers when considering such results. College professors might wax nostalgic about rural simplicity and going back to "basics," but even a week spent living as the traditional Inuit did—as Nansen did for an Arctic winter, chewing seal fat in the dark—would be enough to send the vast majority of Westerners, myself included, hotfoot back to the airline counter, clamoring for a seat on the next flight out.

Bohbot did not advocate going back in time to an Inuit-style way of life, but she was greatly concerned by what happens to a society in which the spatial and mnemonic tasks for which our brains are built and in the use of which they evolved are performed for us by a network of electronic devices and associated systems.

The ease of those devices and systems, and the passive society they sculpt, Bohbot says, are highly addictive. The subtle but extremely powerful result of this passivity, and the manner in which it is sold to us, is a manic optimism. We are conditioned to think no problems exist that our devices and systems cannot solve. By extension, we start to believe we should never have to fail whatever challenges life throws our way. Thus, Bohbot says, we do not easily accept the inevitable opposites of ease: fear and loss, defeat and death.

As I listened to Bohbot and read the material she was showing me to support her arguments, I suddenly experienced an intimation of dread. Bohbot's photos were vistas of an Arctic world that was lovely in its starkness, but inside I felt as cold and threatened as those flat expanses of ice rolling toward the North Pole. Conclusions were slotting home from what she was telling me, from what I'd been thinking about after *Knorr*, and what they all seemed to agree on, loudly, was this ineluctable fact: navigation is dead. We cannot rid ourselves of our addiction to ease and the mechanisms of ease that are killing the parts of us that find our own, personal way around our planet. The parts that not only navigate but look around and interact with the world and surrounding people. The parts that make us human.

It's a given that new technologies always have detractors. Traditionalists once warned of the perils of Gutenberg's printing press, of the typewriter, the telephone. But what we were dealing with here, I thought as I sat in Bohbot's office, was something objectively worrisome: a new atopic human. This is someone who, instead of switching back and forth between active mapmaking (of whatever nature) and creative give-and-take with his environment on one hand; and easy, stimulus-response, relatively passive skills and amusements on the other; has become so reliant on the second category that she has grown uncomfortable with the first, with exploration on any level.

We are all looking around less, asking fewer tough questions, avoiding environments whose paths and shadows we don't know. I thought then of the GPS-bewitched French-woman in Washington Square, of almost everyone I knew: atopic, all of us.

"We have to live consciously," Bohbot said, checking e-mails again, for she could no longer hold her backed-up rendezvous at bay. "It's not good to spend your life reacting to stimuli that are not what you choose. If *we* choose them, that's another story." But what if our brains have become so addicted to the power and coolness of our devices that we've lost even our ability to choose?

CHAPTER EIGHTEEN

The Sail, and the Story of the Sail

The wind increases slowly in strength till midnight, blows steadily for an hour, then begins to wane, so that by 2:30 A.M. it barely fills the sails, and I shake out the reef and start the engine to keep us at the five- to six-knot average I want to maintain to simplify my dead reckoning. I wish to maintain speed, also, so as not to find myself offshore when our window of fair weather slams shut late tomorrow.

The night is split three ways: deep waves rolling purple-ebony valleys under our stern from the south; the metallic glint of moonlight on their crests; and a sky painted in gradients of darkness turning to platinum as they near the moon—a darkness which, even in its most shadowed quarters, the stars cannot muster sufficient energy to pierce. This is very different from the sky in Haiti, under a similar moon. I wonder if pollution from America's industries is masking the constellations here.

Martini has been resting below. When he comes back on deck at 4:00, I ask him if he'll steer while I try to rest. "I don't think I'll sleep," I tell him, "but just in case, wake me before dawn so I can do the sextant thing." I pause before going below, remembering now that I never gave my crew instructions beyond emergency, man-overboard procedures. "Uh, we're fifty miles offshore," I add, "and almost thirty from Matinicus, so we're not going to hit anything. But I should have told you, anyway: look out for the black and white."

Martini gives me his stoic "Just tell me what to do" stare.

"What do you mean, 'black and white'?"

"Well, if you see something that's blacker than normal ahead, it could be land or a ship's hull. If you see white, it could be breakers or a ship's wake, but don't worry—"

"What do you mean, 'don't worry'?" Martini asks, his voice rising.

"It won't happen," I begin, "so—"

"Wait, wait," Martini interrupts, laughing but not laughing really. "Let me get this straight. A *ship's hull*? *Breakers*?"

"It ain't gonna happen," I repeat. "I mean we might see a ship going to Portland, but that's it, and you'll see its lights from miles away tonight. I just forgot to tell you the drill."

"Got it," Martini says, taking the wheel, his jaw set like that of Admiral Nimitz before Midway. "Black and white. *Got* it, George. Have a nice rest."

I lie down in the forward berth trying not to think of black and white and how strange things happen at sea. The even beat

of diesel, the regular wash and run of hull in swells are sooth-
ing, reassuring, the way I suppose one's own pulse is reassuring with its message of "so far, so good"; and to my subsequent
surprise, I do fall asleep. When I wake an hour later and return to the cockpit Martini gives me the mock salute and says
he'll try to sleep, as well, and I tell him I'll have to wake him
at dawn so I can use the sextant and he says, "Aye, aye," and
disappears below. When dawn comes, slowly diluting the
darker end of night's color gradient, like mixing pearl pigment
into designer paint labeled "shadow" and "unknown" and
"unshriven ghost," it hardens the horizon, but almost all the
stars remain invisible against the moon's overarching sheen.
What stars can be seen I don't recognize at all; measuring them
with the sextant would be useless. The bloody moon itself is
so far west at this point that, were I to gauge its altitude and
work out the corresponding line of position, it would give me
a line that won't tell me what I need to know, which is how
far north we've come.

I am getting used to the infernal chain reaction at this
point, I take note of this development calmly. I decide not to
wake Martini, and hold *Odyssey* on her course, northeast
toward an empty horizon across a sea so calm it's hard to
believe it was ever high and angry and crazed with foam. Its
swells look like pooled ceramic.

AT 5:45 I SPOT A black fin, perhaps two feet high, sticking
out of the water to port. Around 6:00 I leave the helm and
quickly check the chart, measuring our distance run from the

last DR estimate. It looks like we're sixteen miles from Matinicus.

A little after 7:30 I become aware of shapes nudging above the horizon forward and to port, northwest, where land should be. As *Odyssey* pounds on the shapes rise higher; they appear to be a line of gray hills in the distance, and at first I smile, thinking we have made landfall and pretty much on time. But the hills are a bit too even, their color is wrong also, the shade of cream flavored with tannin, a greenish tinge. Pus colored, I think. The grim analogy is deliberate and I am not smiling now because I know what those "hills" are.

Fog.

I am not scared. Nervous, perhaps, and this interests me. For weeks, months, I worried about what would happen if we encountered fog on making landfall. Now that fog has happened I am anxious to close with its dun presence and solve, one way or another, the problem it represents.

MARTINI WAKES AT 8:00. "I can't believe I slept so long," he says. I show him the fog. "It's got to be just off the coast," I tell him, "it's exactly where Penobscot Bay should be and it's running at the same angle." Martini takes the wheel, and I update our dead reckoning. If it's accurate, we are now five miles southwest of Matinicus Rock.

Just before 8:30 we spot lobster-trap buoys, which means the water is shoaling. *Thalassa* has become *pelagia* again, we are back in the coastal zone, an estimated 2.5 miles from destination.

Gazing through binoculars at the line of fog I notice it blending, east of north, into something else, a darker, rougher undulation that must be real hills.

I notice something else: the fog has turned lighter, lower, and seems to be imbricating itself into the air we sail in. It is wispier, more bleached, and has tendrils that reach toward us and without further warning all horizon disappears and gray, in fifty shades and more, is all around us.

I slow the engine to near idle. I am no longer calm. Part of my brain indulges in useless anger against fate, the sea, *pelagia;* against Poseidon and his crew. No fog was predicted for this morning in every forecast I consulted.

Another slice of synapses—I assume they lie within the hippocampal formation—is sorting through various navigational options. One thing I can be sure of is that the caudate nucleus is not active at this point since I have zero rote or reactive behaviors to indulge in where fog is concerned: only a few ideas, none of which I much care for.

Martini has been perusing notes I printed out about the Maine coast, and now he reads aloud a passage about Downeast fog that ends: "carelessness is swiftly punished."

"Carelessness is swiftly punished!" Martini repeats, laughing; his laugh is a little wild. "Oh, wow! Oh, great!"

"Don't worry," I tell him, "it'll burn off," though I have no idea if that is true, at least in the foreseeable future.

I go below again to look at the chart. I don't like being close to land in fog this thick, with no recent fix to base a course on. I plot a new course anyway, starting at our estimated position. This will bring us parallel to the run of coast.

A machine noise deeper than our diesel's suddenly vibrates around us, and through the horizon of visibility perhaps fifty yards away, a large white Jonesport lobster boat roars past, heading south. Its crew don't even glance in our direction.

The way fog rubs in its pearly sheen to soften the lobster boat's contours reminds me of my grandfather's etchings.

I tell Martini we have two choices: to sail slowly offshore and wait for the fog to clear, or break out the handheld GPS, find our exact position, and sail north to the broader channel between Isle au Haut and Seal Island and then pick our way to harbor, fix by satellite fix.

I tell him I'd prefer to wait offshore as we are doing now. Offshore, I tell him, will be safe, away from rocks. The lust for *thalassa,* for deep water open and far from land, that I felt when we finally left the Cape behind, returns. "We'll just sail in deep water till the fog clears," I finish dreamily, and Martin asks, "When will that be?" and I say, "I have no idea; usually fog clears sometime during the day, but it might stick around," and he says, "Stick around how long?" and I shrug, and he says, "Ballpark?" and I reply, "Maybe all night."

"Uh-huh," Martini says. He looks me in the eye. Then he says, very firmly, "I have a problem with that, George. I have a real problem with that."

Martini is no chicken. I think his navigational rheostat is set quite a bit higher than mine, though of course this is no great achievement, because he chose to come on this trip in the first place, wanting only a new experience, knowing almost nothing about boats and sea matters except that inevitably they involve a quotient of risk.

We talk it over and amicably reach compromise. We will keep running along the line of coast for a while: then, if the fog looks like it's not going to clear, we'll turn on the GPS.

THE FOG DOESN'T LIFT. Instead it thickens. It's both eerie and boring to sail in this fashion, slaloming around lobster trap buoys, like a plane lost in clouds with no clue to direction but the pink-glowing compass. Garish buoys, dark water, zinc-colored fog. Sometimes, steering without horizon, my balance falters, and I have to steady myself on the wheel.

We run like this for what seems like hours. The thought of waiting all the rest of the day, all night maybe, is daunting, it rises in me like an intimation of sick. "What if this shit doesn't lift?" I mumble to myself. The Weather Service doesn't even deem it worth reporting, maybe because it's chronic around here? And the weather going downhill tonight . . .

"Fuck it," I mumble suddenly. I go down into the cabin, open the box in which it lives, and break out the handheld GPS. The little screen comes alive with graphs, one for each satellite it's acquiring—five are available, it seems—and I see them with a mind's eye sharpened by what I learned at Schriever; twenty thousand kilometers overhead, they shoot their discrete time signals to this tiny instrument in the cockpit of my boat.

After a couple of minutes, the latitude and longitude numbers show up. Forty-three degrees, forty-four minutes north; sixty-eight degrees, forty-eight minutes west. I plot our fix on the sailing chart and smile: we are right on course in terms of longitude, though a couple of miles farther south than my DR put us. Those were, indeed, hills to the northwest. We got to where we were going.

Pleased with the result, calmer now because this experiment is over and we've been told with great authority precisely where we are, I plot a new course for Isle au Haut.

And we sail on, still keeping a slow speed and close lookout because of the buoys, the marauding lobster boats. Soon we see more buoys farther off and before we realize why, the shape of a tiny island materializes out of the cotton horizon to port and then another, bigger island beyond. The fog is lifting. "Land ho!" Martini calls, grinning broadly. The little island is dominated by a tall light tower. After months of imagining it, I am looking at Matinicus Rock.

THE FOG CLEARS FROM NORTH to south, as fast as it enveloped us a few hours ago, and soon we make out a fair wedge of Penobscot Bay. I reverse our course and then, once west of Matinicus, head north toward the Fox Islands. There is good harbor in the thoroughfare between the two islands of Vinalhaven and North Haven.

With the fog gone, the sun shines brightly, the day is near cloudless. Regret must show on my face because Martini says, "It's my fault; you didn't want to use the GPS, you can blame it all on me."

I deny this, politely. In truth it was not Martini's fault. Thinking it over, I realize I wanted to turn on the GPS as much as he did, in good measure because the trip was done. We knew where land was, had navigated here the old way, all that was left was the waiting. This is where the trip has taught me something about my navigational rheostat: the setting can rise sometimes, as evidenced by my willingness to strike out for sea, my capacity to feel happy doing that. It bounces up once the time has finally come to go, to start the trip.

Conversely, waiting for something to happen multiplies stress and the mirror desire for safety and drags my rheostat down.

I remind myself that this trip was planned to model Halvor's, and he did not have the GPS option we had. But I knew all along that the narrative of Halvor's voyage and the story of mine could only crudely parallel each other. Anyway we did get lost to some extent, caught in conditions of poor visibility near a coast fully as dangerous as that off which *Paquet* sank. I knew from the first I was not deliberately going to court storm and shipwreck in the depths of a northern winter. My story was made up and could never be the same as Halvor's. And that was always OK because I figured, if I pursued it long enough, it must become its own story, whatever the initial plot: must fashion its own bash at the ineffable.

The wind strengthens again, and we spend the balance of the day under sail, cutting northward through the glittering chop of Penobscot Bay.

I'M AWARE, FROM WRITING and studying fiction, that stories tend to start with characters getting lost, often literally and always, if they have any gumption to them, emotionally.

E. M. Forster once said that only two plotlines exist: somebody embarks on a journey, or a stranger comes to town. He was deliberately oversimplifying but a measure of truth resides in his aphorism and in the concept of voyage implied in both plots. Travel, with its burden of movement and having to find one's way in a strange environment, is always implicit in narrative. The imbalance that happens at the outset of any tale and the voyage that's required to solve it constitute one of the themes I emphasize in my fiction class. It's another way of saying that the normal, stable world has changed around a character; he or she no longer has solid bearings on which to rely, the landmarks are all unfamiliar or vanished, and the rest of the story must be focused on trying to find other landmarks in order to fix position and bring the voyager safely home.

Many of our archetypal tales revolve around characters getting lost in a quite literal sense. The examples are too numerous to list comprehensively but even a brief scan of the memory banks raises a few, starting (in fiction) with *The Odyssey* and Dante's *Divine Comedy* ("Halfway through life's journey I found myself in a dark wood, the path having been lost"); proceeding through *Robinson Crusoe* and *Gulliver's Travels*. On TV we've seen the *Lost* series, as well as *Lost in Space, Space Family Robinson, Gilligan's Island;* in film, *Lost Horizon, Planet of the Apes, The Vanishing, All Is Lost*. Even that iconic American movie, *The Wizard of Oz,* is based on a child getting blown right out of Kansas into a spatial unknown. Scores of children's stories, such as Hansel and Gretel, Snow White, and Goldilocks, are based on kids losing their bearings in the woods. Children live closer than adults to basic fears and they appreciate the vicarious thrill built into stories about being turned around in strange territory. This in itself is an indication of how deep in our psyche lies the awareness that we are how we find our way. But adults too find themselves drawn to the trope and to real-life navigational disasters such as the *Titanic* sinking or the disappearance in March 2014 of Malaysian Airways Flight 370.

Stories also cement the logical connection between being lost and navigating: between not knowing our position and the necessity to figure out where we are in order to plan further movement. It's a tension that catalyzes action, jump-starts the plot. It's the storm that knocked Bjarni Herjólfsson off course, the social disorientation that leads Scout to find out more about her town in *To Kill a Mockingbird,* the tension between "roving" and coming home in countless folktales and songs. It's what causes us to explore and at the end of exploration sort out how to get back; only to realize that home is but respite, a fleeting second when all bearings and landmarks seem nailed down but which, in a fluid setting like history, the weather, or one's own life, will never stay fixed for long.

We start out wondering where we are as we come out of the womb. Forever after we try to find our way and every time we succeed realize that, simply by virtue of being alive, we must be lost once more. It's a truism implied in Buddhism, in which the cycle of life by definition includes death, the ultimate "lost" place, Hamlet's "undiscovered country from whose bourn no traveler returns." The lines from "Little Gidding"— "the end of our exploring / Will be to arrive where we started"—are well known, but fewer recall the lines that follow:

Through the unknown, unremembered gate
When the last of earth left to discover
Is that which was the beginning . . .
Not known, because not looked for
But heard, half-heard, in the stillness
Between two waves of the sea . . .

Home is a place "not known."

The mingling of navigation and its associated reality—that we cannot *find* our way by definition if we already *know* where we stand; that we must be lost in order to truly navigate—extends into how we talk and think. Who and what we are, what we remember, and how we remember are largely built on language. And even language is built on navigation. Literary historian Paul Zumthor makes the point that every sentence, through the gearing of subject, verb, and object, does something to an aspect of the subject's environment, which as "movement chauvinist" Wolpert has demonstrated, logically implies the subject must be in motion. Equally logically, since there is no point in moving if you don't know where you want to go, movement means that, no matter at how microscopic a level, the subject must be *navigating* motion. I don't think it's too much of a stretch to take it one step further and write that every sentence including this one conceals, in fractal miniature, the story of which it is part, with the subject as character verbally crafting some kind of movement, starting a form of journey into the verbal unknown, searching for a landmark in the following thought.

Researchers have found that the areas of the brain we use to register landmarks, build cognitive maps, and navigate space fire up in an identical process when navigating language. Consider, or perhaps navigate, this sentence from a paper by Leneteo, Adornell, et al.: "Discourse comprehension and production strongly rely on the ability to detect [linguistic] landmarks, sequencing them according to the communicative goal, forming expectations about these landmarks and checking if they have been met or not." The researchers back this up empirically by noting that the same brain areas in and around the hippocampus light up for linguistic as well as for geographical charting.

And what a terrible thing it must be to be lost spatially and at the same time in language, as are the late-stage Alzheimer's patients in Résidence Symphonie, unable even to talk about being lost while shorn of the ability to find one's way out. Because ultimately what saves the rest of us is the process of storytelling and finding in those characters and stories both a certain harmony in the way-finding and an ally against the eternal fear of it.

ODYSSEY ARRIVES AT FOX ISLAND Thoroughfare in late afternoon and we pick up a mooring off Brown's boatyard. The weather, as predicted, deteriorates. Cirrus veils the sun, lower clouds roll over our anchorage after dark. The wind rises from the east and soon is blowing more strongly than it did during our trip, kicking up short waves and whitecaps; we learn later that it gusted to fifty knots. The thoroughfare runs west in North Haven Harbor so the wind has a clear run and even fastened as she is to the solid mooring provided by Brown's, *Odyssey* pitches as if we were sailing. She yaws away from her mooring, first port then starboard, as Circe did before we hauled it aboard. I wrap antichafing gear around the mooring warp and double up lines on the dinghy, which we replaced in the water earlier. Then we break out the rum.

Already we are rearranging the journey linguistically. For Martini, my "black and white" advice, as he puts it, marked the story's climax. It's a monument raised to his courage and the health of his own rheostat that he continued to steer alone through the offshore dark, peering very hard for peril, while allowing me to nap below.

For me, our narrative kicks up two spikes: when I almost fell overboard while bringing Circe on deck; and when we first saw lobster buoys and that glimpse of foggy hills, which meant we had found land. It might be the rum and tonics but despite or because of my exhaustion I suddenly feel very content to be on this boat, in safe harbor with a trusted friend, as the bully gods of weather sling their weight around.

I suspect Martini feels the same way. He stands at the open hatch now, watching rain lash sideways in the orange lights of the ferry terminal. With a rum drink in his hand he taunts the storm, chanting repeatedly in the nya–nya singsong of playground rivalry, "*I'm* on dry *la-and, I'm* on dry *la-and*;" and the wind shrieks back in impotent fury through the shrouds.

CHAPTER NINETEEN

The Politics of Navigation

My original map of where to go once we got to Maine, which included bringing *Odyssey* back to the Cape, no longer suits the temporal terrain. Martini's free week is almost over and I don't have time to bring the boat back single-handed, short hop by short hop; this would take at least four days, even if the weather turns fair, which it's not supposed to do. What is more, due to waiting for crew and winds, I am crowding up against the date when I'll have to leave for Norway. I cannot postpone that trip: I've arranged with the Haugesund wreck diver to take me to where I think *Paquet* went down. Erik Bakkevig has a job running a remotely operated robot to work on underwater gear for British Petroleum, and once that's finished, he'll have time to take me to Espevaer, but his own window of opportunity is not wide.

I ask him, only halfway joking, if he might be able to use BP's submersible to search for *Paquet*'s remains, but he claims the robot is not his to schedule or use for other purposes than BP's.

So I sail in tranquil fashion across Penobscot Bay and leave *Odyssey* in Rockland, to be laid up for the winter at Knight Marine, next to what used to be a herring cannery. After that, I return to New York by bus. In the city, I buy a smartphone. I've been meaning to do this for a while, to continue the experimenting I started with Louis' GPS into how people navigate, or, more accurately, how we are navigated now.

Over the next two weeks, between spending time with my family on the Cape, preparing for Norway, and readying *Odyssey* for her winter layup, I commute back and forth to Maine three times. On one of those trips, I step off the bus in Portland and walk southeast from the Concord Trailways bus station, heeding directions from the Google Maps app on my smartphone, which leads me smoothly to Aunt Imelda's apartment.

Imelda is part Hispanic Texan, part Amerindian, and she possesses a calm, deliberate quality that seems familiar to me from time spent investigating silence among the Plains tribes. In the dining room of her flat she has laid out the artifacts and materials my uncle saved that had to do with our family: a Bible, the sextant, the original painting of *Stavanger Paquet,* and Halvor's sea chest.

The sextant, as I surmised from the photo, is a model Fred used as a naval officer during World War II. The Bible comes from my grandmother's English family. I had high hopes for the sea chest, since my mother told me it was washed ashore when Halvor drowned, then used by his son Thomas, and I reckon an artifact like that is bound to trail strands of information, caught like cobwebs on its sharp corners over the years. It's the usual size, standard issue for nineteenth-century seamen: three and a half feet long by two deep, fashioned of wide, age-darkened hardwood boards. Deep cracks run along boards forming the box's top and sides. A brass plaque set on top bears the name, in elegant copperplate script, "Thos Michelsen." Thomas would have replaced his dad's name with his own, I suggest doubtfully to Imelda, realizing as I do so that I'm still trying to twist family legends to fit the Procrustean matrix of fact.

The chest, in which Imelda usually stores bed linens, is empty. Leather loops screwed into the inside back planks were clearly meant to hold tools. They evoke in me the same feeling of empathy, of a common humanity, that I experience whenever I look at old tools, worn by the grip of hands; when I look at hands themselves, the palms of working people like those of my canvas-repairing friend Laura, calloused and clenched by toil. It's how my own hands used to look when I worked on ships. I assume those cracks in the chest might have occurred in the process of being washed ashore, but there's no way of knowing for sure.

Nor does the *Paquet* painting tell me more than what I learned from the *giclée* copy in my house. Imelda and I pry the frame apart, hoping to find notations inside, some clue about the ship it portrayed. Nothing is marked on the heavy paper. On the painting's front, hidden under the frame, the signature is Halvor's, and that at least is new. I had not realized he was the artist, and I feel increased respect for him. The watercolor, though hardly a masterpiece, is technically good. It interests me that this aptitude for draftsmanship was handed down from Halvor to his grandson; to my daughter as well, judging by the intricate pen-and-ink drawings she's been making most of her life.

Another painting hangs in a hallway next to Imelda's dining room. It was made by Pop, Imelda tells me, and I glance at it casually, then with increasing curiosity. It shows a woman in a long black dress, clutching clasped hands to her breasts in histrionic fashion, a very nineteenth-century-Gothic representation of high emotion. She is looking at—no, more than looking, rushing toward—two men who stand awkwardly by a door to the viewer's left. The men turn slightly away as if embarrassed by the strength of her feelings. Both are bearded, dressed in long seamen's oilskins, and bear the same glum expression. "That's a sad one," Imelda remarks. "Fred said it shows Pop's mother getting the news, when her husband was lost at sea."

I examine the painting more closely. Technically, it's better than Halvor's watercolor. The light from a gas lamp highlights the woman, casting a strong, Titian-esque shadow behind the sailors. The gradients between light and dark on skin and clothes, walls and furniture, are painstakingly rendered.

I am amazed less by the painting itself—it tells me nothing I didn't already know—than by the fact that Pop painted it at all. Clearly the work took days if not weeks to craft, and to spend so much time representing what might well have been the worst moment of his life surely tore him up somewhere deep. I am reminded of the painting back at our house, of the women and children waiting by a jetty, peering at storm waves, which has the same somber tones of black and ochre in the foreground. This one is more specific in the story it tells. I wonder if my grandfather painted it because he was so young when his father died. He must have wanted to fix the story in place and memory and given his talent for images, this was the best way to go about it. In a way, Pop did in that oil painting what I try to do in words: map out the stories of those who are important to me so I can fix their position, so they cannot disappear entirely.

I am impressed by another detail of this painting. Pop's mother—my great-grandmother—has a graceful nose and a delicate, firm chin; she is lovely. If you lightened her hair a bit and swept it to one side, she would be the spit and image of my daughter.

MY NEW SMARTPHONE AMUSES ME. It's not an iPhone of any number or an elite Android, but it still looks cool, this Samsung bought on credit; it is thin and shiny with black-silver trim and stuffed with applications. With it I can speak text messages, play an astonishing number of colorful games, take pictures in back of me, find out to the minute when the next C train is due to arrive at Columbus Circle. The navigation apps, Google Maps in particular, are efficient. As long as I'm not in a tunnel or the equivalent of an Afghan ravine, they tell me exactly where I am with very little lag. Even more importantly, while I'm driving they show me where traffic is building, to a resolution greater than a city block. Google's GPS function works better than Garmin's Imogen, although the process of trying to plot routes beforehand is as clumsy, and just as many fast-food restaurants and other irrelevant chain outlets pop up if I zoom down to a given area.

The more I use the map application, the more I listen to Google's version of Imogen, the more I find myself lusting for the navigation app when I'm traveling without. More and more I desire to watch the little blue circle that represents me gliding steadily along the Cross Bronx Expressway or up Route 1 toward Rockland. I like being told precisely where I am in that bright little square of world. I download a free compass app called Compass 360 Pro that reads the Earth's magnetic field to find north, just as eels and pigeons do. It's supposed to display my latitude and longitude at the same time but for some reason does not, maybe as punishment because I won't download fancier apps being advertised by this one.

Abandoning the compass app, I return to the screen I like best, the maps function; back to the little blue dot that is me in the world. Yet even as I play with it I also feel—there's no other way to say this—castrated. My smartphone, it seems, has already taught me something valuable. The passive/reactive behavior summoned by this sort of tech, the caudate nucleus activity of which Bohbot spoke, is not merely some abstract theory based on statistics and surveys. It occurs as a solid syndrome, hardwired as a virus latching on to cell receptors, when initiative on my part, however wrongheaded or inaccurate, is subsumed by obedience, or strong attention at any rate, to the direction of outside systems.

As fast as I've become addicted to the accuracy of Google Maps, I have also come to feel helpless, controlled, ordered about because I have no personal bearings, no ability to find my way independently, as soon as I start using it. I see cross streets, the outlines of rivers, but so obsessed have I become with the azure circle that I pay little attention to the map's background and forget it as soon as it slides offscreen.

THAT FEELING OF BEING CONTROLLED leads me to wonder about another aspect of modern navigational systems, something that might appear self-evident but the implications of which, I think, too often go unrecognized: if I know exactly where I am at all times thanks to these systems, it follows that the systems, and those who program and control them, also know where I've been, where I am, and where I'm going as long as I am using my device, and even when I'm not. My smartphone, after all, tells service providers my exact location at all times, as long as it's powered up. So does my computer the second it "handshakes" with a modem. The minute I use a credit card, a highway toll pass, or any of the numerous other passes I own that allow me onto public transport, through customs, or into an office, my position is instantly on display for anyone with access to the relevant networks. Is not such knowledge a degradation of privacy and therefore a form, however potential, of control?

I could, of course, escape the grid: cut up all credit and

debit cards, plus any other document with a readable micro-chip; crush my cell phone's SIM with a sledgehammer, pay for everything with cash, and move to a place so isolated it won't have electricity, cable, gas, oil, or telephone utilities. But how long would I last like that? How long before I needed to go into town to buy aspirin, or propane for the camp stove, or sardines? As soon as I emerged from my self-imposed frontier lifestyle, as soon as I parked on Main Street or set foot in a store, the growing web of closed-circuit TV cameras would capture my position for the benefit of whoever might be watching.

I remember my musings in Colorado about the pioneers, the early Americans who defined themselves by how they found their way across the great unmapped spaces of this country, where they could vanish if they had a mind to. That America is gone forever.

THE CRUCIAL IMPORTANCE OF NAVIGATION to memory, identity, and consciousness is hard to refute. So is the idea that navigating for ourselves through direct interaction with our environment must have evolved historically as a vital compo-nent of consciousness.

It follows that anything persuading us to forgo the process must erode our ability to function as conscious, creative individuals.

This decrease in ability happens on a superficial level, through using devices like my Samsung. On a deeper level, however, allowing ourselves to be navigated divides us from a simpler truth, one I've obsessed about lately, which is the unbreakable link between navigation, getting lost, and the fear that happens when we get lost.

The fear, once again, is important. I began this journey because I got scared when I woke up and didn't know where I was at the rest stop in Wareham. That panic had the same frequency and texture as the fright I suffered making navigational mistakes off Hedge Fence shoal in Nantucket Sound and near Goodwin Sands in the North Sea. Whatever it says about my rheostat, such fear makes sense in the most basic of ways, because to not know where we are means we cannot move rightly or act sensibly. That "Oh shit I'm lost" reaction is a rational one and yet—this is important—it's very different from the fear of getting ourselves into a position where *we might become* lost.

This second form of angst: the fear of ever acting in such a way that we could lose track of where we are; is gaining ground in our society. I see it in my fellow passengers, on airplanes that fly over our planet's most gorgeous landscapes, who look at nothing but in-flight videos. I see it in the street, in the subway, where more and more people exist in the mode of texting, playing video games, following MapQuest instructions, their primary relationship always with the little screen that cues them to the next direction they're told to go in: shunning the dramas of ugliness, anger, humor, and harmony visible in the faces and theater of people around them.

I see fear in the downstream effects of screen obsession: less creative thought-processing in the centers Bohbot studies, which might correlate to a decline in overall creativity measured by the Torrance test, since it takes courage to risk new thoughts. I recognize it in rising levels of depression, clinically linked to deterioration in the time sense on which our key position-finding skill, dead reckoning, is based. (The core of our time sense, according to Boston University neurobiologist Howard Eichenbaum, also lies in the hippocampus, which registers the sequence in which spatial events occurred—the basis of temporality—thus tying together even more tightly the navigational triad of speed, course, and time.) I see it in our growing geographical ignorance as American school systems favor more "useful" math and science disciplines that will enable students to score jobs as data-entry clerks and pipeline engineers, even as 50 percent of those students cannot find New York on a map. Thirty-seven percent of them, at the height of the latest Middle Eastern conflict, had no idea how to locate Iraq.

I see fear in many intelligent, educated people I know who flat-out refuse to turn off their device and navigate their own map of whatever nature. Few among them would admit they're scared, but I think they are, and rightly so, because they have largely forgotten how to find their way without being told how to do so. This isn't fear, my friend Mac says. He is one of those who will not turn off his device even during a dinner with friends; the issue, he claims, is one of ease versus effort, of better use of his time. Yet I believe it cuts deeper than that.

I tell Mac about the limits of short-term memory. What happens to our life, I ask him, when we spend so much of it cutting ourselves off from the footling scraps of information we can retain, in favor of those fire-hose volumes of data pumped into us by the systems that control our screens? What happens to personal freedom when the information-tech sector, which in itself constitutes 20 percent of our economy and runs infrastructure for the rest, has a vested interest in boosting consumers' addiction to the tools that navigate us?

What will happen to humans, as economic and political animals, when the exponentially growing networks—already far beyond the capacity of a single human brain to monitor, and placed as a result under the tutelage of various embryonic forms of artificial intelligence—acquire (as inevitably in networks of such complexity they must) their own brand of consciousness and with it the drive to expand their influence even further?

And what happens to this planet, pincered between burgeoning population, rising temperatures, extremist ideologies, and finite resources, when so many of its most educated citizens forget, both literally and metaphorically, how to navigate its complexities?

I describe to my friend Bohbot's idea that we use satellite navigation to travel to a new place, and put it aside to find our way home. Such a balance, I suggest, might answer the question I asked myself earlier about how best to approach these technologies: use the systems when we need them; switch them off when we don't so as to reopen our minds, for once unfiltered and unscreened, to the world around us.

But Mac just laughs and checks his text messages for what must be, given his average rate of checking, the fortieth time today.

TWENTY

Halvor's Wedding

I arrive in Halvor Michelsen's home port on a sunny morning at summer's end. I remember Stavanger only vaguely. The last time I was in this city on Norway's southwestern rim, I couldn't have been more than twelve years old. My strongest impressions then were of a tight harbor crowded with ferries, workboats, and fishing craft; markets with basketfuls of slimy stuff from the deep; sidewalk stalls, white-washed houses, the stink of fish. I remember boredom, because we were visiting family, two elderly spinsters, cousins of Pop's. They lived in a big house with a dumbwaiter, and gooseberry and red-currant bushes in the garden. Another strange, pastel memory, words I only half understood: our mother suffered a miscarriage here.

Since then Marta and Borghild, the cousins, have died. Oil was discovered beneath the North Sea and Stavanger became the chief staging port for massive rigs sucking the rot of Cambrian krill from under the continental shelf. Norway got rich. Office blocks of glass, steel, and ersatz–Le Corbusier design rose on every hand. The fishing boats left. The huddled houses of the old town, rising on hills on each side of the harbor, were not bulldozed but filled with American fast-food restaurants and trendy outlets for Provençal skin cream and Swiss espresso machines.

From my bed-and-breakfast, following a tourist map I found at the airport, I walk to the old town and after a few wrong turns—the smartphone was supposed to work here, but its GPS function reads "No Service"—I locate the *kulturhuset,* the library. It's a three-story modernist building built in slabs of white concrete on the southeast slope of the old town. The ground floor includes a movie theater and café and is full of people, many of them middle-aged bearded men. The latter are accompanied by young women with glasses, clipboards, and intense expressions. Posters announce something important in Norwegian, which I don't understand because my Norwegian is limited to a few phrases in Stavanger dialect gleaned from cousins way back when, on the order of *takk for maden* ("Thanks for the meal"), *e' du galen* ("Are you nuts?"), and *ha' du hår i armhølen* ("Do you have hairy armpits?"). I learn later that Stavanger, and the library in particular, are hosting an international gathering of refugee writers, scribblers turfed out of their homeland for political reasons.

The librarian in charge of newspaper archives is Egil

Henriksen. I find him working at a desk on the top floor, a quiet, slim, white-bearded man who, in accordance with a strict regulation affecting all Norwegians, speaks fluent English. Henriksen leads me to the microfilm room, finds the right box—*Amstidende og Adresseavis* 1844—and threads the film into an old-fashioned reader. The wreck happened in February: I spool to the beginning of April, then scroll backward slowly.

Amstidende was a weekly, roughly twelve pages per edition, which means there are far fewer pages to flip through than would be the case with a daily. That's a good thing since everything is written, for some damn reason, in Norwegian, and not only Norwegian but an archaic version of the language extant in the mid-nineteenth century. This translates, font-wise, into an imposing but hard-to-read variation of German Gothic: *s* like *f,* for example, as in Hanoverian English. All I can do is scan painstakingly for such keywords as *Paquet,* and *skip,* which means "ship," and Halvor Michelsen of course; and *forlis,* which Henriksen told me to look out for and means shipwreck or sinking.

Nothing shows up in April or March.

The combination of backlit screen, tiny font, and fuzzy, heavily serifed characters soon makes my eyeballs feel as if they've been popped by nutcrackers. I reach February, when the ship went down, starting to wonder if despite all evidence this event I'm trying to research might be a complete fabrication, a family fable. It feels a little like the day I stood on the beach, at high noon, and despite astronomical data, the sun seemed to keep right on climbing.

Suddenly it's there in front of me, in the issue of February 29, a tiny notice between an ad for what must be gravestones (*Grav Monumenten*) and auction reports: A *Dodesalt,* which might mean "death notice," for "skipper Halvor Michelsen" of the *Stavanger Paquet.* The announcement is dated February 27 and signed by Dorothea Michelsen, née Eeg, who I know from Imelda's papers was Halvor's wife.

I keep scrolling, still reversing time's arrow back to the issue of "Torsdagen, den 22 Februar." Here the *Stavanger Paquet* surfaces, so to speak, again. The ship's sinking was front-page news that week, topping the right-hand column. From the text I put together the words *forlis, sluppen* ("sloop"), *fart ab Hamburg* which means "trip from Hamburg," also Espevaer and "Grøttefjord." I print out both notices and show them to Henriksen, who strings the words together and comes up with little more than I did. The sentence at the end of Halvor's death notice, Henriksen says, means "The ocean was his grave, and the *Paquet* was his coffin." Oh, I think, how cheerful.

I reverse the film's direction now, reading forward into the year past April, looking for any report of investigation into the shipwreck. The shirr and flash of microfilm, the slide of white letters on black, are addictive. I go through the whole year and find nothing more. Obsessively, I do it again, to no avail.

In the men's room mirror my eyes are pink as boiled shrimp. When I walk outside at dusk, the refugee writers are funneling toward a conference room and a meeting titled "Words Will Break Cement."

. . .

MY HOTEL PUTS OUT AN excellent breakfast buffet that includes pickled herring and a brown goat cheese called *gjetost,*
both of which I liked to eat when we visited as kids but which
my brother, who didn't care for Norwegian cooking, despised.
I smile, thinking of Louis here. Then I walk to the old harbor
and the maritime museum. It's an amazingly beautiful day
for a North Sea port in September. Fusillades of sunlight
ricochet off everything glass or metal or wet, and it's warm.
Even wearing a light jacket I work up a sweat. Despite the
fair weather, walking the quays of the old harbor confirms
my initial impression of change, of strong memories swept
away. The fish smell is gone and with it the associated flavors
and textures of a working port: paint, tar, varnish, sewage,
old beer, diesel, seaweed. Clearly the tourist board has won,
big oil has triumphed, the area has been cleaned up and it
smells of nothing now except money, which only smells if
you trace its origins and effects: every other atom of dirt has
been removed and the port cleaned and what everyone forgot
was that life is smelly, work is grimy, and once you sterilize it
all the way, you have, by definition, killed it.

I notice before walking into the Sjøfartsmuseum that the
neighboring building displays a large sign for a lawyer whose
name, Helliesen, is the same as the *Paquet*'s owners'.

The museum inhabits a couple of ancient buildings, four-
story warehouses with an overhanging, dovecote-like peak
built on the top floor to shelter pulleys that once lifted ships'

cargoes in and out. The current exhibition, appropriately enough given what I'm doing here, is called *Forlis*. It centers around the loss of the *Colibri,* a Norwegian coaster only slightly bigger than *Tower Helen,* that disappeared with all hands on a trip to Iceland in 1904. Storms had reamed the area at that time and the presumption was *Colibri* had foundered in heavy seas, but no one knew for sure until a year later, when a bottle containing a last message from the ship's crew washed ashore on a Norwegian beach. "It's all over for us," the message read. "Wheelhouse broken by wave, no rescue. God help us."

Inside, I ask to speak to Harald Hamre, with whom I had earlier corresponded by e-mail. Hamre is middle aged and bearded, like the librarian, like the refugee writers. It feels like most of the adult males in Stavanger, myself included, resemble each other. In his office, Harald and I go over the Grøttefjord/Grøtle/Grutlefjorden issue once more. He is not familiar with the Grutlefjorden marked on modern charts; however Harald knows everything there is to know about the nineteenth-century herring trade in and around Stavanger. He tells me the 1840s constituted the peak of the so-called herring boom, when the fish were plentiful in southern Norway and much in demand in Germany and the Baltic. It was the equivalent in those days of North Sea oil now, the wealth of whole towns depended on the trade, and Halvor was probably surfing that wave. *Paquet,* on her regular run to Hamburg, most likely transported not only immigrants but barrels of herring. Espevaer and nearby harbors were centers of the fishery, adding to the probability that Grutlefjorden, just north of Espevaer, was the port *Paquet* left from on her last trip.

Hamre knows nothing more than what he has already told me about the shipwreck. He did not know about the *Amstidende* article, though it adds little solid information. *Paquet* was not a large ship and her sinking, while a major news story in February 1844, wasn't important in the bigger picture. I mention Ole Helliesen, who was probably Halvor's step-grandfather, and ask whether the lawyer in the next building might be related. Hamre nods. "They were one of the most important shipowners in Stavanger," he says. "This building was their headquarters."

"This one?" I ask, surprised. "The one we're in now was their headquarters in 1844?" He nods again.

I walk around the museum on my way out. I find a room that holds models of ships like *Paquet*. A caption reads, "In the 1800s the main proportion of local and coastal transport was carried out by single-masted sloops . . ." Several rooms have been restored to resemble the headquarters of a nineteenth-century shipping firm, and I psych myself into an illusion of time travel, standing in the building Halvor knew, where he must have climbed the stairs, cap in hand, reporting to some bean counter with a fancy mustache to get his orders: "Sail to Grutlefjorden," so the accountant might have said, "and pick up a cargo of herring from Peter Köhler's outfit; here's the name of his agent there. Once you've loaded up, sail to Stavanger [or straight to Hamburg] . . . and why did you file a request for another coir of manila rope?" I remember that Halvor, according to family legend, died because he went back for the ship's papers. Was this accountant a stickler for forms? Did that broad wooden banker's desk under the oil lamp once carry paperwork for *Paquet*'s master?

The restored rooms are evocative. What impresses me more, however, is the unrenovated inner courtyard, all clapboard and peeling paint, which looks like no one has touched it for two hundred years; and a workshop with a huge, old-fashioned fireplace on the ground floor, full of tools and lumber used for repairing exhibits. Looking at the tools, remembering the leather loops in the family sea chest, I think, It's the work that ties all this together, the shared knowledge of navigation and seamanship and cargo; not the sociological background or words in history books.

THE FOLLOWING MORNING I MEET Ola Myrvold and Greta Falkenberg. They are distant cousins and I have never seen them before, but Ola, with whom I've corresponded, is interested in family history, and Greta was a good friend of my mother's. Both have traveled by air, Ola from Sweden, Greta from north of Bergen, to see me for an afternoon, and I am touched by their interest and the effort they made. Ola is in his early seventies, of moderate height and friendly demeanor, with glasses and a small mustache. Greta is the same age, thin, elegantly dressed, pretty. I show them the research I have accumulated on Halvor and the *Stavanger Paquet*. Ola is mostly interested in family connections. The handwritten genealogy Imelda sent me fills gaps in his timeline. He hands me a copy of a church record noting the marriage of Halvor's son, Thomas, in Stavanger cathedral. As I spread the various letters and photocopies before them, I realize I never fully translated the paragraph in the lineage chart that refers to Halvor, and Ola does so now: stuff about Halvor's marriage to Dorothea, which also, almost certainly, took place in the cathedral, especially if they were related to an influential family like the Helliesens. And at last I get a full read of the sentence describing the shipwreck: "[Halvor] sailed *Stavanger Paquet,* which sank in a storm off Kleven. He was lost going back for the ship's papers, at thirty-one years of age."

"Wait a minute," I say. " 'Off Kleven'—what's that?"

"It's a place," Ola says. "It could be Klaven, it's either *e* or *a. Utfor* means 'off of.' "

"There's a Kleven near Christiansand," Greta says doubtfully. "It's nowhere near here, though."

On my laptop I call up photos of the King's Point chart, and zoom in on the images. There is no "Klaven" to be seen, or "Kleven" either.

WE WALK AROUND STAVANGER, Greta, Ola, and I. The oldest part of town, built on both sides of the main harbor, opens to the north onto Stavangerfjord. At the southern end, inland of a short rise now choking under glass/steel offices, lies the Breiavatnet, a small, heart-shaped lake surrounded by an elegant promenade and a few pretty, white-painted mansions. After the fish stink, now expunged; after Marta and Borghild's house on Eigenes Vei, this lake harbors my strongest memory of childhood visits to Stavanger. Louis and I had been given locally carved toy boats, double-ended sloops with green topsides, red bottoms, and cotton sails, which we launched on the shoreline here and controlled with sticks; except sometimes the boats sailed off by themselves. And so we watched, two boys in awkward shorts elated and also horrified as one of their boats tacked randomly toward the lake's center and was inspected by the large, pugnacious swans whose domain Breiavatnet is still.

Between harbor and lake rises the Domkirke, the city cathedral. Greta and Ola want to find a plaque commemorating my grandparents, who donated money for the cathedral's maintenance. I find an entrance on the side. If Halvor and Dorothea married here, surely his death must also be mentioned in the archives. In a basement function room, I scare up a woman dressed in black clerical robes who tells me the archives have been moved to the diocesan offices, located in the business district.

In the church proper, Ola and Greta have found the plaque. The nave is tall, dark, and quiet; what afternoon light has the gall to make it into this sanctuary is muted by the various stained-glass windows, allowed to evoke only cooler notes in the intricately carved, painted scenes adorning pulpit and side chapels. I imagine Halvor and Dorothea standing in the transept, a couple in their twenties filled to bursting with all the imagined joys of the life they will make together, utterly unconscious of what will happen in three years' time to shatter that life into a hundred shards of heartbreak. The sight of the flagstones they stood on somehow adds just enough detail to the brain files

Halvor has filled in my cortex to give them shape, because suddenly I am filled with sadness for this man and his wife, a feeling strong enough to register as pressure in the gut.

The sadness is largely false, of course, since I never met him and know so little about him. Yet a bond exists in the trade we share, in the feeling I had when I married Liz on a knoll overlooking Nantucket Sound, the memory that hit me on Saint Mark's Place of when we brought our first baby home; all places that anchor and enhance the memories that have become my life, as the corresponding places must have anchored and enhanced Halvor's.

I remain aware of an earlier thought, from my subway ride after Lucien's: that loss is cousin to loss. My brother's death, the loss of my parents, losing Olivier—even the prospect of giving up, sometime soon, our family's home on the Cape (for I am struggling to pay the taxes, which are high)—have a hand in molding the container of emotion into which I pour this dubious empathy.

But it would be just as false completely to deny connection to Halvor, and not only because he is my ancestor. I can feel for him on the same basis that humans fashion empathy for each other, because ultimately we want the same things, to love and be loved, to see sunlight drive in sapphire rays through stained-glass windows, to walk under cold drizzle then warm ourselves at a fire; to not lose those we care for.

IT'S TRUE THAT AFTER Olivier died I decided that missing, this consciousness of loss, was something to be welcomed in that it keeps the person who died alive. And as I imagined in Haiti while thinking about my brother, the lost person survives in a very real sense because even when he's alive, unless we are with him all the time, we go about most of our daily business without his actual presence but accompanied by the memory of him, which in turn is tied navigationally to the places we were together in the past. When someone is gone forever, though, it turns too hard. Sometimes the brain's maps and images are not enough, you long to go back to the flesh, and that longing hurts.

This imagined loss of Halvor teaches me something, precisely because in his case I never had the flesh, the material presence against which to reset my dead reckoning. What is left is this navigational process that seems to hold true both for those I've known and loved and those I've only imagined. It backs up the conclusion I arrived at earlier, on *Odyssey*: that the process of trying to end dead reckoning and find sure position: the process, then, of navigation itself; is *dependent* on loss. Loss is what inevitably must happen when we move forward. Living, no matter how much it hurts, comes down to losing landmarks: loved ones, homes, lighthouses; and then striving to find where we are again. Always we must measure how far we've traveled, whom we've voyaged with, and to what extent we've been shifted from the course we planned, until we find a steady star, a loyal friend, a beloved garden to show us where we are now—but for an instant only—before starting the process over again.

And it comes clear to me, standing on the stone floor where he and Dorothea were married, that finding out what

happened to Halvor was always more than an exercise in foren-
sic navigation. All along I've been doing what I strive to do in
writing, which is to solve the problem, a deeply navigational
problem, of where we were, where we are, where we're going.
In Halvor's fate, through the details of navigation attached to
it, I will reacquaint myself with something I already know,
but which in the rough-and-tumble of living I forget also
every day: that movement is the point, and the position we
seek lies just as much in realizing we're lost as working out,
for a fleet second, where we stand.

OUTSIDE THE DOMKIRKE, ROMANI WOMEN sell magazines.
Children feed cake to crows: the birds boast gray trim feath-
ers that make them look like they're wearing morning coats.
I call a number I found earlier for Torfinn Bei, who conducts
tours of something called the Badehuset, which is all Espevaer
Island possesses in the way of a museum.

At the cathedral offices downtown I learn that church
records have all been digitized and transferred to the state
archives. When I search the archives online I find no trace of
either Halvor's death or Thomas's marriage.

ERIK BAKKEVIG CALLS ME THAT night. His work for BP has
ended on schedule. The weather forecast for the day after tomorrow looks good. He has lined up a contact on Espevaer,
he tells me, who might help us figure out what happened
to *Paquet*.

The news about the weather forecast reminds me of a response I got recently from Magnar Reistad, of the Norwegian Meteorological Institute, and I read it over. It tells me that, while they've been unable to find data for Espevaer proper, NMI does have records from the nearby Slatterøy lighthouse, which indicate the most prevalent storm pattern in the area, in February, is a blow starting from the southwest, which soon turns northwest as the wind rises. That's when the heavy snow starts, Reistad says.

ANOTHER COUSIN TAKES ME OUT to a fancy country club in Sola, near the airport; after dinner, Helge drives me to a building where, according to family tradition, Halvor's wife started a grocery business that sold supplies to seamen to keep the family fed following her husband's death. It's a former warehouse, with the same dovecote arrangement at the peak that adorned the ex–Helliesen headquarters. It now belongs to Stavanger's one badass bike gang, the Devil's Choice MC. A banner in front shows a logo of a winged Satan over a sign: "Harley Parking Only." From what I can see of the clubhouse it's as clean, neatly furnished, and empty as a midwestern community center, and I smile. I think of the Base Vampire gangbangers in Wharf Jérémie, those sullen kids in dark glasses and torn T-shirts, and the smile dwindles. My friend Daniel, who took me there, told me last month that two gangs, the Dessalines and Croix des Brossailles, fought a pitched battle at the wharf in which ten of them died. It happened three months after I left.

ON A TABLE IN THE empty dining room of the B&B I spread my printed-out photos of the charts showing Espevaer and the neighboring coast. I consult the official Norwegian survey, called Norgeskart, magnifying its online maps of southwestern Norway to a point where I could almost spot lemming. I zero in on the tiniest islands of the Espevaer archipelago and search for names that might resemble Kleven or Klaven, bearing in mind, yet again, the perils of transcription and the loose standards of nineteenth-century orthography. The only places that come close are the islands of Klovning and Store Klovning, just southeast of Espevaer; and Upsøy Kalven, the smaller in a pair of tiny islands on the archipelago's northeastern end.

Something about that smaller, northernmost island, Upsøy Kalven, scares me. Perhaps the fear here is a clue. The meteorological institute says the most common snowstorms in February start southwest, then swing around till the heaviest snow and wind are blowing from the northwest.

A skipper sailing southward down the coast from Grutlefjorden in a snowstorm, disoriented, trying to steer clear of the whole hellish mess of these islands, would probably try to claw off westward toward open sea. If anything went wrong, the odds are he would get tangled up in the northern, outer edge of these islands first—off Upsøy Kalven—rather than farther south on Klovning, near the archipelago's center.

CHAPTER TWENTY-ONE

Finding North

E arly on an overcast morning on the cusp of fall I leave Stavanger for Haugesund. The bus trip north up the coast takes a couple of hours. We run past suburbs that seem designed by the architectural firm of Ikea & Lego; then islands, inlets of tinfoil water, fields dotted with sheep and bales of shrink-wrapped hay. The bus dives into long tunnels, surges over low hills, reminding me a little of the diving, surfacing pilot whales in Cape Cod Bay. At one point we drive onto a whale-backed ferry that churns us across Boknafjord.

Erik Bakkevig meets me at the Haugesund bus station. He is in his seventies, of medium height and build, with a monkish fringe of white hair. He wears a baseball cap that reads "Wreck." The e-mails I've received from him have been terse, even dour, and I was expecting someone irascible, like the

Quint character in *Jaws*. I am nervous anyway. My research into *Paquet* has lasted over a year, and its success or failure is now compressed into a single day with this man and his boat.

But Erik—though like most Norwegians, not exactly an exuberant, outgoing, singing-dancing fool—is friendly and obliging. He has kind blue eyes. He reminds me of yet another Norwegian cousin, Eivind Bornholdt, the father of Reidar who helped me with research at the very start of this undertaking. Eivind, like Ole Krosvik on the Cape, was an object of my childhood worship because he was a skilled woodworker, and a captain on United Fruit banana ships as well. He carved, in the workshop of his house in Tenafly, New Jersey, beautiful toy boats for Louis and me.

Erik's house is set on a steep bluff on the very edge of Haugesund's old harbor. It's a copy of an old warehouse, with the same dovecote peak, and so resembles the Devil's Choice headquarters, and the Sjøfartsmuseum. His dive boat, the *Risøygutt,* is moored at a dock so close it's practically in the basement, and I experience a brief pang of jealousy. How fine it must feel to walk downstairs in the morning, in pajamas even, open a door, and step straight onto your boat.

Risøygutt is the same length as *Odyssey,* only much broader. She is heavily built in steel, with commercial-grade hatches and winches. Her wheelhouse is roomy and includes a broad wooden dive table, a settee, and handmade racks for pencils, dividers, and other navigational equipment. The boat's smell is similar to that on *Knorr,* on my dad's liners: oil and salt, coffee and paint. Erik starts the engine, casts off, and we move up a narrow inlet, much of which has been converted to swank restaurants and office buildings but that is lined with enough old warehouses, some of them still reading "Sild," or herring, to confirm what Hamre said about the size and power of the herring industry in southwest Norway.

The rest of the harbor has become an oil port, like Stavanger. *Risøygutt* turns north up the coast, rolling slightly in a long swell. Erik's electronic chart display hangs above the wheel. On its brightly hued screen the cursor stabs straight into a cluster of islands at the top edge, almost eleven miles away. The twisted-butterfly outline of Espevaer is now as familiar to me as my own face.

Erik pours coffee, and I go out on deck with my cup. The coast to our right, north of Haugesund, is low, gray, rolling. It reminds me of Penobscot and the trend of land under fog, except nothing here is blurred: sea, rocks, cliffs, the sanded-down shapes of glacial hills, clouds drifting eastward are all sharply defined against each other. To the north and west low islands peek over a gray horizon. From a distance the Espevaer archipelago resembles dark sea monsters, crocodile-like profiles with occipital ridges, serrated backs just breaking the water . . . or like the backs of whales. The smaller ones especially appear streamlined like cetaceans, breaching the surface as whales do.

My chest feels fizzy, a symptom of nerves and of an astonishment I've felt before when I finally reach a place I've been thinking about and recognize it because I know what it looks like theoretically and I know my course and speed and it has all shown up on time. Also I don't recognize it at all because it's different, has to be different since any environment is so vast and complex, so crammed with billions of details that will never come across in photos or text. These glacial hills seem lower than I thought, and the islands group closer than I imagined. From far off they appeared smooth, yet as we approach they are revealed to be scored with myriad fissures, most running diagonally from low on the southern end to high in the north, with points of dark-green grass or lichen on ledges and rocks above the reach of waves. They are brown with seaweed below. It's clear to me now, observing them from five miles away, then three, then one, how hard they would be to spot when iron seas rise above the horizon on every side, topped with blown spume in gray-white blizzard: a flock of fog-hued islands, ridged and cracked like waves, crowned with snow and surrounded by the wrack and crash of seas of the same color. It must have been flat-out impossible to see them from any distance or be certain where they were.

Espevaer itself draws closer, and the rocky sides of the island rise fast; they are now higher than I imagined earlier. Erik steers us carefully into a fjord so narrow that *Risøygutt* has only ten feet worth of clearance on either side. And yet the depth sounder shows twenty meters, or sixty feet, apt illustration of how close deep water is to these rocks, how savagely scored the channels between. The midget fjord opens into a small oval harbor. Wooden houses painted white and russet cluster near the docks; a few perch on surrounding slopes. Hedges and flowers are planted on rocky ledges. Almost no trees grow here. A chain ferry: a tiny barge with an electric motor that, once you feed a krone coin into its mechanism, pulls itself link by link along a submerged chain; connects one wing of the island to the other.

We moor at the town dock. It is very quiet in this tiny harbor once the diesel is switched off. I call Torfinn Bei, and Erik phones his contact who lives across the harbor. Torfinn shows up first and leads me to an old building with a thick-walled cellar out of which his ancestors, like mine, once sold provisions to seamen and herring fishermen. So many herring boats came here in the nineteenth century, Torfinn says, that at times two thousand men used the island as base. Groups of sailors would sleep in the store's attic, which has since been set up as a museum, with items of seagoing gear lined up haphazardly on shelves or floorboards: tools, tackle, a taffrail log. I pick up an octant, a form of sextant made of tropical wood and ivory, old enough to have been part of *Paquet*'s navigational gear. Few of the exhibits are captioned, and no one knows where this one came from.

We return to *Risøygutt*. An outboard drones closer, and Erik's contact climbs aboard, tying his boat to our side. Kåre Mahle, a compact man with a thin, lined face and big glasses, looks more like a research chemist than what he is, a native Espevaerian who like many islanders does a bit of everything, boatbuilding and fishing in particular. He is courteous and interested, even voluble when he gets going. We cluster in the wheelhouse, where Erik has laid out a chart of the archipelago and surrounding waters, including Grutlefjorden, on the dive table. I repeat for Kåre's benefit the clues I have to go on:

the *Paquet* was lost off Espevaer in February, probably disoriented in a snowstorm. She was most likely coming from the north, from this harbor: I point out Grutlefjorden. I think of the meteorological institute information, the southeast wind strengthening to northwest with snow. The Swedish newspaper spoke of northeast gales. Either way, a northerly component. That storm must have come up fast, I continue, speculating a bit (but these men will understand the underpinnings of what I say): why else would Halvor, whom that Swedish article praised as being one of the city's top skippers, have put to sea at all?

Kåre and Erik are leaning over the chart, touching it with their fingers as I speak. I think *Paquet* must have encountered much bigger waves than expected, I tell them. Anyway, her cargo shifted, causing her to capsize or at any rate to lie on her side; the cargo hatch was stove in, the ship started to sink. Halvor stayed aboard, or left the safety of a lifeboat, to retrieve the ship's log. He went down with *Paquet* as she sank, supposedly in eighty fathoms of water.

Now the three of us are leaning close to the chart. I trace with one finger the eighty-fathom contour, which defines a channel leading from the north end of the strait between Espevaer proper and Bømlo, the mainland. "The family papers say the *Paquet* sank near Kleven or Klaven," I tell Kåre. "But I cannot find any place with that name here."

Kåre's English is not great. Erik repeats what I said in Norwegian. The islander shakes his head firmly: there is no place with that name around here.

The two keep talking in Norwegian, leaning on crossed arms even closer to the chart, then opening their hands, pointing along the eighty-fathom line. Both men have rough hands, meaty, with stubby fingers, scratched and lined and calloused. Their fingernails are dirty. And I am seized again with my old affection for hands and the men who own them or rather— since I've known Erik only half a day, and Kåre I don't know at all—for all men and women with hands like these, Kåre and Erik and Laura, people who work on sea things and share this craft, this body of navigational knowledge that rests on a deep understanding of the saltwater environment; this environment that, even when someone has spent her or his life on the ocean and has grown resentful of its cruelty and sick of its monotony, still becomes part of his rhythms and movements, her way of perceiving everything else; offers also alliance, comradeship, if only in the way that soldiers in the same platoon feel an opportunistic love for each other because in wartime, during those seconds of fright and weeks of ennui, they must trust each other with their lives; as the crew of *Tower Helen* trusted me when I navigated our ship, for better for worse, around this same North Sea in which Halvor and his son both drowned; as Martini trusted me with his life on *Odyssey.* And I smile inwardly, thinking of his plea: "Just tell me what to do."

Kåre is still talking, and after a minute or so Erik turns back to me. "He says he has never known a shipwreck to come except with a wind from the northwest. That is always the direction of storms in winter."

Kåre nods and talks further in Norwegian.

"He says, with a northwest wind, when the current comes from the south—here—that is very bad."

I lean forward with the chest fizz happening harder. I open my own hand and plant my index next to Erik's.

"Here?"

Kåre nods.

Our fingers are pointing at the eighty-fathom channel just off Upsøy Kalven, on the northeast tip of the archipelago. Kåre is talking about the effect that happens when a current runs in the opposite direction from a strong wind, kicking waves sometimes to double their usual size and steepness.

Kåre's fingers move, indicating two other places where opposed current and wind will stir up rips and higher waves, but both are far from the two names that are anagrams of "Klaven," and they are not close to the eighty-fathom contour, either.

"But this could be it," I tell Erik excitedly, my finger still stuck on the spot. "I mean, this is the one place where all the facts match. It's near Kalven—which had to be transcribed wrong, nothing else in this whole area comes even close. Kalven," I continue more slowly, to give Erik time to translate, "is also the first part of the archipelago he would hit, coming from Grutlefjorden with a northerly wind; and it's right on the eighty-fathom line, where you get the wind and current thing." . . . I don't have to go on, the chain of events is implied. Higher waves than usual most likely shifted the freight. Anyone who has worked on a cargo ship is deeply aware of what happens when the center of gravity moves too far off the ship's middle line. The ship starts to tilt. And this cargo was trickier than most. I know this because, when we were talking earlier, Erik passed on a couple of additional facts.

First, the herring were almost certainly loaded raw into *Paquet,* netful by netful in a rush of tiny bodies poured wriggling straight into the ship's hold. Apparently this was the usual method, in winter at least. The seething silvery mass would have been subdivided within the sloop by checking boards, timbers slotted vertically to define smaller compartments inside the hold. But wet, live herring would have been, essentially, liquid cargo, which shifts easily in a hold. Just as the "watertight" bulkheads on *Titanic* did not extend all the way to deck level so that once incoming water flooded to a certain height it flowed over those bulkheads to the rest of the ship, the checking boards on *Paquet* probably did not reach all the way to her hatch. At least, that's been true of checking boards on all the fishing boats I've worked on and seen. Once *Paquet* tilted beyond normal, the whole slimy cargo would pour to whichever side was lowest, shifting her center of gravity even farther, which caused her to tilt more, and so on until eventually she capsized.

The other piece of information Erik imparted had to do with Peter Köhler, whom he knows, from research on other ships, was the leading herring merchant in Stavanger. Köhler must have contracted Helliesen's *Paquet* to bring the fish to Stavanger, where they would then be salted or pickled in his warehouses and packed in barrels for transport to the German market. Köhler's fishing boats were all local, Erik says, which means it's now a virtual certainty that Grutlefjorden, six miles north-northeast of here, rather than that Grøttefjord halfway to the North Pole, is the port from which *Paquet* sailed.

For a while, Erik, Kåre, and I debate why Halvor left when bad weather was looming. While we were looking at the chart and talking about the northwest wind a new theory formed in my head. If winter storms tended to kick off with a south/ southeast component, as the meteorological institute says they do, it would mean that when bad weather first showed up, Grutlefjorden was no longer a secure anchorage since the wind would have been blowing straight up the inlet from the southeast: as that wind screamed straight up Fox Island Thoroughfare the night *Odyssey* took shelter there. Might this have been the reason Halvor put to sea—only to watch the wind veer northwest, pushing him toward Espevaer?

RISØYGUTT RUMBLES NORTHEAST. ERIK WANTS first to swing toward Grutlefjorden, then come back along the route Halvor would have taken. The Upsøy skerries of which Kalven is part are a few miles away, but from this angle I can't tell which is which.

Then Erik turns to port, southwest, and his ECDIS cursor lines up with the skerries. One islet, maybe a hundred yards long, lies at the tip of this formation. A few hundred yards to the south is a larger island. Erik confirms that the smaller is Kalven; the name means "outlying islet," he notes, and that seems accurate enough. I go out on deck.

Kalven is not much to look at. It too resembles a whale, of

the stylized type that appeared on old charts with the legend "Leviathan" or "Here Bee Monsteres." The higher part, the leviathan's head, is perhaps thirty feet high and faces south, while the body tapers smoothly northward a hundred yards toward the "tail." The side closest to us flattens at one point like a fin at water level. The monster's skin, like the surface of all the other islands around here, is scaly and gray.

The sea is still calm with low, widely spaced swells. A breeze blows from the west and lightly cards the clouds into the blue-white ribbed pattern known as mackerel. Everything looks peaceful.

But I imagine this place in February, Halvor sailing out of Grutlefjorden without benefit of a forecast, thinking he needs to lam out of this crap anchorage so vulnerable to a southeast wind; probably yearning to get home to Dorothea and their child; believing, an hour later when the wind shifts northwest, this is just another variation in the ongoing symphony of western winds, stronger than usual but he can weather it, and if not he'll find shelter. Once out of harbor it feels good because the wind is stronger than we thought, and since it's coming from the northwest now we're sailing like all the trolls were after us, *Paquet*'s blunt bow smashing into and over the high swells, her long hull easily riding the waves. It feels bad also because already we are out of the fjord, exposed to the ocean, and that wind is suddenly too high for this mainsail which has no reef points and can't be shortened. The ship is leaning well to port. And the wind hesitates, then strengthens. We'll be heading for shelter east of Kalven and Upsøya and down the channel behind Espevaer, the decision made now not to switch to a smaller mainsail, it's best to hustle as fast as possible for a protected channel; which will prove to be a mistake, one in the chain of small mistakes that lead to disaster.

The helmsman is told to steer a more southerly course, heading for the gap between the Upsøy skerries and the mainland. The gap is faint in wind-driven seas confused by spume, it seems to fade in and out. Now snow is starting to fall. The wind blows stronger yet and the snow grows thicker; it resembles an infinite number of white diagonal hash marks jotted upon darkness, for in this storm daylight has leaked away. Snow begins to pile up on deck, turning into slush where the waves come aboard through the freeing ports, making it hard to stand upright.

We post a lookout forward, our position now unsure, and in this visibility we would get only minimal warning before butting into one of the rocks and islands north of Espevaer. Perhaps a decision is made at this point to change tactics, to head straight west and out to sea, avoid the islands altogether. Once clear of Kalven we'll keep sailing westward and, when the weather settles, break out sextant and almanacs, shoot the sun, and find our way back from that position. . . . Whatever decision is made suddenly feels urgent. Without knowing exactly where we are or where the rocks and islands lie, the navigational panic is strong and smothering and rises further with every minute we sail into waters we can only guess at, and no time anyway to go below and check chronometer and chart or recalculate our dead-reckoning position.

The wind, ever stronger, wails in the rigging. Though her crew are not aware of the fact, *Paquet* has reached the point where the southerly current, now pumping north and west out of the channel between Espevaer and the mainland, meets the wind full on. Suddenly the waves, already six feet high, rise to ten, twelve from the northwest, their steeper sides veined in cold green drool. *Paquet* takes one off her stern, almost surfs, overtakes the wave she slid off fifteen seconds earlier. Then, too quickly, comes another, which pushes her rear end leftward. The helmsman is slow to react; he should steer *Paquet* to port also to keep the ship moving in line with these crazed seas. The skipper yells, and finally the helmsman spins the wheel counterclockwise, but the waves have grabbed hold of *Paquet's* stern and heaved it sideways and without further notice she is broadside to the waves and listing to port under their smash. The wind now shoving at her mainsail compounds the list, and she tilts even farther.

That is when we hear the crack from below; one of the checking boards has given way. The cargo is shifting. *Paquet* dips another ten degrees to port. Crewmen, struggling too late to cut the mainsail down, lose their footing on the snowy decks and slide into waves now surging over the port side. One of the boards covering the cargo hold is broken by the weight of slopping fish, then another, and seawater starts to pour into the *Paquet's* gut. Orders are shouted to cut loose the ship's tender, and maybe the crew succeed in doing so because some at least live to tell what happened. Perhaps the boat is swamped as soon as it's cut loose, the news that reached our family later was unclear on that score. Is it guilt, then—guilt from the mistakes he's made, shame at the panic he felt when he realized he was lost; the overall humiliation because of what seems, though he would not express it so, the mediocre setting on his navigational rheostat—that sends Halvor down the accommodations companionway into the cabin, up to his waist in flooding, icy seawater to rescue the ship's log for that fucking anal accountant back at Helliesen's?

I have never thought as far as what happens next, the ship finally turning turtle or, filled now past neutral buoyancy, melting into the sea, her starboard side heaving over two, three more waves—and then, suddenly, gone. Halvor in utter darkness in his cabin, or in the ship's office, the water like a huge, cold animal squeezing the breath out of him; lost within the greater disorientation of how his ship wound up like this, still clutching the logbook as water rises past his mouth; fighting to find a way out as *Paquet* sinks and the sea closes over his head.

I feel sad for him once more. I sense the same weird connection I had earlier, only stronger—something that allows me to pity this man, a grandfather twice removed yet close now because we are both in the same place: I am pretty sure I've found where he drowned, where his bones must lie.

I want to tell someone I've made it here. I'd like to tell my brother, who would want to know this. He'd have taken pleasure in hearing me talk about it, might have mixed into the tale his own memories of Norway, and the *Paquet* painting, and images of our mother and all of us into this new memory place that positions lost and found again, of sea and memory, have woven together here off Upsøy Kalven. The imagined feel of losing Halvor blends with the very solid sense of loss from losing Louis, our parents. It's the same feeling I received loud and clear in the subway, after Lucien's, with one difference: I have nowhere left to go with this. I know exactly where I am, in this minute, I know in my gut this is *Paquet*'s grave, there are no more bearings I can take, no sun line or GPS coordinates will pin down this place more exactly. All I can do now is tell their story; all I can do is write about Halvor and Thomas and my brother and Olivier as well. All I can do is paint some small picture of them and how much I loved, not the people I never met but those I knew, by describing them and also the process by which they navigated their places and emotions, which is the same as describing how they loved me back. It doesn't feel like enough, it will never even be close to enough, but it's all that lies within my power.

And it must suffice. The full sense I had in Domkirke comes back to me, that this is what navigation and the disorientation that's part of it have taught me: we cannot live *without* loss. We lose our childhood, our grandparents, lover, parents, brother, and this is not what matters, it's how we loved them and what we make of that process of losing and loving again that counts, it's how we thereby craft our lives and why: in this, too, we are unsure of where we are, and therefore we are forced to look hard around this world, its every speck of filth and loveliness, to fix a new position, set a new course. In that act lies all the pain and joy we'll ever need.

We are abeam of Kalven. I realize, having come this far, I should have brought something to leave at *Paquet*'s grave: that shell from Samothrace, for example. I climb back into the wheelhouse. Erik points to the depth sounder, which shows, still around eighty fathoms, a series of regular east-west undulations such as occur on sandy bottom when a current runs across it. I point at a red blip near the trough of one un-dulation. "There she is," I say, smiling because I know this is rubbish, as Erik told me long ago nothing can possibly be left of *Paquet* but a few metal parts, the anchor, the ship's bell, all of which would be covered by 150 years' worth of mud or silt. Erik shrugs, but inwardly I'm thinking, *Damn, that could be the anchor, this is exactly the point where all the data meet.* I fum-ble in my shoulder bag, looking for some memento to throw overboard. My fingers encounter a pack of cigarillos I bought in Frankfurt airport on my way here. I grab two cigarillos and leave the wheelhouse again.

From the stern deck I glance at Kalven. The island is a couple of hundred yards off. I toss the first cigarillo. "Here you go, Halvor," I mutter, hoping the diesel's noise will cover my words, for this would surely seem like weird behavior to Erik. "Here you go" . . . I'm reluctant to believe this is over, that nothing is left to find, I'm trying to pad out the ceremony and I throw the second cigar: "Here you go, Dioskuri"—though they hardly deserve tribute, having failed here most abysmally.

The cigarillos dance in the boiling white of the boat's wake; they spin, then disappear.

We have reached the southern end of Kalven now. Erik twists the dial on his autopilot until the cursor points south-ward.

Risøygutt heads home.

ACKNOWLEDGMENTS

Thanks to everyone who helped in preparing this book, which includes those given voice within its pages as well as: Farley Chase, Thomas H. Cook, Jasmine Faustino, Dr. Hope Iglehart, Dr. Rosamund F. Langston, Dr. Lindsey J. McCunn, Kristin Powers, Jenny Reiner, Seth Rolbein, Prof. John F. Skoyles, and Prof. Stephen Small. Their counsel was in all cases informed and wise; any inaccuracies or imbalances in the text, of course, are mine and mine alone. I should also like to thank the Royal Institute of Navigation for its support of this project, and the Hungarian Pastry Shop of Morningside Heights, Manhattan, for granting me a place to write and to fix my position in a disorienting city.

SELECTED BIBLIOGRAPHY

The Environment and Social Behavior, Irwin Altman, Wadsworth Publishing, Belmont California, 1975.

The Hippocampus Book, Per Anderson et al., ed.; Oxford University Press, 2006.

"UPDATE: Northwest Airline Overshoots Airport," Associated Press/NBC/WMTV, March 15, 2010.

"Cognitive Processes and Spatial Orientation in Animal and Man," *NATO ASI Proceedings,* Vol. 11, P. Ellen and C. Thinus Blanc, June-July 1985.

Celestial Navigation for the Yachtsman, Mary Blewitt, International Marine Publishing, Camden, Maine, 1995.

Vanishing Point: How to Disappear in America Without a Trace, Suzanne Bürner, ed., Revolver Publishing, 2009.

"Transcripts of Criminal Trial Against Triangle Owners," Cornell University ILR School, Kheel Center for Labor Management Documentation, Ithaca, NY.

"Phones Blamed as Mountain Alerts Hit Peak: Relying on Navigation Apps Is Leading to More People Getting Lost, Rescue Workers Say," *Daily Mail,* London, August 29, 2015.

"Navigation in the ancient eastern Mediterranean," Danny Lee Davis, MA thesis, Texas A&M University, 2001.

"The New Age of Exploration: Restless Genes," David Dobbs, *National Geographic Magazine*, January 2013.

Spatial Cognition, Spatial Perception: Mapping the Self and Space, Francine L. Dolins and Robert W. Mitchell, ed., Cambridge University Press, NY, 2010.

Cruising Guide to the New England Coast, Duncan, Ware, Fenn, W.W. Norton, New York, 1936, revised 1995.

"Discourse Processing and Spatial Navigation," Francesco Ferretti, Ines Adornetti, in *European Perspectives on Cognitive Science*, Kokinov et al. ed., 2001.

East Is a Big Bird: Navigation and Logic on Puluwat Atoll, Thomas Gladwin, Harvard University Press, Cambridge, 1970.

You Are Here: Personal Geographies and Other Maps of the Imagination, Katharine Harmon, Princeton Architectural Press, New York, 2004.

"The Well-Worn Route and the Path Less Traveled: Distinct Neural Bases of Route Following and Wayfinding in Humans," Hartley, Maguire, Spiers, Burgess: *Neuron*, Vol. 37, 877–888, March 2003.

"How to Disappear: 9 Ways to Avoid the Creepy Surveillance Systems All Around You," Betsy Isaacson, Huffington Post, September 18, 2012.

Inner Navigation, Erik G. Jonsson, Scribner, New York, 2002.

The Genetic Architecture of Selection at the Human Dopamine Receptor D4 (DRD4) Gene Locus, Kenneth Kidd et al., *American Journal of Human Genetics*, April 9, 2004.

Samothrace: A Guide to the Excavations and the Museum, K. Lehman (6th ed.), rev. by J. R. McCredie, Thessaloniki, 1998.

We, the Navigators: The Ancient Art of Landfinding in the Pacific, David Lewis, University of Hawai'i Press, Honolulu, 1994.

Proceedings of the 12th International Symposium on Aviation Psychology, Loukopoulos et al., Dayton, Ohio, April 2003.

"Grounding of the Panamanian Passenger Ship *Royal Majesty* on Rose and Crown Shoal, Nantucket, Massachusetts," Marine Accident Report, NTSB, Washington DC, April 2, 1997.

Stavanger Sjøfarts Historie, M.L. Michaelson, Deyers Grafiske Anstalt, Stavanger, 1927.

A Primer of Navigation (6th edition), George Mixter, Van Nostrand Reinhold, New York, 1943.

"GPS Addict? It May Be Eroding Your Brain," NBC.com, November 2010, http://www.nbcnews.com/id/40138522/ns/health-mental_health/t/gps-addict-it-may-be-eroding-your-brain/#.Ve72tM4d-lg.

"Rose Freedman, Last Survivor of Triangle Fire, Dies at 107," *New York Times*, February 17, 2001.

"The World as They Knew It: The Legacy of Greco-Roman Mapmaking," *New York Times*, January 10, 2013.

U.S. Coast Pilot: Eastport, ME, to Cape Cod, MA, NOAA, 44th edition, 2014.

"Traditional Navigation in the Western Pacific," Penn Museum, 1997, http://www.penn.museum/sites/Navigation/Misc/contents.html.

"Interactive Memory Systems in the Human Brain," Poldrack et al., *Nature*, Nov. 2001.

"Questions Asked about Volvo Ocean Race Accident," *Scuttlebutt Sailing News*, April 2014: http://www.sailingscuttlebutt.com/2014/11/30/questions-asked-volvo-ocean-race-accident.

Up from Dragons: The Evolution of Human Intelligence, John R. Skoyles, Dorion Sagan, McGraw-Hill, NY, 2002.

Personal Space, Robert Sommer, Prentice-Hall, New Jersey, 1969.

"Media multitaskers pay mental price, Stanford study shows," *Stanford News*, August 24, 2009.

"Genetics of morphogen gradients," Tetsuya Tabata, *Nature Reviews / Genetics*, August 2001.

A Very Necessarie and Profitable Booke Concerning Navigation, Joannes Taisnier, facsimile edition, John Carter Brown Library, ca. 1579.

Green Badge Knowledge, Free Session: Taxi Trade Promotions, http://www.taxitradepromotions.co.uk/green-badge-knowledge-free-introductory-ses.html.

Maps of the Imagination: The Writer as Cartographer, Peter Turchi, Trinity University Press, San Antonio, 2004.

Alone Together, Sherry Turkle, Basic Books, New York, 2011.

The Haven-Finding Art: A History of Navigation from Odysseus to Captain Cook, EGR Taylor, Abelard Shulman Ltd., NY, 1957.

"The real reason for brains," Prof. Daniel Wolpert, TED.com, http://www.ted.com/talks/daniel_wolpert_the_real_reason_for_brains?language=en#t-1133831.

La Mesure du Monde; Représentation de l'espace au moyen-age, Paul Zumthor, Seuil, Paris, 2014.